THE THEMES OF ELIZABETH GASKELL

By the same author

L'influence du symbolisme français dans le
renouveau poétique de l'Allemagne

Passages from French literature for analysis and comparison

The foreign vision of Charlotte Brontë

THE THEMES OF ELIZABETH GASKELL

Enid L. Duthie

ROWMAN AND LITTLEFIELD
Totowa, New Jersey

First published in the United States 1980
By Rowman andLittlefield, Totowa, N.J.

Printed in Hong Kong

Library of Congress Cataloging in Publication Data

Duthie, Enid Lowry.
    The themes of Elizabeth Gaskell.

    Bibliography: p.
    Includes index.
    1. Gaskell, Elizabeth Cleghorn Stevenson, 1810–1865 —
Criticism and interpretation.   I.   Title.
PR4711.D85   1980   823'.8   80–10235
ISBN 0–8476–6224–1

To the memory of my parents,
Arthur and Gertrude Duthie

Contents

List of abbreviations

The edition used for the works of Mrs Gaskell, with the exception of her biography of Charlotte Brontë, is the Knutsford edition, with introductions by A. W. Ward, published by Smith, Elder & Co., 1906, and reprinted by John Murray, 1919–20. Reference to individual works is given under the title of the volume in which they appear. This title has been abbreviated to that of the main work contained in that volume; for example, a reference to 'Half a Lifetime Ago' would be given to *My Lady Ludlow*, the title story of the volume concerned. The abbreviations used, and the full titles, with the list of the complete contents of each volume, are as follows:

Mary Barton	*Mary Barton and Other Tales* (Libbie Marsh's Three Eras, The Sexton's Hero, Clopton House).
Cranford	*Cranford and Other Tales* (Christmas Storms and Sunshine, Lizzie Leigh, The Well of Pen-Morfa, The Moorland Cottage, The Heart of John Middleton, Disappearances, The Old Nurse's Story, Morton Hall, Traits and Stories of the Huguenots, My French Master, The Squire's Story).
Ruth	*Ruth and Other Tales* (Cumberland Sheep-Shearers, Modern Greek Songs, Company Manners, Bessy's Troubles at Home, Hand and Heart).
North and South	*North and South*.
My Lady Ludlow	*My Lady Ludlow and Other Tales* (Round the Sofa, An Accursed Race, The Doom of the Griffiths, Half a Lifetime Ago, The Poor Clare, The Half-Brothers, Mr Harrison's Confessions, The Manchester Marriage).
Sylvia's Lovers	*Sylvia's Lovers, etc.* (An Italian Institution).

Cousin Phillis	*Cousin Phillis and Other Tales* (Lois the Witch, The Crooked Branch, Curious if True, Right at Last, The Grey Woman, Six Weeks at Heppenheim, A Dark Night's Work, The Shah's English Gardener, French Life, Crowley Castle, Two Fragments of Ghost Stories).
Wives and Daughters	*Wives and Daughters, an Every-Day Story.*

References to *Life of Charlotte Brontë* are to the Haworth edition, edited by C. K. Shorter (reprinted by John Murray, 1920–2). The title has been abbreviated to *Life*.

In references to *The Letters of Mrs Gaskell*, edited by J.A.V. Chapple and Arthur Pollard and published by the Manchester University Press, the title has been abbreviated to L, followed by the letter number.

Introduction

Some writers have to wait longer than others to receive their due from posterity, even when they have been widely acclaimed in their own generation. The lack of adequate appreciation from which Elizabeth Gaskell has suffered has been due largely to the scope and variety of her work. Each of her short stories has its own distinctive qualities, still more each of her novels. And she wrote a large number of tales, of varying length, as well as essays of diverse character, in addition to the five full-length novels and the biography of Charlotte Brontë.

It is true that she has never lacked enthusiastic readers ever since the publication of *Mary Barton*. Each generation has found something to admire in her, but no generation has done justice to her total achievement. It has even been claimed that *Cranford* was harmful to its author's reputation by its very success, throwing into shadow works of deeper import. In recent years the social realism of the novels set in Victorian Manchester has received the renewed attention natural in an era of industrial unrest. In a more general context, *Wives and Daughters* has at length come to be recognised for what it is, one of the great novels of any age. And *The Life of Charlotte Brontë* continues to be one of the most widely read of all biographies. Yet the approach to Elizabeth Gaskell remains to some extent incomplete, because the very individuality of the separate works tends to obscure the essential qualities that unite them in a harmonious totality.

Like Charlotte Brontë and George Eliot, she orchestrated themes which belonged both to her age and to her personal experience, themes which recur, with variations, in the tales and essays as well as in the full-length novels. In his valuable *Mrs Gaskell: The Basis for Reassessment*, published in 1965, Edgar Wright adopted an approach which was partly thematic and partly chronological. In the present study, though the chronological factor cannot, of course, be ignored, a thematic approach is used throughout in an attempt to show the basic unity of Elizabeth Gaskell's total achievement. The main stress must always fall on the major creative work, the novels and the biography—which has close links with the novelist's art—but it frequently happens that the lesser known works provide interesting illustrations of the way in which the main themes are understood and handled. She was naturally attracted by variety of form, as well as by variety of subject. Her style indeed took its shape from her themes, and increasingly achieved a similar harmony underlying its diversity.

Any consideration of those themes today must be indebted to the publication of *The Letters of Mrs Gaskell*, under the editorship of Professor J. A. V. Chapple and Professor Arthur Pollard, which revealed the richness of the experience on which she was able to draw, as well as to the wide-ranging *Mrs Gaskell's Observation and Invention* of Mr J. G. Sharps.

Elizabeth Gaskell died before she could complete the final pages of her last novel, and as certainly before she realised her full potential, for *Wives and Daughters* shows her at the height of her powers, yet hers was no unfinished symphony. Few writers leave us with such a sense of fulfilment; few have sought it less for themselves, or better succeeded in leaving to their readers a lasting legacy of beauty and truth.

My thanks are due to Professor J. A. V. Chapple and Professor Arthur Pollard, and to the Manchester University Press, for kindly permitting quotation from *The Letters of Mrs Gaskell*. My acknowledgements are also due to John Murray for quotations from the Knutsford edition of Elizabeth Gaskell's works, and from the Haworth edition of her *Life of Charlotte Brontë*. The Brontë Society kindly permitted me to use material from my article in *Transactions* in 1977 on 'Henry James's "The Turn of the Screw" and Mrs Gaskell's "The Old Nurse's Story"'. Finally I should like to express my sincere gratitude to the staff of the University Library, Exeter.

1 Biographical background

Elizabeth Gaskell once expressed her belief that to live an active and sympathetic life was the indispensable prelude to producing fiction which had strength and vitality in it. This was certainly true in her own case. By the time *Mary Barton* appeared in 1848, she had a wide experience of the areas of life which were to provide her major themes. Nor did literary fame prevent her from continuing to take part in the spheres of activity to which she was already committed. Neither her temperament nor her circumstances inclined her to the self-absorption which is the pleasure and the peril of a different order of genius. She was receptive to the atmosphere of her age as well as to the varied happenings which filled her busy days. Before considering the themes of her work, it is desirable to look briefly at the sources, personal and social, from which they evolved.

Her father William Stevenson, born at Berwick-on-Tweed in 1772, belonged to a naval family. By temperament, however, he was a scholar, not a sailor, though he had a hereditary love of the sea. As the family were Dissenters, Oxford and Cambridge were closed to him, but he became a divinity student at Manchester Academy and subsequently minister at the Unitarian chapel at Failsworth, near Manchester. It was while there that he met Elizabeth Holland, who belonged to a long-established Cheshire yeoman family, whom he married in 1797. He had resigned from the ministry before his marriage and was soon to begin the erratic career in which his many talents were never to find full scope. He became an experimental farmer at Laughton Mills, near Edinburgh, but the venture failed. The Stevensons moved to Edinburgh where he was private tutor, journalist and editor of the *Scots Magazine*. In 1806 the family moved to London in the hope of a brighter future, Lord Lauderdale having invited Stevenson to accompany him to India, on his appointment as Governor-General, as his private secretary. The project never materialised, as Lord Lauderdale's appointment was not confirmed by the East India Company, but he secured a post for Stevenson as Keeper of the Treasury Records, an occupation which allowed him time to contribute to many of the leading periodicals. His daughter Elizabeth was born in Chelsea in 1810, the last of eight children and, with her eldest brother, the only one to survive infancy. Her mother died thirteen months later, and an elder sister of her mother, Mrs Lumb, who lived in Knutsford in Cheshire, took the motherless infant into her care. The child was therefore brought up in a small country town, and under the aegis of the Hollands, and both facts were important for her future development.

Her deep love of the country had its roots in her early familiarity with rural Cheshire. Sandlebridge, the family home of the Hollands, four miles from Knutsford, both farm and country house, came to represent for her the epitome of pastoral peace. In Knutsford itself her aunt's house faced the open common, and Mrs Lumb kept a couple of cows, poultry, geese and ducks on the pasture behind. The child also became familiar from an early age with the pattern of life in a traditional society. In Knutsford, her 'dear adopted native town', the social hierarchy was firmly established and ensured a stable community, in which the Hollands, as a family of substantial yeoman stock, which had been fixed in the county for generations, had a recognised status.

That they were Dissenters, of Unitarian belief, no longer represented a barrier to social recognition, and their position was made more secure by the fact that they were related by marriage to some of the most important and influential Unitarian families. The Brook Street Unitarian Chapel at Knutsford, to which the young Elizabeth Stevenson was taken regularly, had been built, as we are reminded in *Ruth* (where it features as Thurstan Benson's chapel at Eccleston) 'about the time of Matthew and Philip Henry, when the Dissenters were afraid of attracting attention or observation, and hid their places of worship in obscure and out-of-the-way parts of the towns in which they were built'.[1] But the late eighteenth and early nineteenth century saw the growth and consolidation of the Unitarian movement in England. Religion, as it was presented in Brook Street, was the strongest of all the influences that moulded Elizabeth's youth. It involved a close personal knowledge of the Bible—particularly the New Testament—practical help to one's neighbour, tolerance and open-mindedness and the belief that there is in all men the spark of divinity.

Meanwhile in distant London William Stevenson married again, in 1814. There were two children of the second marriage, but his daughter Elizabeth remained in Knutsford. Her only contact with her own family was through the occasional visits and lively letters of her brother John, twelve years older than she. He entered the Merchant Navy, and it was to say goodbye to him on his departure on his first voyage that she returned to Chelsea on a visit in 1822. This first visit was followed at intervals by others, but they were never enjoyable experiences. '. . . *very, very* unhappy I used to be'[2] was her recollection of them many years later.

In the August of 1822 she left Knutsford again, this time to spend five years at boarding-school. The school chosen was at Barford in Warwickshire and later moved to Stratford. It was run on liberal lines by the Miss Byerleys, who had Unitarian connections, being related to the Wedgwoods. Her years at this school, in pleasant rural surroundings, were happy ones. She returned to Knutsford in 1827 and soon after enjoyed a holiday in Wales which initiated her into the beauties of a new type of scenery, more awe-inspiring than the pastoral.

The next year brought unexpected calamity. John Stevenson sailed for India in that summer, as he had done several times before, but he never returned from this voyage and his family never knew whether he was actually lost at sea or disappeared after landing. The traumatic effect of the loss of this loved and admired sailor brother was to be reflected in his sister's works. She returned to Chelsea because of this family tragedy and remained with her father, now in failing health, till his death from a stroke in March 1829. Her helpfulness during these difficult months was later praised by her stepmother, in a letter to her aunt Mrs Lumb.[3] But their relationship remained superficial and, after her father's death, she returned to the orbit of the Holland family.

She did not, however, return immediately to Knutsford. Two of her relatives with established positions in London society invited her to visit them, her uncle Swinton Holland, a banker with a house in Park Lane and her cousin Henry Holland, son of the Knutsford surgeon and an eminent London doctor. After a brief contact with a milieu wealthier and more sophisticated than any she had yet known, she went on a long visit to family friends at Newcastle. The impressions received during her stay with the Revd William Turner, Unitarian minister at Newcastle, and his daughter Anne are reflected in her sympathetic portrayal of the Benson household in *Ruth*. Turner's religion represented the same practical and charitable ideals as those of Brook Street Chapel and he also had the intellectual culture and interests characteristic of Unitarians, and

was active in 'every benevolent and scientific interest in the town'.[4]
His daughter Mary had married John Gooch Robberds, minister of
Cross Street Unitarian Chapel in Manchester, and Elizabeth
Stevenson accompanied Anne Turner on a visit to the Robberds in
the autumn of 1831. It was while staying with them that she met
William Gaskell, the assistant minister at Cross Street, whom she
married at Knutsford in August 1832.

William Gaskell, five years older than she, was the son of a
Warrington manufacturer. He had graduated at Glasgow
University and trained for the Unitarian ministry at Manchester
New College, then at York. He was, like William Turner,
intellectual and cultured and, like him, a tireless worker for social
causes. The marriage was based on shared ideals and in many ways
similar tastes, as well as on physical attraction. In temperament
they were very different; her fundamental seriousness was overlaid
with a charming gaiety and she was as naturally exuberant as he
was naturally grave.

After a honeymoon in Wales, they began their married life in a
house in Dover Street, conveniently near to Cross Street Chapel.
Here after the loss of a daughter, stillborn, in 1833, two children
were born: Marianne in 1834 and Margaret Emily (Meta) in 1837.
In 1842 they moved to a larger house close by in Upper Rumford
Street, where a third daughter, Florence, was born the same year
and William, the only son, in 1844. Their life was already a busy
one. William Gaskell's enthusiasm for education and social reforms
involved him in many commitments, as well as his ministerial
duties. His wife proved a most devoted mother, as well as showing
hospitality to their relatives and friends, though Mrs Lumb died in
1837. She was proud of her husband's social work and herself took
an active part in the Cross Street Chapel's Sunday and Day Schools
in Lower Mosley Street, directed by Travers Madge. Through this,
and her visits to the poor families she befriended, she gradually
came to know much of the conditions in which the Manchester
workers lived.

The city had by then come to be considered representative, more
than any other, of the social ferment caused by the industrial
revolution. The development of the cotton industry had trans-
formed it, in the latter part of the eighteenth century, into a vast
manufacturing centre and by 1831 the population had increased
almost six times in sixty years. But the growing distance between the
manufacturers and the workers led to increasing social unrest. The

1819 'massacre of Peterloo' was far from forgotten when the Gaskells settled in Manchester in 1832. In the 1830s and 1840s, the decades when Elizabeth Gaskell grew familiar by personal contact with conditions in the dingy courts and slums, there were recurrent economic depressions. The most severe of these followed the financial crisis of 1836 and, coupled with bad harvests, reached its height during the years 1839–42. Elizabeth Gaskell was appalled by the squalor and misery she saw, and Engels's descriptions are hardly grimmer than some of those she was to give in *Mary Barton*. With virtually no drainage and no pure water supply, epidemics were rife. The fever from which Davenport, one of the mill-workers in *Mary Barton*, dies, is 'of a low, putrid, typhoid kind; brought on by miserable living, filthy neighbourhood, and great depression of mind and body'.[5] The factories, no less than the slums, took their toll of health and life through excessive working hours, unguarded machinery and ill-ventilated work-rooms. Attempts at industrial legislation were still inadequate, though a series of Factory Acts, from 1833 onwards, tried to improve conditions for children, and later for women, in the mills. In their misery during the depression Manchester workers supported the Chartist movement, which hoped to secure political representation for the working classes. The 'People's Charter', which stated the aims of the movement, was published in 1838 and delegates from all parts of the country joined in presenting it to Parliament in June 1839, but Parliament refused to consider it. The rejection of the Chartist petition was to be used by Elizabeth Gaskell as the turning-point in the life of her hero in *Mary Barton*.

But Elizabeth Gaskell also knew the other side of industrial Manchester, the side probably considered most characteristic in the forties. This was the Manchester of the manufacturers and merchants, the new aristocracy of commerce. She recognised, like Engels, the extent of their power, though, unlike him, she considered the lack of communication between them and their operatives, so different from the relationship between rich and poor in the traditionalist society to which she was accustomed, as an unmitigated evil, which called urgently for redress and remedy. Some of Manchester's wealthy businessmen were known to her personally because they and their families formed a considerable part of the congregation of Cross Street Chapel. There were for example the Potters, rich calico-printers, the Schwabes, also calico-printers, who belonged to the German colony in the city and Robert and Samuel Greg, who were cotton-spinners. This wealthy congreg-ation had their philanthropic interests, but frequently their laissez-faire individualism in industry and economics was in opposition to the 'Christian interventionism' desired by Elizabeth Gaskell. The critic W. R. Greg, brother of Robert and Samuel, was to attack *Mary Barton* bitterly as unfair to the manufacturers. In some, however, she did find the concern for their workers' welfare which was ultimately to be shown by Thornton in *North and South*. Samuel Greg sincerely desired to improve their condition, though his efforts on behalf of his Bollington workers were not repaid with success in business and he became bankrupt in 1847. It was to Samuel Greg's wife that Elizabeth Gaskell was to write explaining her motives in *Mary Barton*.[6]

In this restless but dynamic atmosphere both she and her husband had many demands to meet on their time and attention, but their family life remained a happy one, never so happy, indeed, for Elizabeth Gaskell, as after the birth of her son in 1844. Her happiness was abruptly shattered when the child died of scarlet fever at the age of ten months. It was to divert her thoughts from this overwhelming sorrow that her husband suggested she should attempt to write 'a work of some length'.[7] Clearly the suggestion would not have been made if she had not already given evidence of her literary ability. She had kept a private diary of the first years of her two elder children and no doubt written short stories like 'The Doom of the Griffiths', begun, on her own admission, when her first child was a baby though not published till much later.[8] But in 1845 only two of her writings had been published, a poem in collabor-ation with her husband—the first and only example of a projected series 'Sketches among the Poor'—and an account of her visit as a schoolgirl to Clopton House, included by William Howitt in his *Visits to Remarkable Places* in 1840. She may also have composed by this time the three short stories that appeared in *Howitt's Journal* in 1847 and 1848 under the pseudonym 'Cotton Mather Mills'—'Libbie Marsh's Three Eras', 'The Sexton's Hero' and 'Christmas Storms and Sunshine'. But she did not give the full measure of her capacities till she began work, probably in the last months of 1845, on the full-length novel that appeared in 1848 with the title *Mary Barton: A Tale of Manchester Life*.

In *Mary Barton* she did not so much escape from her own sorrow as identify herself with the sorrows of the working poor of Manchester. The result was a work of compelling power, if uneven construction.

It aroused anger among some of the Manchester mill-owners, but at once reached a wider public and made of her a well-known writer instead of an anonymous one. It also introduced her, on her visit to London in 1849, to the literary society of her day. Though too well-balanced to be spoiled by 'lionising', she enjoyed the hospitality lavished on her, including a dinner given by Dickens. The contact with Dickens helped to establish her as a writer, for she became a frequent contributor to his new weekly journal, *Household Words*, when it began to appear in 1850.

1850 was another landmark in the history of the Gaskells, for it saw their establishment in the house in Plymouth Grove that was to become a centre of hospitality and cultural life in Manchester. There were now four daughters, for another child, Julia, had been born in 1846. In addition to the care of her growing family, Elizabeth Gaskell now had the entertainment of frequent guests to occupy her, as well as her writing. But she had not lost her concern for the victims of the industrial society, and it was this that provided the starting-point for her next novel *Ruth*.

Among the occupations open to working women, that of seamstress was one of the worst paid and worst organised. The most wretched were those working at home but, in spite of the efforts of Lord Ashley, those who were apprenticed to dressmakers often fared little better. The conditions frequently amounted to sweated labour of the worst kind and, because of the starvation wages, dressmaking was one of the trades often associated with prostitution. The plight of a sixteen-year-old dressmaker's apprentice, seduced, abandoned and imprisoned for theft, whom she visited at the request of her friend Thomas Wright, the prison philanthropist,[9] suggested to Elizabeth Gaskell the first chapters of *Ruth*. The book is, however, chiefly concerned with the moral recovery and social reintegration of the heroine and develops into a powerful plea for a more compassionate attitude to the unmarried mother and her child. Its reception, when published in 1853, was even more hostile than the author had feared but its admirers included Dickens, Kingsley, Mrs Browning and Florence Nightingale.

By now Elizabeth Gaskell was also contributing stories and sketches to *Household Words*. The setting of these was by no means limited to the industrial city, being as often Wales or Cumbria or Silverdale on Morecambe Bay, the Gaskells' favourite country home. Knutsford reappeared as Combehurst of 'The Moorland Cottage', Duncombe of 'Mr Harrison's Confessions' and, above all, in *Cranford*, serialised in *Household Words* before appearing in book form in 1853, when it aroused no such hostile reactions as its controversial predecessors.

In *North and South*, also serialised in *Household Words* before publication in 1855, Elizabeth Gaskell returned to the industrial scene, this time allowing both master and workers to state their case. The period of the action was more or less contemporary. By the 1850s Chartism was no longer the same active force, and the Public Health Act of 1848 and the Factory Act of 1850 had done something to improve conditions for the workers. Yet they remained grim enough. Bessy Higgins dies of tuberculosis contracted in the ill-ventilated carding-room, where the air was full of cotton fluff. Relations between masters and workers are still stormy, and strikes sufficiently frequent for Bessy to have seen three in the course of her short life. Elizabeth Gaskell does not gloss over the problems of the industrialist society, even though she now allows more scope to the forces of conciliation. Her second industrial novel met with general approval, even from W. R. Greg, the most severe censor of *Mary Barton*.

Its completion left its author temporarily exhausted, but writing was now part of the pattern of her life. She did not allow it to interfere with her care of her family or her contacts with an ever widening circle of friends and acquaintances. These included the Nightingales, F. D. Maurice, Kingsley, John Forster, the Arnolds and the Kay-Shuttleworths. It was on a visit to the Kay-Shuttleworths that she met Charlotte Brontë in 1850 and their close friendship began. Charlotte visited her in Manchester in 1851—the year of the Great Exhibition—and in 1853, and Elizabeth Gaskell visited Haworth in September of the same year. Charlotte came again to Manchester shortly before her marriage in 1854. It was their last meeting, for she died in 1855.

The news caused Elizabeth Gaskell deep sorrow and when Mr Brontë asked her to write the official biography of her friend, she at once agreed. Characteristically she thought of it as a portrait of the woman, of which the development of the artist was only a part. Her biography, inspired by true friendship as well as admiration, was universally praised on its appearance in March 1857. Unfortunately she had allowed her indignation on Charlotte's behalf to outrun caution in speaking of the woman—transparently alluded to though not named—whom she held responsible for Branwell's downfall. The consequence soon became apparent with the threat of legal action from the solicitors of the former Mrs Robinson, now Lady Scott. There were also protests from the Carus-Wilsons about Cowan Bridge, and from a number of others, though Mr Brontë, whose eccentricities she had exaggerated on insufficient evidence, took it in good part, only asking for the most obvious exaggerations to be omitted from the next edition. A second edition was in fact out, but it had to be withdrawn by the publisher, George Smith, and a third, amended, version got ready. Elizabeth Gaskell, on holiday in Italy when the biography appeared, returned to be greeted with an avalanche of bad news which both wounded and exasperated her, but did not shake her belief that she had come as near the truth as it was possible to do.

The tensions of an exceptionally busy life had by this time made more frequent periods of change and relaxation a necessity. Holidays abroad played an increasing part in her life. In 1854 she began her close friendship with the Parisian hostess Mme Mohl, at whose flat in the Rue du Bac she first stayed in 1855. Mme Mohl was English by birth but had lived in France since childhood and had married the Orientalist Julius Mohl. Though she was a declared Orleanist, her salon retained its popularity after the re-establishment of the Empire in 1852. Among its habitués were Guizot, Montalembert, Victor Cousin and Geoffroy St Hilaire, son of the great naturalist. Thanks to her friendship with Mme Mohl, Elizabeth Gaskell gained a more intimate understanding of France than of the other countries she visited.

None of her trips abroad, however, rivalled in sheer enjoyment her visit to Italy, with her two elder daughters, in 1857. Financed by advance royalties from *The Life of Charlotte Brontë* and in happy ignorance of troubles ahead, she and her two elder daughters passed there an idyllic two months. Her pleasure was increased by finding herself in an environment of artists. Her hosts were the American sculptor William Wetmore Story and his wife, and the Storys' friend Charles Eliot Norton, later professor of the history of art at Harvard, proved the ideal guide to the art treasures of Rome. Norton was already an admirer of her books and, though he was sixteen years younger than she, their congeniality of taste and temperament was the foundation of a lasting friendship. He visited the Gaskells in Manchester before returning to America, and the friendship was continued by correspondence till her death.

On her return from Italy Elizabeth Gaskell found other problems as well as the revision of her biography awaiting her. The Art

Exhibition held in Manchester that year—a sequel to the Great Exhibition of 1851—attracted visitors from all quarters and even her hospitable nature was daunted by the influx of guests at Plymouth Grove. Circumstances were not propitious for another full-length novel and *My Lady Ludlow*, serialised in *Household Words* during 1858, is a sequence of episodes rather than a novel. It was published in 1859 as the first part of a two-volume collection *Round the Sofa*. The other volume was made up of five tales, three of which had previously appeared in *Household Words*. The whole was given a rather artificial unity by an introductory sketch of an Edinburgh drawing-room where story-telling is part of the entertainment, the various tales being ascribed to the hostess, herself the narrator of *My Lady Ludlow*, and others of the guests. The Edinburgh background owed something to the author's memories of staying there in her youth with Anne Turner and to her friendship with Mrs Fletcher, once a noted Edinburgh hostess, who had entertained her parents.

A visit to Germany in 1858, spent chiefly in Heidelberg, had not the same ecstatic quality of discovery as the visit to Rome, for she had visited Heidelberg already, with her husband, in 1841. This visit was in fact undertaken to provide a change of scene for her second daughter, Meta, who had recently broken off her engagement to an army officer. But, as always, she was intensely sensitive to landscape and atmosphere, and her knowledge of Germany (which she visited again in 1860) was to be reflected in the stories 'The Grey Woman' and 'Six Weeks at Heppenheim'.

Not till 1859 did she begin another full-length novel, *Sylvia's Lovers*. She chose the closing years of the eighteenth century for the period of the action and North Yorkshire for its location. She visited Whitby in the autumn of 1859, but she was no stranger to the north-east coast after the months spent in Newcastle in her youth. For the life of the whaling-port and the activities of the press-gang she could consult a still living tradition as well as documentary sources. When *Sylvia's Lovers* eventually appeared in 1863, the book had a mixed reception, but some discerned its epic quality and it has been increasingly appreciated, both as a historical novel of stature and one of Elizabeth Gaskell's richest works.

The delay in finishing *Sylvia's Lovers* was chiefly due to the busy life she continued to lead, though during the years 1859–63 she also published several tales in Dickens' *All the Year Round* and George Smith's *Cornhill Magazine*. They included 'Lois the Witch', a powerful tale of a witch-hunt in seventeenth-century New England,

and 'A Dark Night's Work', in which, with the exception of the Roman episode, the scene is set in small-town society in rural England. In the spring of 1862 she and her daughter Meta had a holiday in France, intended to provide material for a book on the life and times of Mme de Sévigné, which unfortunately was never written. But in the autumn and winter of that year the social distress caused among the workers of Manchester by the effects of the American Civil War on the cotton mills became the major concern of herself and her family, taking precedence over everything else. This time of acute strain was followed, in 1863, by another visit to France, and to Italy. Recent memories of France were to inspire the sketches which make up 'French Life'. In September 1863, the marriage of Florence, the Gaskells' third daughter, to Charles Crompton, a barrister, took place and the following year saw the engagement of Marianne, the eldest, to her second cousin Thurstan Holland.

The serialisation in the *Cornhill Magazine* of the prose idyll *Cousin Phillis* from 1863 to 1864 marked Elizabeth Gaskell's return in imagination to the farm of Sandlebridge, near Knutsford, the Arcadia of her youth. It was to Knutsford itself that her thoughts turned when she planned to write the 'story of country-town life 40 years ago'[10] which became *Wives and Daughters*. It began to be serialised in the *Cornhill* in August 1864. Its underlying serenity shows no trace of the physical exhaustion which was becoming increasingly evident in its author. Part of the novel was written abroad, at Pontresina in Switzerland and in Paris. But, tired as she was, Elizabeth Gaskell gave much of her energy at the same time to realising her project of buying a house in the country to be a home for her husband in his retirement—though he was not yet to know of the plan—and for her unmarried daughters. A house was found, in the village of Holybourne near Alton in Hampshire. Her intention was to furnish it and let it to tenants for a few preliminary years. By October the house was ready for occupation, thanks to the help of her daughters, and she went there with Meta and Julia for a short visit. They were joined by Florence and her husband, while Marianne remained in Manchester. Elizabeth Gaskell was still working on her novel, but only the last instalment remained to be written when she died suddenly, on Sunday 12 November 1865. The country home was never to be occupied by the Gaskells, but everything it stood for is perpetuated in *Wives and Daughters*.

Elizabeth Gaskell's was an exceptionally rich nature. She once

spoke in a letter of the different 'selves' within her: the 'true
Christian (only people call her socialist and communist)',[11] the wife
and mother, the lover of beauty. She could not have tolerated an
existence which suppressed any one of them, but she did not manage
to 'reconcile all these warring members' without cost to herself. It
was not that she felt there was any basic incompatibility between
them. She believed, like her husband, not in a religion that was
gloomy and oppressive but in one which was, by definition, 'a
constant presence of comfort and joy'.[12] It enjoined neither celibacy
nor the suppression of her gift as a creative artist. Art, like marriage
and motherhood, was at its best a sharing of the personality with
others. But she always put real people before fictional ones. At
Plymouth Grove she had no study of her own: her writing was done
in the family dining-room with its three doors, where she was
constantly called upon to attend to the needs of her children and the
household in general. Vital as she was, however, and gifted with a
natural ease in writing as in speech, she became increasingly
conscious of the limitations of her strength, as well as of her time.
Changes of scene and air became a necessity, but she was usually
accompanied by her family, when away from Manchester. They
remained her constant concern, though she also managed to show
understanding and sympathy to a wide circle of friends, the most
intimate of whom, like the Winkworths, Eliza Fox and later
Charlotte Brontë, she treated almost as younger sisters.

She was unquestionably successful in her relationship with her
children, whom she passionately loved, and who found in her a
mother, a companion and a friend. Her surviving letters, the
majority of which are to her daughter Marianne, bear witness to her
understanding of them at each stage of their development and her
respect for them as individuals. No letters to her husband survive
but her references to him in her correspondence, especially to her
sister-in-law Nancy Robson, convey the idea of a marriage securely
based on deep mutual affection, though not immune from the
occasional misunderstanding inevitable between two extremely
busy people of contrasting temperament. There was nothing of the
domestic tyrant about William Gaskell. He was devoted to his
children, if not usually demonstrative towards them, and both fond
and proud of his wife. But by the time she established herself as a
writer, he was becoming one of the outstanding figures in ministerial
and academic as well as philanthropic circles in Manchester.
Lecturer at the new Owen's College, opened in 1851, as well as at

Mechanics' Institutes, lecturer on the staff of the Unitarian Home Missionary Board, founded in 1854, senior minister of Cross Street Chapel in 1855, editor of the *Unitarian Herald* from 1861, serving on committees for sanitary reform as well as popular education, he was ceaselessly occupied when away from home and, when there, frequently sought the peace of his study. He was not naturally gregarious and did not welcome constant guests as much as his wife, though he did not oppose her in her hospitality. When it came to holidays, however, though sharing the family affection for Silverdale, he preferred, instead of accompanying his wife and daughters on their journeys further afield, to remain independent and, unlike them, rarely went abroad, though he was once persuaded to visit the Storys in Italy.

He was not opposed to his wife's writing, which he had indeed encouraged in the first place, rightly believing that she would find comfort in this way after their son's death. He did not attempt to control her earnings, though he has been accused of doing so on account of her humorous reference to the £20 cheque for 'Lizzie Leigh' which he 'buttoned up in his pocket', a fact explained by her having, as a married woman, no bank account of her own. The continental holidays she was able to afford for herself and her daughters testify to her economic independence. But though the reverse of a domineering husband, he did intervene on her behalf when he felt her interest demanded it: he persuaded her to control her grief at the hostile reception of *Ruth*, he intervened in the controversial correspondence with Dickens over the serialisation of *North and South* and, during her absence in Italy, took immediate action to deal with the threat of court proceedings after the publication of *The Life of Charlotte Brontë*. Elizabeth Gaskell herself knew her husband's worth. She constantly thought of his welfare and happiness. She praised his kindness, and his goodness to his children, in conversation with Charlotte Brontë, after twenty-two years of marriage, and, two years before her death, dedicated *Sylvia's Lovers* to 'My dear husband, by her who best knows his value'. After her death the family in which her deepest affections had centred remained a united one. She would probably have desired no better memorial, though it was not only her family who mourned her loss. In her husband's words, she was 'widely honoured for her genius and the spirit in which it was exercised'.

2 The natural scene

Elizabeth Gaskell's works most often have their inception in an Arcadia which is either real or nostalgically remembered. Even *Mary Barton* begins with an excursion to Green Heys Fields, and all the sombreness of the succeeding action in industrial Manchester cannot quite obliterate the memory of that May afternoon. The countrybred heroine of *Ruth*, first seen as a dressmaker's apprentice in a decayed urban setting, chooses to sit where she can look at the flowers painted on the panels of a once beautiful room. Such beginnings were natural to Elizabeth Gaskell because her earliest recollections were of such an Arcadia and because it continued to represent, throughout her life, the most satisfying form of existence that she knew.

Biographers have made us familiar with the pastoral setting of her childhood: her aunt's house on the edge of the heath at Knutsford, Church House with its secluded garden, the home of her uncle the Knutsford surgeon, Sandlebridge, her grandfather's farm, and the rich countryside that enfolds them all. It was a countryside where her mother's family, the Hollands, had lived for generations. Sandlebridge, which had belonged to the Hollands since 1718, represented a way of life which was not that of the rich landowner but of the substantial yeoman farming his own land. This was the way of life which Elizabeth unconsciously absorbed in childhood as the norm of a satisfying existence. Later it was what she desired for her own children, and she tried to find some kind of substitute for a country childhood in the unpropitious environment of Manchester. She was thankful that they could see cows milked and hay made in summer in the fields near their Manchester home in Upper Rumford Street, 'the last house countrywards of an interminably long street'.[1] When the family moved to Plymouth Grove, they were at least some degrees nearer to what was for her the only natural environment, for the house stood in what was then almost a country district, on the outskirts of the city. It had its flowerbeds and its kitchen garden, and in the adjoining field, which they rented, its mistress kept her cow, pigs and poultry, as her aunt had done behind the house facing the heath at Knutsford.

The central position of the yeoman farmer in Elizabeth Gaskell's Arcadia had important consequences for her work. Her most sympathetic presentations of country life are based on the small farm which is a busy and usually a thriving world of its own. The Hope Farm of *Cousin Phillis*, considered to be founded on Sandlebridge, is the most idyllic example. The Woodley of *Cranford* belongs to the same category. Not all examples, however, stem from the same locality. In the 'statesman' of Cumberland and Westmoreland Elizabeth Gaskell recognised the compeer of the yeoman farmer. It is by the invitation of a 'statesman' that she and her family are privileged to witness the idyll described in 'Cumberland Sheep-Shearers', and a 'stateswoman' is the leading character in the more sombre 'Half a Lifetime Ago'. *Sylvia's Lovers*, which contains many of her most unforgettable pictures of life on a small farm, is set in North Yorkshire. In this case, however, the farmer, who has been a sailor, is tenant, not owner, a fact which means less security for his family, though they feel Haytersbank to be their home.

There is nothing vague about the pattern of daily life in this small agricultural community. Elizabeth Gaskell knew the routine of the harvest field or the dairy as Constable knew each detail of the hay wain or the barges on the Stour. *Cousin Phillis* gives a spectrum of the activities of Hope Farm from haymaking to apple gathering. The master of the farm is up at three in the morning, and his daughter enlightens her town-bred cousin as to all the tasks that have to be attended to before the early breakfast. In the Westmoreland farm of 'Half a Lifetime Ago' the breeding and rearing of sheep and cattle is the first consideration, but the daily routine is equally strenuous. 'Cumberland Sheep-Shearers', a delightful account of a visit on a July day to a farm on the high fells near Derwentwater, is also a microcosm of the pastoral world. The farm on its rocky ledge far above the lake, the toil and expertise of the sheep-shearers, the lavish Lakeland hospitality are caught with a clarity of detail and vividness of touch which show an intimate knowledge of the rural scene. But the description does not end with the festivities of the July day; the master of the farm is persuaded to discuss his methods and problems, and finally the conversation widens to embrace the whole cycle of the shepherd's year, from early spring when the ewes are brought down from the high fells to the home pastures until, with the end of another winter, 'the Shepherd's Calender works round to yeaning time again!'[2]

In the life of the farm women play an active and competent part. Phillis and Sylvia are as much at home in a pastoral world as the bearers of such names should be. Phillis leads the farm servants in the hayfield; Sylvia runs out into the fields to bring up the cows. The countrywomen of the short stories and sketches are equally able to share in the field work and Susan Dixon of 'Half a Lifetime Ago', when forced by circumstances to run the family farm herself, proves fully capable of meeting the challenge. But it is in the dairy or the poultry-yard or at work on household tasks that the women are most frequently found, and it is their presence and busy domesticity which give colour and warmth to the interiors of Hope Farm or Haytersbank, Yew Nook or Nab-End. Sylvia never appears more enchanting than when seated at her spinning-wheel, or pouring the new milk into the shining cans in the chill of the dairy. Bessy, the farmer's loyal niece in 'The Crooked Branch', excels at butter-making though, like the rest, she can put her hand to anything, if need arises, and 'would either do field-work, or attend to the cows and the shippon, or churn, or make cheese; she did all well . . .'[3]

The farm interiors come convincingly to life in the many descriptions which show Elizabeth Gaskell's obvious delight in their comfort, their picturesqueness and their inherent dignity. She was herself a 'notable' housewife, and her distaste of the slovenly housekeeping of Sylvia's neighbours the Corneys at Moss Brow is as marked as her approval of the immaculate interior of Haytersbank. She reminded an inexperienced young housewife, inclined to be scornful of 'the various household arts', that 'there is plenty of poetry and association about them—remember how the Greek princesses in Homer washed the clothes . . .'[4] There is both poetry and patriarchal dignity in the 'house-place' she so often describes, where the light from the hospitable fireplace shines on the oak dresser and the polished pewter, and the small diamond panes of the windows glitter with cleanliness. The country fare contributes to the general atmosphere of warmth and comfort. Sylvia's mother, a Cumberland woman, always has a store of 'clap-bread' and flitches of bacon, and the honoured guest is regaled with 'turf-cakes' and 'singing hinnies'. Christmas and New Year are occasions for feasting on a grand scale, and so are events like the sheep-shearing on the farm above Derwentwater where, after a liberal Dale tea-drinking for the women and children, a still more substantial meal is prepared for those who have taken part in the 'rural Olympics'.

Animals play an important part in the life of the community. When Sylvia leaves the farm to live in the town of Monkshaven, she misses their familiar presence: 'She sometimes thought to herself that it was a strange kind of life, where there were no outdoor animals to look after; "the ox and the ass" had hitherto come into all her ideas of humanity . . .'⁵ For Phillis the inhabitants of the poultry-yard have personalities of their own: '. . . she showed me the hens that were good mothers, and told me the characters of all the poultry with the utmost good-faith; and in all good-faith I listened, for I believe that there was a great deal of truth in all she said.'⁶ At Haytersbank Farmer Robson's Lassie is a sort of dumb confidante to her master. At Hope Farm old Rover is both confidant and comforter to Phillis. Equally convincing is the less fortunate sheepdog Lassie in 'The Half-Brothers' who belongs to the farmer's unloved stepson and is habitually kicked for that reason. When the farmer's own son is lost in a snowstorm on the fells, his half-brother goes in search of him, but it is Lassie who guides him to the right spot. This time the dog is welcomed by the half-frozen boy who has never shown her kindness before: 'It was Lassie's bark! . . . Another moment, and the great white-faced Lassie was curving and gambolling with delight round my feet and legs, looking, however, up in my face with her intelligent, apprehensive eyes, as if fearing lest I might greet her with a blow, as I had done oftentimes before.'⁷ It is no accident that, where the normal good relations do not exist between the members of the farmer's family, the animals should suffer in the prevalent disharmony. But such unhappy conditions are the exception in the farmsteads described by Elizabeth Gaskell.

In these small agricultural communities there is no artificial distinction of class. The farmer and his wife naturally take precedence, but all are bound together by their common interests and duties, and there is no social barrier between master and men. During meal-times at Hope Farm the door is usually left open between the 'house-place' and the kitchen, and Holman talks to the men and maids as much as to his wife and daughter. At Haytersbank Kester eats with the family, helping himself from the same central dish; his master treats him with 'the rough kindness of fellowship', his mistress with generosity and consideration. In such a community something like an extended family relationship unites all the members. Even a thoroughly incompetent labourer, whom Holman has been driven to dismiss because of the damage he does, shows deep concern when his master's daughter is seriously ill, and is reinstated on that account. Kester shows an almost paternal concern for Sylvia, and gives her shrewd advice, and it is part of the tragedy of Ruth that she would not have lacked help at a critical juncture, had she taken refuge, as instinct warned her to do, at her former home of Milham Grange, where her father's old farm servant and his wife were still living.

It was this kind of pastoral existence, of which *Cousin Phillis* offers the most finished example, which recalled to Mrs Gaskell the happy memories of her youth, and with which she re-established contact whenever she could. She was never happier than when revisiting the Holland farm at Sandlebridge after her marriage and watching her little daughter's delight in the milieu so familiar to herself: 'Baby is at the very tip-top of bliss . . . There are chickens, and little childish pigs, and cows and calves and horses, and *baby-horses*, and fish in the pond, and ducks in the lane, and the mill and the smithy, and sheep and baby-sheep, and flowers . . .'[8]

None the less, she does not paint a scene of unrealistic perfection. She mentioned Crabbe as part inspirer of her first poetic 'sketch' of an old countrywoman in exile, which she wrote in collaboration with her husband. Although she aimed at 'a more seeing-beauty spirit' than the author of *The Village*, she never distorted facts or allowed her country scenes to become blurred by a golden haze of unreality. Her agricultural settings belong chiefly to the northern counties of England, which suffered less than the southern in the depression which followed the end of the Napoleonic Wars, and she is concerned with the farmstead rather than with the labourer's cottage. It would therefore have been in general unrealistic for her to have described rural life in the accusing terms of Kingsley or Disraeli, but she knows that it can be darkly shadowed. In *North and South* Margaret Hale discourages the factory worker Higgins in no uncertain terms from migrating to the South and attempting to earn his living as a hired labourer. Lady Ludlow is shocked when she sees at firsthand the conditions in the squatters' cottages on Hareman's Common. But the farmers and feudal tenants of her tales are in a more favoured position. Nevertheless they have their problems, which she does not attempt to minimise; there are poor harvests, pests which infect the flocks and economic problems. There do not appear to be any pressing financial worries at Hope Farm, but all are not equally fortunate. Daniel Robson is unable to leave his widow and daughter adequately provided for. Nathan Huntroyd, who has the small dairy farm of Nab-End, lives, like Wordsworth's Michael—with whom he has been compared—to see the security of his old age undermined by a dissolute son. Above all, Elizabeth Gaskell shows her realism in the recognition that the human factor operates in Arcadia as surely as it does elsewhere. An ineffectual man like Ruth's father cannot hope for success as a farmer, nor can an unpractical one like the narrator's father in 'My French Master', whose wife derives positive satisfaction from the small scale of his operations, reflecting to herself: 'If on twelve acres he manages to lose a hundred pounds a year, what would our loss be on a hundred and fifty?'[9] A selfish lover destroys the peace of Yew Nook in 'Half a Lifetime Ago', and a thoughtless one almost shatters the stability of life at Hope Farm. Far more tragically, Daniel Robson, who has succeeded as a farmer while remaining a sailor at heart, ends by sacrificing his farm, his family and his own life to his obsessive hatred of the press-gang.

Yet Arcadia retains its essential qualities; the farmstead still stands guardian of peace and beauty. The reason lies partly in the beauty of nature herself, partly also in the hardy response of these countryfolk to misfortune: farm work goes on, family loyalties endure, in some form life begins again. *Cousin Phillis*, the most mature study of the pastoral milieu, subsumes the qualities which Elizabeth Gaskell most admires in it. Life in such a milieu ensures, when it is successful, the co-operation of man with the healthful activity of nature. There is a symbolic rightness about Edward Holdsworth's desire to paint the daughter of Hope Farm as Ceres. The farmer's task of collaborating with nature in the feeding of the human family seemed an essentially satisfying one to Elizabeth Gaskell. The fact it called for arduous labour, carefully planned ahead, made it all the more valuable in her eyes. She distrusted idle dreaming and abstract speculation and the farmer has no time for either. If Holman does snatch time to dip into Virgil's *Georgics* it is not only for the beauty of his 'enduring epithets' but because Virgil understands agriculture and his shrewd advice to the farmer is still 'living truth'. But just as the *Georgics* are more than an agricultural treatise, so the country life at its best produces not only harvests but virtues like patience, loyalty, generosity and the contentment that comes from belonging to a community safely rooted in the friendly earth.

This patriarchal setting is not, however, the whole of the country world, though it is the friendliest and most intimate part of it. The squire's hall and the nobleman's mansion, in their ancestral acres, were also part of Elizabeth Gaskell's memories. Her earliest published writing, under her own name, was a description of Clopton House, visited during her schooldays in Warwickshire. Adjoining Knutsford itself were the broad acres of Tatton Park, and in the neighbourhood was Tabley, the old house with a moat within a park which was the goal of many holiday outings in her youth. The country landscape of *Wives and Daughters* has its stately home, Cumnor Towers, and its old manor-house, Hamley Hall, while in *My Lady Ludlow*, which has a Warwickshire setting, the action centres round the life of Hanbury Court.

Inevitably there is not as close a contact between the owner of the great house and the countryside as there is in the case of the yeoman farmer. In *My Lady Ludlow*, where the action takes place at the turn of the century, the great lady prides herself on her superintendence of her own estate, but she actually sees it chiefly from the interior of her coach and four, though her tenants are able to come to see her, at an appointed time each week, dressed in their Sunday clothes. When the old steward dies, his successor tells her bluntly that the land is in a poor state, and that more modern methods of agriculture must be introduced. The Cumnors and the Hamleys of *Wives and Daughters*, who belong to the first half of the nineteenth century, are more enlightened and recognise the importance of up-to-date methods on their land. But it is only the wealthy Earl of Cumnor who can afford to employ them. Squire Hamley tries to take advantage of the new methods of drainage on his land, with the help of a government loan, but cannot afford to continue the work. Both landowners are genuinely interested in the welfare of their estate, but Hamley in his 'old red-brick hall', which is approached not through a deer-park but through 'meadow-grass, ripening for hay', is in closer touch with the country scene than his richer and more influential neighbour. Hamley farms the land which has belonged to his family since the Heptarchy, prizes his woods and fields for themselves and personally supervises his labourers. Lord Cumnor likes to 'potter' round his estate and among his tenantry, but for much of the year he is not there to do so and the authority is vested in his agent.

The pastoral milieu, with the farm house at its centre and the manor-house somewhere on the horizon, among its ancestral trees, is what most appeals to Elizabeth Gaskell in the natural scene. So successful are her reconstructions of this milieu, so deep her penetration of its essential qualities that there is a danger of forgetting that her treatment of the natural setting is not limited to this rural Arcadia, though it was her starting-point and always remained the haven to which she periodically returned, both in her life and her art, for rest and renewal.

In *Ruth* the first sight of the Welsh mountains means 'opening a new sense'[10] for the heroine, at first almost overpowered by their grandeur. They made a similar impression on Elizabeth Gaskell when she first visited Wales at the end of her schooldays and she remembered how, on her return, she used to climb to a spot from which she 'could see the Welsh hills, and think of the places beyond again'.[11] The Welsh landscape remained familiar to her, for she frequently visited her uncle Samuel Holland at his home, 'Plas Penrhyn', on Portmadoc estuary. It was intimately associated with her personal life, for it was in North Wales that she and her husband spent their honeymoon and, thirteen years later, it was at Festiniog, where they had been on their honeymoon, that their eldest daughter caught scarlet fever and at Portmadoc, where she had been taken to convalesce, that the Gaskells' ten-month-old only son died of the same disease. The double memory of happiness and tragedy seems to permeate Mrs Gaskell's reconstructions of the Welsh mountain setting. In the early story 'The Well of Pen-Morfa' the beautiful Nest Gwynn looks forward to becoming mistress of a farm under the shadow of the mountains, but is crippled for life by an accident. Misfortune pursues the ill-fated heir in 'The Doom of the Griffiths', who lives in a wild valley running down from the mountains to Tremadoc Bay. The finest descriptions of mountain scenery, and the most abrupt transition from joy to despair, are found in the early chapters of *Ruth*, where the heroine is abandoned by her lover in a Welsh village reminiscent of Festiniog. It is, on her own admission, not of Ruth but of her personal memories that the author is thinking when she describes the room at the inn, with its magnificent view, into which Ruth is led by her lover, 'a large bow-windowed room, which looked gloomy enough that afternoon, but which I have seen bright and buoyant with youth and hope within, and sunny lights creeping down the purple mountain slope, and stealing over the green, soft meadows, till they reached the little garden, full of roses and lavender-bushes, lying close under the window. I have seen— but I shall see no more'.[12]

It was not only from the Welsh hills that Elizabeth Gaskell derived a firsthand knowledge of the wilder and grander aspects of nature. She and her family often went on holiday to North Lancashire and the Lake District and sometimes into Yorkshire, and the Cumbrian fells and the Yorkshire moors made their contribution to the rich store of memories she amassed through her penetrating observation and her keen sensibility to natural beauty. The Lakeland farms with their bustle of rural activity and their hospitable interiors made an irresistible appeal to her, and were part of her Arcadia. She loved to walk over the fells that rose behind them. They make an attractive background to the busy scene in the 'Cumberland Sheep-Shearers', where their austerity is softened by the summer warmth. In general, however, her tales show the fells in their bleak winter aspect; they are the scene of disaster in 'The Half-Brothers' and they form a grim background to the haunting in 'The Old Nurse's Story'. Her pictures of moorland life also suggest as a rule an awe-inspiring but inhospitable environment. 'The Moorland Cottage', in spite of its title, belongs to Arcadia: on one side of the cottage is the open moor, but on the other is a common not unlike the heath at Knutsford, and only a few miles separate it from a friendly little market town. But in the *Life of Charlotte Brontë* the grey-stone parsonage and the village are dominated by the moors and it is the sombre impression which Mrs Gaskell received on first approaching Haworth from Keighley which continues to colour her view of them, 'wild bleak moors—grand from the ideas of solitude and loneliness which they suggest, or oppressive from the feeling which they give of being pent up by some monotonous and illimitable barrier, according to the mood of mind in which the spectator may be'.[13] She knew that the heather could become for a brief spell the 'blaze of purple glory' Emily Brontë loved, but when she paid her visit to the parsonage it had been blighted by a thunderstorm and her memory of the moors remained a sombre one: 'Oh! those high, wild, desolate moors, up above the whole world, and the very realms of silence!'[14] The same idea of desolation is given by the description of the barren hinterland in *Sylvia's Lovers*, 'wild, bleak moors, that shut in Monkshaven almost as effectually on the land side as ever the waters did on the sea-board'.[15] The overall impression of sombreness given by these fell and moorland settings cannot be ascribed, as in the case of the Welsh mountains, to memories of personal sorrow. It seems rather that though Elizabeth Gaskell, with her acute sensibility, felt to the full their picturesque qualities, she instinctively preferred a fertile countryside which bears the visible impress of man's collaboration with nature in its very shape, in hedges and lanes, meadows alternating with cornfields, prosperous farms and stately manors.

She appears more truly exhilerated in the presence of a more untameable element, the sea. Hereditary influence had something to do with this. On her father's side she came of a sea-faring family; her grandfather, a native of Berwick-on-Tweed, and two of her uncles were naval officers and her only brother was in the merchant service till his mysterious disappearance in 1828. Her father shared the family affection for the sea; while holding the post of Keeper of the Records at the Treasury he published in 1824 an important work, *The Historical Sketch of Discovery, Navigation and Commerce*. His daughter came to know the sea first through her holidays in North Wales, and wrote nostalgically from Manchester: 'I *long* to be in those wild places again, with the fresh sea breeze round me . . .'[16] Her visits before her marriage to Newcastle and Edinburgh brought her into contact with the bleaker north-east coast, which she saw again when she visited Whitby. After her marriage she often spent holidays with her family on the shores of Morecambe Bay, especially at their favourite Silverdale.

For her, however, the sea is seen primarily from the shore. On the rare occasions when the action moves from shore to open sea, as in the melodramatic dénouement to 'The Moorland Cottage', the scene is less convincing. Far more effective is the account in *Mary Barton* of the chase by a river boat down the Mersey in pursuit of a passenger aboard a ship about to sail, but the boat returns to the quayside once its task is accomplished. The wider horizons of the sailor's world are suggested, none the less, at one remove from reality, through the medium of travellers' tales. If Elizabeth Gaskell did not herself know life at sea, she did know sailors. She had talked in her youth with characters like old Captain Barton in Anglesey and a man who had fought on the *Victory* with Nelson.[17] She was personally acquainted with the former captain of a Greenland whaler, later vicar of Bradford, Dr Scoresby, whose published account of the northern whale fisheries helped to provide material for the nautical background in *Sylvia's Lovers*.[18] Most of all she was inspired and haunted by the memory of her own lost sailor brother. The tales of Will Wilson in *Mary Barton*, of Daniel Robson and Charlie Kinraid in *Sylvia's Lovers* suggest an unknown and fascinating world to fireside listeners. Sylvia is at first almost as much in love with visions of the icy Greenland seas as she is with Kinraid himself.

But it is the seacoast which she knows at first hand and which is the setting of some of her most dramatic episodes. In 'The Sexton's Hero' the sands of Morecambe Bay bring tragedy to belated travellers overtaken by the swift incoming tide. The sea-shore is the place of decision in *Ruth*, where Abermouth sands, at the turn of the tide, are the fitting stage for the climactic scene. It features again in a brief interlude in *North and South* where the transition from their southern home is temporarily softened, for the Hale family, by a few days in a little northern watering-place where they can watch 'the great long misty sea-line touching the tender-coloured sky'. Above all in *Sylvia's Lovers* it becomes at intervals the arena of the principal action, and at no time can the reader forget the proximity of the sea.

It is noticeable, however, that in her work Elizabeth Gaskell rarely seems to disassociate the maritime element completely from the pastoral. She herself, when mentioning to a friend the family's 'annual migration to the sea-side', immediately added: 'Silverdale can hardly be called the sea-side, as it is a little dale running down to Morecambe Bay. . . . And we are keeping holiday in most rural farm-house lodgings, so that our children learn country interests, and ways of living and thinking.'[19] In *Sylvia's Lovers*, her one full-scale presentation of a sea-faring community, the whale fishers of Monkshaven certainly pass the most adventurous part of their lives at sea, but from October to March they are ashore, involved in the winter activity in the melting-sheds. The whole town has an 'amphibious appearance', and if 'in this country sea-thoughts followed the thinker far inland', it is equally true that the farms on the cliffs are as indispensable as the whale fishing to the total life of the community. Daniel Robson is a sailor turned farmer and Sylvia his daughter loves both sea and farm.

No one can question the importance of the natural scene in Elizabeth Gaskell's work. Her country people, farmers, squires or labourers, and her fisherfolk are seen in their native countryside and would not usually be at home in any other. It follows that the countryside itself is an integral part of her work. The reader comes to know it as well as he knows the people in it. This knowledge is made possible by the descriptions which are part of the fabric of her narration, but so unobtrusively are they introduced that one hardly realises, except in retrospect, how essential a part they play in her art. Yet it was in this field that she most quickly approached perfection. Here she rarely uses a word too much or spoils a picture by the intrusion of moralistic comment. Because of what has been called her 'naked sensibility' she could recapture immediately that freshness of perception which writers like Proust or Baudelaire prized as the supreme gift of the artist but only attained by more circuitous routes. Many writers have painted the countryside; she does more, she takes us into it.

Her inborn mastery of description can be seen from the first. The brief pastoral overture to her first novel *Mary Barton* shows her already in perfect control of her descriptive powers:

> It was an early May evening—the April of the poets; for heavy showers had fallen all the morning, and the round, soft, white clouds which were blown by a west wind over the dark blue sky, were sometimes varied by one blacker and more threatening. The softness of the day tempted forth the young green leaves, which almost visibly fluttered into life; and the willows, which that morning had only a brown reflection in the water below, were now of that tender grey-green which blends so delicately with the spring harmony of colours. (Ch. 1)

Here, like Constable, she paints not only the view but the season, the weather, the time of day. This picture of the English rural scene might be described in the same terms which he used to describe one of his own—'lively and soothing, calm and exhilerating, fresh and blowing'.[20] One can recognise here the salient features of her landscapes: the keen observation, the effortless selection of concrete detail, the instinct for composition which blends them into a harmonious unity, the sense of movement which permeates the whole.

The freshness which characterises her descriptions owes much to the keenness of her sensory perception. She herself said that she liked 'a smelling and singing world',[21] instinctively giving priority to the sense which has the fewest 'literary' associations. Her country gardens are full of the fragrance of flowers and the pungent odour of herbs. The sweet smells of the hayfield at Hope Farm are 'a balm in themselves', and the clover-field bordering the forest in 'My French Master' has 'its one pure fragrance'. The country scenes have their appropriate sounds: the lowing of cattle, the clatter and cackle of poultry, the humming of bees, the 'gentle perpetual sounds, such as mill-wheels and bubbling springs', bird song in its infinite variety, from the dawn chorus and the full-throated tones of lark or thrush to the last song of the robin before he goes away into the stillness of night. Taste and touch contribute to the sensory power of these vivid evocations of nature. The pears that grow on the south wall in the Helstone garden are 'crisp, juicy fruit, warmed and scented by the sun'. In the sterner climate of Monkshaven the salt tang of winter is vividly suggested: '. . . the sharp air was filled, as it were, with saline particles in a freezing state; little pungent crystals of sea-salt, burning lips and cheeks with their cold keenness'.[22]

Elizabeth Gaskell's descriptions compose an admirable gallery of landscapes, or of more rapid but always vivid sketches, all vibrant with life. But when considered simply in themselves they reveal only part of their significance, for they are inseparably connected with the lives of her characters. The correlation between the natural scene and the fictional is established so effortlessly that it is easy to underestimate how much each owes to the other. In a variety of ways, unobtrusively or simply by implication, she indicates the correspondences between them which give another dimension to her descriptions.

One of the most evident points of contact between nature and human life comes through the influence of the seasons. It is a commonplace that there is a natural affinity between spring and youthful happiness, or between autumn and melancholy, but a commonplace which has always inspired poets, because it is a matter of universal experience. One of the best known eighteenth-century exponents of the theme was the Scottish poet James Thomson, author of *The Seasons*, who was a connection of Elizabeth Gaskell's family on her father's side. She herself was keenly susceptible to such influences. Writing nostalgically from Manchester, she confessed that 'the bursting leaves and sweet earthy smells' of early spring made her long 'to be off into the deep grassy solitudes of the country, just like a bird wakens up from its content at the change of the seasons . . .'[23] Her novels and stories abound in harmonies between the seasonal environment and the experience of the characters. Phillis's love ripens with the June days, it is winter when she gives way to her grief after Holdsworth's departure and spring again when her renewed, if illusory, confidence in his love makes her rejoice afresh with the opening year. The long hard frosts on the north-east coast have broken and early spring has succeeded when Sylvia plights her troth to Kinraid. The period of heaviest sorrow, for Maggie of 'The Moorland Cottage', is ushered in by a November of incessant rain, closing-in mists and sodden leaves. In the more sophisticated but still pastoral ambience of *Wives and Daughters* there are less evident but persisting affinities between the lives of the characters and the seasons. The country surgeon's sensitivity to their beauty is illustrated by his unspoken appreciation of a lovely day in early autumn, when the leaves are still on the trees and the hedges full of ripening blackberries, though here and there a leaf flutters to the ground without a breath of wind. The autumnal décor unobtrusively corresponds to the stage of life he himself has reached, still fruitful but far removed from the ecstasy of spring; it also corresponds to his immediate preoccupation, the premature death threatening the Squire's elder son Osborne Hamley, young but already marked to fall.

It need hardly be said that Elizabeth Gaskell is realistically aware that sometimes the relation between human life and the seasons is one not of harmony but of contrast. In times of grief spring brings 'all the contrasts which spring alone can bring to add to the heaviness of the soul'.[24] There is no more quietly tragic description in literature than the scene in *Sylvia's Lovers* where Daniel Robson's widow and daughter return to Haytersbank Farm after his death on the gallows at York. It is a sunny April afternoon and 'the air was full of pleasant sounds, prophesying of the coming summer . . . the song of the lark . . . the bleat of the lambs calling to their mothers . . .' But the spring is no spring to Sylvia and her mother, any more than it is to Kester, the old farm servant, who cannot forget his dead master:

There he was in the farm-yard, leaning over the gate that opened into the home-field, apparently watching the poultry that scratched and pecked at the new-springing grass with the utmost relish. A little farther off were the ewes with their new-dropped lambs; beyond that was the great old thorn-tree with its round fresh clusters of buds; again beyond that there was a glimpse of the vast sunny rippling sea; but Sylvia knew well that Kester was looking at none of those things. (Ch. 28)

The seasonal environment, whether it harmonises or contrasts with the lives of the characters, is an integral part of them. The same may be said of the landscape. There are natural correspondences between setting and mood, though here too the law of contrast also operates. Deserted by her lover in a lovely Welsh valley, Ruth learns the truth that 'earth has no barrier which avails against agony'. But Margaret Hale's youthful happiness is in tune with the beauty of the New Forest, as much as poor Lois Barclay's instinctive depression corresponds with her bleak surroundings when she sits in the sea mist on Boston pier. Certain types of landscape tend to become associated with certain patterns of feeling and action. Fine wood-lands are a source of calm and relaxation, as in 'Libbie Marsh's Three Eras', where the climax of happiness is reached with an excursion to Dunham Park. Neglected and encroaching forest trees suggest physical and mental decay; such is the background to the family mansions in 'The Old Nurse's Story', 'The Poor Clare' and 'The Doom of the Griffiths'. Ageing trees may themselves indicate the scene of some fatality: a sinister history is known to the two gnarled hollies in 'The Old Nurse's Story' and to the group of old trees in 'A Dark Night's Work'; in 'Half a Lifetime Ago' the essence of Susan Dixon's tragic life is anticipated in the initial description of the yew which gives its name to the farm, 'a mighty, funereal umbrageous yew, making a solemn shadow, as of death, in the very centre of the light and heat of the brightest summer day';[25] the old snow-covered larch close to the dismal house where Ruth works, which had once stood on a pleasant lawn but is now 'pent up and girded about with flagstones', is a mirror image of her own imprisonment in alien surroundings. An often recurring feature of the country landscapes is the breezy upland common, bordered with firs and golden with flowering gorse, which opens up a fresh stage in the action; Maggie traverses such a spot on her way to the wider horizons of Combemere, it is from there that Ruth ac-companies her lover to London and there that Paul Manning first becomes aware of the growing attraction between Phillis and Holdsworth. The pond which is a common feature of rural scenes can also have its unobtrusive symbolic significance: the solitary pool where Owen Griffiths instinctively goes for refuge after the death of his child reflects only dark and slaty clouds; the mountain pond in which Ruth sees her reflection, crowned with water-lilies, mirrors also a sky which is 'clear and dark, a blue which looked as if a black void lay behind'.

This natural symbolism is seen at its most effective in *Ruth* and *Sylvia's Lovers*, because Ruth is the most sensitive to natural beauty of all the Gaskell heroines, and Sylvia the closest to nature. In *Ruth* the successive settings correspond to the successive stages of her development. In each of them, till the last, nature counts for most: in the assize town Ruth lives on memories of the country till she can revisit it; in Wales her love and her delight in nature temporarily fuse; in her first years at Eccleston she is happiest in the Bensons' small garden; at Abermouth the seacoast is the stage for the crisis of her life; only in the last Eccleston section does the city dominate Ruth's life, but never her affections. Each individual setting, until the last, is rich in correspondences between nature and feeling, from Ruth's delight in the flowers on the wall panel, which remind her of her country home, to her moment of utter despair, after the ordeal on Abermouth sands, when 'the expanse of grey, wild, bleak moors, stretching away below a sunless sky, seemed only an outward sign of the waste world within her heart . . .'[26] In *Sylvia's Lovers* nature and life are interwoven from the start, effortlessly and inevitably. The whole tragedy of Sylvia's marriage is implicit in the difference between the 'lazy pleasure' with which she watches the sea from the cliff top in her heedless youth and the 'sad dreaminess of thought' with which she looks at it when, escaping from the 'comfortable imprisonment' of her home, she sometimes mounts the cliffs to sit there again.

The correspondences between nature and human life, in Elizabeth Gaskell's work, operate not only on the individual level but in a more universal sense. The frequent emphasis on autumn, in her descriptions of the seasons and on sunset, in her descriptions of the time of day, illuminates more than the immediate context: it reflects her constant underlying awareness of the passage of time and the immanence of mortality. Occasionally the connection becomes explicit: autumn is described in an early scene of *Sylvia's Lovers*—the sailor's funeral—as a time when old people are 'weaning themselves away from the earth, which probably many may never see dressed in her summer glory again'. For human life, as it passes, knows no such renewal as the glad earth. Although, to Elizabeth Gaskell's happy and genial nature, 'this lovely earth' is and remains Arcadia—even if, as in *Sylvia's Lovers*, Arcadia is only a wind-swept farm sheltering in a slight green hollow near a cliff top— she faces the fact that man's final destiny must be played out on a wider and more mysterious stage.

In her descriptions it is the sea that best typifies that mystery. In the scene of the sailor's funeral at Monkshaven she refers to 'the busy, crowded little town, the port, the shipping, and the bar on the one hand, and the wide, illimitable, tranquil sea on the other' as 'types of life and eternity'. Though the sea, in her work, never ceases to be the living element in which she delighted, it can also suggest the unknown and the infinite. There is a hint of this at the end of 'The Doom of the Griffiths' when the ill-fated Owen and his family

seem to become engulfed not in the waters of Tremadoc Bay but in a
more mysterious destiny: 'They sailed into the tossing darkness, and
were never more seen of men.'[27] In the Abermouth section of *Ruth*
the seashore where Ruth meets her former lover epitomises
loneliness; there is no sign of human life except for the black posts
which rise above the water, marking the place of the fishermen's
nets, no sound but the 'eternal moan' of the waves. Later, in her
dreams, the sea becomes a symbol both of human cruelty and of a
yet more terrible unknown. Carrying her son in her arms, she seems
to be pursued both by her former lover, determined to claim his
child, and by the unrelenting tide. 'All at once, just near the shore, a
great black whirlwind of waves clutched her back to her pursuer;
she threw Leonard on to land, which was safety; but whether he
reached it or no, or was swept back like her into a mysterious
something too dreadful to be borne, she did not know, for the terror
awakened her.'[28]

In *Sylvia's Lovers* the sea fills a dual role; it is the Protean element,
always alive and always beautiful, and it is, more mysteriously, the
'type of eternity'. In the opening scene of the novel one is made
conscious of its vigorous eruption into the more sheltered world of
the little port: 'The fresh salt breeze was bringing up the lashing,
leaping tide from the blue sea beyond the bar.'[29] Its very
neighbourhood spells exhilaration, and even though Sylvia con-
nects it later with the loss of her lover she still sometimes finds solace
in watching from the shore 'the advancing waves catching the
sunlight on their crests, advancing, receding, for ever and for ever,
as they had done all her life long . . .'[30] But it is this ceaseless
advancing and receding of the waves which, throughout the novel,
acts as a symbol of eternity and counterpoints the accidents of
mortal existence. The theme is orchestrated with all the variations
appropriate to the course of the inner action. To the inhabitants of
Haytersbank Farm there is something reassuring in the sound of the
sea far below, but the same waves are breaking on the shore when
Kinraid is carried off by the press-gang under the eyes of his rival. It
is to the sound of the 'passionate rush and rebound of many waters',
at 'high-water at the highest tide', that the ship carrying Kinraid
back to Monkshaven finally struggles into harbour, but it brings
disaster to Sylvia and her husband, and from this climactic point
onwards, their destiny seems to be ever more closely menaced by the
tide which will ultimately bear them away. The temporary shifting
of the action from Monkshaven to the siege of Acre, where Sylvia's

husband saves the life of his rival, retains the archetypal presence of
the sea. But this is the least successful variation on a theme otherwise
superbly handled—the tideless Mediterranean is no substitute for
the boundless ocean. With Philip's return to Monkshaven come the
great closing chords in this sea symphony. Haytersbank Farm, the
cliff-top Arcadia, is deserted for ever and the final scenes take place
at the foot of the cliffs, where the river coming from the moors runs
into the open sea. The mountainous waves of the spring-tide
threaten to carry off the child of Sylvia and Philip; her father saves
her, but at the cost of his life, and is carried back by his rescuers to
die in a cottage close to the shore. Before his death, Sylvia and he are
reconciled and, in the pauses between life and death, he listens to
the ever recurrent sound which is to become his requiem, 'the
lapping of the ceaseless waves as they came up close on the shelving
shore'.

There is deep sadness here—Elizabeth Gaskell called this tale
'the saddest story I ever wrote'—but it should be noticed that it is
not the sadness of fatalism. Sylvia and Philip are not the victims of
an inhuman cosmos. The sea is a symbol of eternity in its incessant
rhythm and its infinite expanse, but it is itself a part of nature and
subject to the laws given it by nature's Creator. Waves may appear
cruel or relentless, but Elizabeth Gaskell knows that in themselves
they are neither; the cruelty and relentlessness in *Sylvia's Lovers* come
from man, not nature, and death comes to all men, whether on land
or sea. In the realistic view of the sailor Kinraid: '. . . I reckon we a'
must die some way; and I'd as soon go down into the deep waters as
be choked wi' moulds.'[31]

Realism is in the essence of Elizabeth Gaskell's view of nature. It
is a poetic realism which allows her to make exquisite use of natural
symbolism, as well as to take a Wordsworthian pleasure in the life
which animates plants and animals and gives movement to the
cosmos. It is also a realism compatible with her belief in an ordered
universe where all natural phenomena, from the greatest to the
least, are part of the same beneficent design. The accuracy of her
descriptions, where the smallest flower grows in the soil and
situation suited to it, bears witness not only to her powers of
observation but to her sense of the laws inherent in the natural
scene. Job Legh, the amateur naturalist in *Mary Barton*, rejects with
scorn the sailor Will Wilson's tale of a mermaid, but greets his
account of having himself seen flying fish in other latitudes with the

approving comment: 'Ay! ay! young man. Now you're speaking truth.'

Job Legh, the Manchester cotton-spinner who, like many of his kind, makes natural history his hobby, represents the scientific approach to nature in a manner particularly congenial to Elizabeth Gaskell. This character in her first novel has, however, no true successor till the professional naturalist of her last novel, Roger Hamley. In the interval the influence of science on agriculture is sometimes reflected in the conversation of her farmers or landlords, who are usually not without their suspicions of the viability of the new methods. Lady Ludlow doubts the wisdom of her new agent's admiration for Coke of Holkham. In 'Mr Harrison's Confessions' a knowledge of Liebig's agricultural chemistry is rated less of an asset than practical knowledge and experience, where success in farming is the issue. As one with a first-hand knowledge of farming communities, Elizabeth Gaskell may have shared this cautious approach. But there is no doubt about the significance, and the value to society in general, of the figure of the young naturalist Roger Hamley in her last novel. Here nature and science are seen in truly happy and fruitful combination.

It has been pointed out that Roger Hamley's career, though not his personality, has analogies with that of Charles Darwin, who was a relative by marriage of Elizabeth Gaskell and personally known to her. His voyage in the *Beagle* was in her mind when, writing to her publisher George Smith about the plot of her new novel, she mentioned that Roger was 'to go round the world (like Charles Darwin) as naturalist'.[32] Roger, whom his family considers unintellectual in comparison with his supposedly brilliant brother Osborne, is from boyhood a dedicated student of nature who, on his country walks, sees twenty things where the uninitiated see only one. It is he, not Osborne, who becomes Fellow at Trinity and is subsequently chosen to go on a scientific expedition from which he returns as a distinguished traveller and naturalist, with a great career ahead of him. Some indication of the bias of his views as naturalist is given by the fact that he introduces Molly Gibson to passages from Cuvier's *Le Règne animal* and, more significantly, publishes articles advocating the views of the French naturalist 'M. Geoffroi de St. H' (Geoffroy St Hilaire), whose fundamental idea was the unity of all animal life. Such a background seems in harmony with emergent Darwinism, though as the action of the novel—loosely indicated—appears to take place between the eighteen-twenties and the late eighteen-thirties, it would be anachronistic to suppose that Roger, any more than Darwin at the same age, was yet in a position to formulate his final theory. The *Origin of Species* had, however, appeared by the time Elizabeth Gaskell began to write her last novel. But she clearly saw no reason why a resemblance in any point to the author of this controversial work should disqualify Roger from being one of the pivotal and certainly one of the most sympathetic characters in *Wives and Daughters*.

In fact, the exact nature of Roger's views as a naturalist is unimportant in her work, though there is no reason to suppose that she, any more than Kingsley, whom she admired, shared the antagonism to Darwinism felt by many of her contemporaries. She belonged to a circle where independent thought and scientific enquiry were encouraged, and her religious faith was too firmly grounded for evolutionary theories to affect her basic belief in a beneficent Creator behind all the unfolding mysteries of the universe. Yet the fact of Roger Hamley's profession is important in itself for it shows how nature can, in her view, be most happily assimilated with science. Roger is a scientist, but he is also a countryman, intelligently interested in farming and able to enter without effort into the interests of the old Squire, his father. His concern with the affairs of the estate does not, however, imply any egoistic interest in them: he does everything he can to ensure the succession of his brother's infant son. His own interest in nature is not limited by personal considerations; it is enough for him to explore her infinite riches, and his exploration is no ill-planned venture but a methodical progress, based on that observation of facts which Elizabeth Gaskell judged indispensable to all true knowledge, though not excluding those intuitive discoveries which only a preliminary mastery of facts makes possible. Those who, like Roger Hamley, study nature for herself establish a link between her infinite beauty and the marvels of an expanding universe of which the mid-Victorian era was increasingly conscious. But their deepening knowledge of her is compatible with unfailing respect for her inherent majesty. Roger, the future explorer, never forgets to tread carefully in the Hamley woods. 'He was so great a lover of nature that, without any thought, but habitually, he always avoided treading unnecessarily on any plant; who knew what long-sought growth or insect might develop itself in that which now appeared but insignificant?'[33]

The natural scene can thus expand, in the closing achievement of Elizabeth Gaskell's career, to include contemporary science. Yet in many ways it is timeless. The sense of stability inherent in the countryside and its life provides an element of continuity in the troubled perspective of history. It is for this reason, as well as because of the fascination the past always possessed for her, that she shows a liking, in her tales and essays, for collecting information on country customs, folklore and songs of the countryside. They may be indigenous or foreign; their value for her stems from their popular origin.

It was their mutual interest in such subjects which prompted her, while still unknown as an author, to write to William and Mary Howitt, whose appreciation of her description of Clopton House helped to determine her literary vocation. A second letter, to Mary Howitt, is dedicated to an account of country customs, especially those prevalent in the district round Knutsford.[34] One of the most charming was that of 'sanding' the houses on any occasion for rejoicing, red sand being strewed in front of them and sprinkled with white, so as to produce a pattern of flowers. She remembered how, when she was married, nearly all the houses in the town were sanded. In such an environment folklore was still a living reality; like the Brontës' servant Tabby, she could boast of knowing a man 'who has seen the Fairies' and point out the entrance to the cave on Alderley Edge where King Arthur and his knights lie sleeping. In her novels and tales old customs and poetical beliefs play their part in her reconstruction of rural life as naturally as they did in her own experience. Thurstan Benson tells Ruth, as Elizabeth Gaskell had herself been told by an old blind countrywoman, that the foxglove has 'knowledge' and knows when a spirit passes by. Lois Barclay tells her New England cousins of the Hallowe'en customs familiar to her from childhood, unhappily without foreseeing the sinister interpretation which will be put on them in her new home. Inevitably there is a crude side to some of these traditional usages. In Cheshire a penance for a shrewish woman was to parade her through the nearest village or town, seated astride an old horse with her face to the tail, 'drowning her scolding and clamour with the noise of frying pans, etc.'—a process known as making her 'ride stang'. It is typical of Elizabeth Gaskell's realism that she mentions this custom in the same letter where she speaks of more poetic ones, affirming that she knew it to have been followed in a number of cases and adding the matter-of-fact observation: 'I never knew the woman seek any redress, or the avengers proceed to any more disorderly conduct after they had once made the guilty one "ride stang" '.[35]

Ballads and folk songs made a keen appeal to her as an organic part of the life of the people. Margaret Hale prefers 'Chevy Chase' to cog-wheels; the returning whalers in *Sylvia's Lovers* are greeted by the singing of 'Weel may the keel row', and it is to the accompaniment of this North Country song that Kinraid leads his men when they land on the beach at Acre. There is a basic kinship between such songs in all countries, and it was the consciousness of this that prompted Elizabeth Gaskell to give an account, in her 'Modern Greek Songs', of Claude Fauriel's *Chants populaires de la Grèce moderne*, which she compares, in her opening lines, with Scott's *Border Minstrelsy*. On its original appearance in 1824 Fauriel's work had owed its success largely to its topical interest, at the time of the Greek War of Independence, but its lasting value was in the timeless appeal of 'la poésie naturelle et populaire'. The Greek songs had an added attraction in the fact that they represented an oral tradition which was still being actively continued. They celebrated the great events of domestic life—birth, marriage and death—and the most stirring events in the life of the people. The myrologia or funeral songs made a special appeal to the sympathies of Elizabeth Gaskell. The popular songs of modern Greece had as their favourite subject the deeds of the Klephts, in whom she was quick to see 'the Adam Bells, and Clyne o' the Cloughs, or perhaps still more the Robin Hoods, of Greece'.[36] She was conscious, too, that the modern Greek songs and the accompanying ceremonial still retained much of the spirit of Homeric Greece, the true home of the pastoral tradition, which she had more than once invoked in describing the 'rural Olympics' of her own 'Cumberland Sheep-shearers'. But what she prized above all in these popular songs was their directness, vitality and lack of self-consciousness: 'They are full of colour; there is no description of feeling; the actions of the *dramatis personae* tell plainly enough how they felt. Reading any good ballad is like eating game; and almost everything else seems poor and tasteless after it.'[37]

Ballads and folklore have their own language, the language of the people. Elizabeth Gaskell, like the Brontës, grew up in close touch with a countryside which had its own dialect and she always retained a keen ear for the resonances of local speech. She was aware that dialect, like the ballads in which it is used as a means of communication, was itself a part of the country's living history, containing precious survivals from the successive strata of its development, even to the earliest. She was not herself erudite, but in this she owed much to the erudition of her husband, whose careful footnotes to *Mary Barton* were intended to reveal the true dignity of the vernacular: the Anglo-Saxon of their forefathers lives on in the speech of the country race which industry has crowded into a Manchester slum. And with its historic authenticity this language has retained the colour and the flavour which Elizabeth Gaskell savoured in the ballads. Her country people speak in their natural idiom, which adapts itself as effortlessly to tragedy as to comedy, and is as simple and profound as their own lives. As her art developed, so did her skill in the use of this medium. She did not reproduce all the passages in dialect verbatim—such a procedure would be impossible for any novelist—but she kept near enough to the original idiom of the region in question to ensure that its essential characteristics survived.[38] Sometimes the dialect of the rustic characters is contrasted with the more conventional speech of those coming from a different cultural background. But her greatest triumph in the use of the regional idiom is in *Sylvia's Lovers* where all the main characters, in varying degrees, express themselves in the Yorkshire of the North Riding. Sylvia can neither read nor write, but she never lacks words that express her meaning far more accurately than the more extended vocabulary her cousin vainly tries to teach her. For she is mistress of a strong and simple idiom that harmonises with her simple environment and can yet ring the changes on love and hate and all the infinite gradations between them.

3 The social scene

Not every lover of country life enjoys society, but Elizabeth Gaskell was as much at home in the haunts of men as in a rural landscape, and for a good reason: she loved people, wherever they were. Yet an important reservation must be made: the society she most enjoyed had country roots. She is one of the most faithful painters of the countryside: she is also one of the most admirable painters of the little country town. If, for many, her name still suggests Cranford, it is because Cranford stands for more than masterful spinsters and recipes for washing old lace; it is a part of the history of English provincial life, as vital and enduring as the hawthorn in the hedgerows or the tower of the centuries-old church.

Cranford, as has been said, derived as an artistic creation from the author's love of the little town of Knutsford, where she grew up, just as Sandlebridge farm, a few miles distant, provided the initial inspiration for her pastoral settings. The genesis of Cranford, and all its counterparts, is to be found in the essay 'The Last Generation in England',[1] published the year after *Mary Barton*. The 'last generation' live in a small country town, whose close relationship to Knutsford is established beyond dispute by various details and anecdotes. In this article, which is the preliminary sketch for all her future treatment of the subject, Elizabeth Gaskell outlines the firmly established social hierarchy on which society was based in the agricultural shires in the first part of the nineteenth century, from the landed proprietors in the highest grade to 'the poor, respectable and disrespectable' in the lowest. With her historical sense and her love of continuity, she takes a natural interest in what is most traditional in the social hierarchy, just as she was drawn to the traditional in country customs and beliefs. The accent on tradition is perceptible when she states her wish 'to put upon record some of the details of country town life, either observed by myself, or handed down to me by older relations'.[2] At the same time she shows her awareness that all is not immutable, even in this basically stable environment. It is her sense of inevitable change, no less than her appreciation of stability, which impels her to put on record what she observes, for she realises that 'even in small towns, scarcely removed from villages, the phases of society are rapidly changing; and much will appear strange, which yet occurred only in the generation immediately preceding ours'.[3] When she creates Cranford and its counterparts, she is handling a theme more complex than the evocation of the natural scene; the wind of change is already beginning to ruffle the quiet waters. It is the measure of her achievement that she manages to convey the sense of movement, while preserving enough of mirror-like calmness to reflect the unchanging outlines of the age-old civilisation of rural England.

The anonymous town of 'The Last Generation in England' soon acquired an identity and a name. Combehurst of 'The Moorland Cottage' is a quiet little place, which represents the country metropolis to Maggie and her brother as children, when they emerge from the secluded green hollow where they live. There is more animation in the Duncombe of 'Mr Harrison's Confessions', which already gives a spectrum of small town society. The same year—1851—the first episode of *Cranford* made its appearance in Dickens' *Household Words*, with the title 'Our Society at Cranford'. On her own admission Elizabeth Gaskell 'never meant to write more',[4] but Dickens and his readers refused to be satisfied without further chronicles of the little town, and *Cranford* finally appeared in book form in 1853. Its popularity was and has remained such that 'Cranford' has become almost a generic term, and 'Cranfordian' a qualification applicable to any of the small towns that recur in her work. Barford of 'The Squire's Story', Hamley of 'A Dark Night's Work', Hollingford of *Wives and Daughters* all belong essentially to the same pattern. Hanbury of *My Lady Ludlow* and Helstone of *North and South*, though villages rather than small towns, are substantially variants of the same theme.

In every case, the countryside forms the indispensable frame-work. Cranford is only twenty miles from the commercial city of Drumble, but it is surrounded by meadows and farmsteads, and in summer the fragrant smell of the neighbouring hayfields is borne on the breeze through the open windows that look on to the principal street. When the young doctor Harrison exchanges his London lodgings for a room in Duncombe, he finds that even in the centre of the town the window admits scents from the mignonette boxes on the sill. The 'little straggling town' of Hollingford fades away into country on one side. Country-folk, like the countryside itself, are unobtrusively necessary to the proper functioning of society in these small towns. The little maidservant who is indispensable to any household with pretensions to gentility is usually countrybred, like Miss Matty's devoted Martha. When Miss Matty is in urgent need of financial help, it is the widowed daughter of a well-to-do farmer who makes the most substantial contribution to the fund secretly established by her friends, at the same time apologising for presuming to help the daughter of the rector, whom she re-membered as 'such a fine young lady when I was nothing but a country girl, coming to market with eggs and butter and such like things'.[5]

In this society of rural origin the social hierarchy provides the basic pattern. But there has to be an eye to detect the pattern, and whether the results of the observation are recorded at first hand, as in *Cranford*, or in a third-person narrative, the standpoint is usually that of the middle-class observer. Just as much is normally seen of the lower orders as would be seen by the ladies of Cranford and their extensive sisterhood. They show 'kindness (somewhat dictatorial)' to the respectable poor and manage as a rule to avoid contact with the 'disrespectable', though the existence of the latter is vouched for, even in *Cranford*, by the one or two 'real *bona fide* robberies' which breed panic in the district. There is, however, a notable exception to this inevitably superficial view of the lower orders in *My Lady Ludlow*, where the evangelical clergyman Mr Gray has a closer contact with the realities in his parish. By allowing his words and actions to be reported by a young first-hand narrator, Margaret Dawson, who is herself startled by his unorthodox behaviour, Elizabeth Gaskell preserves the essential realism of her own approach. Gray is painfully aware of the ignorance, bad language and cruelty behind the façade of respect that the children of his parishioners show to their social superiors. He knows also the miserable living conditions of the vagrants beyond the parish bounds who, like Job Gregson, subsist by poaching. It is true that these conditions belong to the early part of the century, but even in *North and South*, where the action is roughly contemporary, Margaret Hale is startled to find, on revisiting Helstone, what superstition and brutality can coexist with up-to-date schooling and building improvements. Such glimpses of a darker reality behind the decent poverty of the lower orders in the small country town are, however, exceptional. In Hollingford, which is the most complete presentation of this way of life, the poor are the least visible, or audible, members of the community. Mr Gibson is as kind to his pauper patients as to the profitable ones, but none of them acquire a separate identity or play any part in the action.

Between the lower orders and the gentlefolk comes the intermediate class of shopkeepers. Financially they are frequently better off than the grade above them, but any friendship, still more any family connection with them, is considered socially compromising. Miss Jenkyns is horrified when Miss Jessie Brown mentions in her drawing-room that her uncle is a shopkeeper, and Mrs Gibson is indignant when her stepdaughter dances with a Hollingford bookseller. One is not much surprised that Margaret Hale, the fastidious daughter of the Helstone vicar, should disdain 'butchers and bakers and candlestick-makers', but one feels the full weight of the social ostracism of trade when one learns that even the gentle Miss Matty might have felt her dignity compromised by 'the slightest expression of surprise, dismay or any similar feeling to an inferior in station, or in a public shop'.[6] Yet, when she has lost most of her money in the failure of the provincial joint-stock bank, she is persuaded by practical friends from commercial Drumble to add to her resources by selling tea. It is true that the conversion of her small dining-parlour into a shop is done as unobtrusively as possible, with a table instead of the obnoxious counter. Even so, it takes Mrs Jamieson, the social oracle of Cranford, several days' consideration to decide whether or not Miss Matty should forfeit her right to the privileges of society by her action, though ultimately the decision is in her favour. The gap between trade and gentility is bridged in a more striking manner when the retired Dissenting baker from Birmingham, Mr Brooke, who, like some other successful tradesmen, has bought the estate on which he was born, is finally received at Hanbury Court by the lady of the manor, Lady Ludlow. Brooke really owes his rise in the social scale to a happy coincidence; his flourishing estate attracts the attention of Lady Ludlow's new and inexperienced agent, a retired naval man, and the two strike up a friendship which her ladyship cannot very well ignore, especially when Captain James falls in love with the baker's daughter. Such cases show that trade will not always remain an impregnable barrier to entry into society, but they are the exception, not the rule. Only in *Sylvia's Lovers* is one of the leading characters, Philip Hepburn, a shopkeeper by trade. The principal accent is on his relations with Sylvia, not on his business life, but enough is said to show that he has outstanding business ability and would have been able to graduate into the middle-class circles of Monkshaven, had personal tragedy not intervened to cut short his career. As it is, the money he has made serves to keep his wife and child in comfort, after his disappearance, but to Sylvia, a farmer's daughter, the dark house behind the shop is as uncongenial a dwelling-place as it would have been to the daughter of any Yorkshire squire.

Above trade come those who qualify for immediate admission to the privileges of society. These are the middle classes, to whom Elizabeth Gaskell herself belonged and who furnish the majority of her characters. Among them it is probably the group of widows and spinsters that comes most immediately to mind when her picture of society is considered, because she immortalised them in *Cranford* and because they play a considerable part in her other versions of small town existence. Undoubtedly her personal memories of Knutsford contributed to this. She was brought up by a widowed aunt, and the two unmarried daughters of her uncle Peter Holland, the Knutsford surgeon, by his first marriage, Mary and Lucy, are usually thought to have supplied some of the traits of Miss Deborah and Miss Matty Jenkyns. After her marriage she sometimes stayed at her uncle's house on visits to Knutsford, and it was doubtless no coincidence that the first episode of *Cranford* was written, as Winifred Gérin has pointed out, after she had returned from such a visit.[7] But, unlike the narrator of *Cranford*, Mary Smith, she was not, in her youth, surrounded by a society almost exclusively feminine and middle-aged. Her uncle counted for much in her life and in the holidays young cousins of her own generation enlivened the Knutsford scene. Duncombe and Hollingford, which are not entirely in possession of the Amazons, must be taken into account, as well as Cranford, where the widows and spinsters are concerned, though Cranford is admittedly their territory par excellence.

It was certainly not unrealistic to show their numbers as considerable in any country town. The surplus of women over men was a large one in the first half of the nineteenth century, and middle-class widows and spinsters, who had no profession and could not seek employment in industry, naturally congregated there. Many were widows or orphans of professional men who had been well known locally, and their importance was frequently in proportion to the importance and length of the family connection with the district rather than to the smallness of their income or their house. Miss Jenkyns, the original leader of Cranford society, if not its social oracle, is the daughter of a former rector; Miss Browning,

who has a similar position among the older generation at
Hollingford, is a vicar's daughter and Mrs Munton, who enjoys
much the same pre-eminence at Duncombe, is a rector's widow.
The significance of these ladies for the community stems from the
fact that they are the hereditary guardians of its traditions, its
manners and its morals. They may be dowdy and elderly, and their
innate conservatism has its amusing aspects, but they have an
unassailable dignity, which is at once sensed by the young doctor,
Harrison, on first sight of Mrs Munton: 'I saw a homely, talkative,
elderly person, with a keen observant eye, and marks of suffering on
her face; plain in manner and dress, but still unmistakably a lady.'[8]
In any crisis, it is they who take the initiative. Mrs Munton
endeavours, though admittedly much handicapped by deafness, to
investigate the rumours about the young doctor's engagement. Miss
Jenkyns intervenes at once, on the death of Captain Brown, to help
his orphaned family. Miss Browning takes upon herself the difficult
task of telling Mr Gibson of the scandal which is being circulated
about his only daughter.

The knowledge of 'the strict code of gentility' originates in the
circles dominated by such ladies, and the observance of it is a serious
matter. The rules for visiting and calls are announced to the young
Mary Smith from Drumble 'with all the solemnity with which the
old Manx laws were read once a year on the Tinwald Mount'. Tea-
drinkings and card parties are the recognised forms of social
intercourse. The catering at these evening occasions is never of a
lavish nature. Unlike the shopkeepers who 'dare to be original' and
give comfortable suppers, the genteel hostess normally provides
only tea and wafer slices of bread and butter. It is true that the guests
can at the same time feast their eyes on old plate and delicate china.
In Cranford only the semi-genteel Miss Barker provides a generous
tea, followed, after cards, by a loaded supper tray, and has the
satisfaction of seeing her guests, even the aristocratic Mrs Jamieson,
do justice to both: '. . . Mrs Jamieson was kindly indulgent to Miss
Barker's want of knowledge of the customs of high life; and, to spare
her feelings, ate three large pieces of seed-cake, with a placid,
ruminating expression of countenance, not unlike a cow's.'[9] In
Hollingford such small parties are a part of Molly Gibson's life, and
it is a sign of the alterations slowly taking place in the existence of the
country town that her stepmother, aspiring to 'county' standards,
should decide to adopt late dinner, thus producing 'a great lull of
invitations for the Gibsons to Hollingford tea-parties', because of

the complications involved by the change of time: 'How ask people
to tea at six, who dined at that hour?'

The code of gentility has a more serious side to it. It involves
morals as well as manners. When the ladies of Cranford speak in
praise of 'elegant economy', it is obviously a euphemism for the
poverty which really underlies the simplicity of their entertaining
and much else, but the phrase shows that they have resigned
themselves to their situation with cheerfulness: 'There, economy
was always "elegant", and money-spending always "vulgar and
ostentatious"; a sort of sour grapeism, which made us very peaceful
and satisfied.'[10] Their acceptance goes deeper than mere sour
grapeism; they really believe that there are more important values
in life than money. Miss Matty's first reaction, when she hears of the
failure of her bank, is to try to help a fellow victim, whose plight
seems to her more undeserved than her own. Her friends combine to
establish a fund for her, of whose existence she is not to know, and
the poorest of them, Mrs Forrester, is deeply concerned lest anyone
should think the smallness of her contribution (which is actually far
more than she can comfortably afford) bears any proportion to her
love and regard for Miss Matty. Their kindness to those in
misfortune is seen at its best when shown to those of their own circle,
for there it is accompanied by the tact bred by genuine understanding, but they acknowledge the claims of any in the community who
are in need of help. When John Brounckner, the jobbing gardener
at Duncombe, is seriously ill, his cottage at once becomes the focus
of kindly activity, not unmixed with officiousness, for all the ladies of
the neighbourhood. When Signor Brunoni, the mysterious conjurer
who has alarmed Cranford, proves to be Samuel Brown, a penniless
ex-soldier with a wife and child, who has been injured in an
accident, all Cranford unites to help the unfortunate family in every
way they can.

There are family resemblances between the 'Amazons' in the
various country towns portrayed by Elizabeth Gaskell; but Miss
Deborah and Miss Matty Jenkyns, Miss Pole and the Honourable
Mrs Jamieson are known to many more readers than Mrs Munton,
or the inimitable Miss Galindo of *My Lady Ludlow*, or even the Miss
Brownings of *Wives and Daughters*. The reason seems to be less in the
ladies themselves than in the perspective in which they are seen.
Cranford is situated both in the present and the past; the age of
railroads has begun, people are reading *Pickwick Papers* and young
Mary Smith, the narrator, knows that gigot sleeves and straight

skirts went out of fashion years ago, but they are still worn in the little town, which had vehemently petitioned against the coming of the railroad, and Miss Jenkyns still reveres Dr Johnson as a model of style. As the cycle of Cranford unfolds, it does so at first in reverse, so that the reader is taken back to the far off days of Miss Matty's courtship and farther back still to the eighteenth century and the courting days of her parents, before returning to the present again. As a result the present is seen in the light of the past and, thus seen, it acquires a double significance. When Miss Matty mourns Holbrook, she mourns both a reality and a dream. Cranford is a quiet place, with an autumnal tranquillity. But this autumn is a mellow one, with late flowers and harvest fields and laughter. Elizabeth Gaskell must have found a similarly pleasant and tranquillising atmosphere at Knutsford, when she left her busy life in Manchester for short spells to relax in the home of her childhood. It explains why she wrote of *Cranford*: 'It is the only one of my own books that I can read again . . . whenever I am ailing or ill, I take "Cranford" and—I was going to say, *enjoy* it! (but that would not be pretty!) laugh over it afresh!'[11]

But Cranford is privileged territory. At Duncombe things are less happy for the 'widows and old maids in rich abundance' who form the majority of the population. Hollingford, the final variation on the 'Cranford' theme, shows them still an essential part of the community, but no longer such a prominent one. The younger generation, wholly absent from Cranford except for the visitor Mary Smith, are here as important as their elders, and the Miss Brownings and the Mrs Goodenoughs no longer occupy the centre of the stage. There is still 'a long habit of reverence' for the formidable elder Miss Browning, and Mr Gibson consults her and values her friendship, but Lady Harriet, daughter of the great landowner of the district, irreverently refers to her and her sister as 'Pecksy and Flapsy', and even the loyal Molly Gibson becomes gradually aware of the limitations of their mental horizon, though she continues to feel deep affection and respect for both Miss Brownings.

In contrast to the group of widows and spinsters, the professional men and their wives, if they have wives, are much less numerous, but an important part of country town society. 'The three black graces, Law, Physic and Divinity' are all essential to its working. Of their representatives, the clergyman was first to gain an assured social position. Elizabeth Gaskell, a Unitarian and married to a

Unitarian minister, had the tolerance and breadth of sympathy which qualified her to portray not only the Dissenting clergyman but the parish priest.

The social status of the parish priest was unquestioned in the first half of the nineteenth century, though it was of relatively recent growth. Lady Ludlow can remember the sycophantic parson of her grandfather's day, who was also the family chaplain and dined at the Hall every Sunday, once receiving a memorable practical rebuke for his greediness from his formidable patron. The parson's circumstances vary with the size of the living, and with his private means; Mr Mountford of Hanbury is comfortably off, but Mr Hale has a small living and only a small income to supplement it, though he and his family are recognised as belonging to the gentry in virtue of their position. The part the parish priest plays in the life of the community depends very much on his personality. In Cranford, where so much happens in the past, we hear much more of the former rector, Dr Jenkyns, than of the present one. Dr Jenkyns belongs to the eighteenth century, with his 'huge full-bottomed wig' and his sermons against Bonaparte, but it is he whom the reader remembers rather than his mild successor, who is accorded only a passing mention. There is a good deal of the eighteenth century also about Mr Mountford, who succeeded the servile family parson at Hanbury, having won Lord Ludlow's favour by his excellent horsemanship. By the time the narration begins, he is old and stout and no longer addicted to hunting, which is in any case discouraged by the bishop of the diocese, but very fond of good living. He is a lazy but essentially kindly man who prefers to remain in ignorance of uncomfortable realities, but does his best to relieve cases of hardship when they are actually brought to his notice.

The parsons in Elizabeth Gaskell's work tend in general to be either austere, like Dr Jenkyns, or lazy but kindly, like Mr Mountford. Mr Hutton, the vicar of Duncombe, is a dignified and hard-working priest, whose presence seems to produce a certain constraint in social gatherings. Mr Ashton of Hollingford is courteous and good-natured, ready to help his poorer parishioners financially but disinclined for the effort of visiting them very frequently. Good nature and reluctance to exert himself unduly also characterise Mr Ness, the vicar of Hamley, though he is more of an intellectual and does take trouble to help the pupils who come to read with him and to work at his new edition of one of the classics. He can also exert himself to help a friend in need. Mr Hale must have been a kind and understanding friend, if not a very assured counsellor, to his parishioners at Helstone, but since he feels himself obliged, on doctrinal grounds, to resign his living, he can hardly qualify as a typical parish priest. Much the most effective of the country vicars portrayed by Elizabeth Gaskell is the young evangelical clergyman Mr Gray, who cares intensely both for the spiritual and the material welfare of his people at Hanbury and ends by earning their affection as well as their respect.

The country doctor's status in provincial society is less assured than that of the parish priest. Medicine was not considered as eligible a profession as the Church for younger sons of good families. The country doctor was partly what his antecedents made him, as far as social standing was concerned, though a good deal depended on his personal fitness or otherwise for polite society. Mr Hoggins of Cranford is a farmer's son but a clever doctor, who might have been admitted to select circles if he had made any attempt to qualify for them. As it is, he is tabooed by Mrs Jamieson as 'vulgar, and inadmissible to Cranford society, not merely on account of his name, but because of his voice, his complexion, his boots, smelling of the stable, and himself, smelling of drugs'. The young doctor at Duncombe, Mr Harrison, is a shopkeeper's son, but he is tutored in the social graces by his dapper and experienced senior partner. Nothing definite is known by the people of Hollingford about the antecedents of their clever surgeon, but his natural distinction of manner and bearing, as well as his outstanding skill, earn him an assured position within a remarkably short period. He is even welcomed, not only as physician but as dinner guest, at the Towers, the great house of the neighbourhood. There is no question, however, of his marrying into county circles when he thinks of choosing a second wife, and Squire Hamley, though a personal friend, warns him that he would not wish either of his sons to marry the doctor's daughter.

If, however, the country doctor's social status is less assured than the parson's, his importance to the community and his place in its respect and affection admit of no question. Elizabeth Gaskell knew this from experience, for she had as a child accompanied her uncle the Knutsford surgeon on his rounds. It is noticeable that she never shows an ineffectual country doctor. The only one who is ever spoken of in derogatory terms is Mr Prince of Hanbury, but since his detractor is Miss Galindo, who insists on doctoring the cottagers with her own prescriptions, thus not unnaturally provoking him to fury, her opinion is obviously biassed. Young Mr Harrison's modern methods are looked on at first with suspicion, even by his senior partner, but they are triumphantly vindicated by the test of experience. Mr Gibson is a clever doctor, whose diagnosis, in the case of Osborne Hamley, proves more correct than that of Dr Nicholls, 'the great physician of the county'. Such men are welcome visitors to all households, because their presence brings comfort and help at times of anxiety and distress. No superhuman skill is claimed for them; gone are the days remembered by the old servant Nancy in 'The Moorland Cottage', when doctors were credited with being able to 'charm away illness', but, as Molly, the doctor's daughter knows, they wage a courageous war against disease and death, sometimes successfully, always with compassion. Their loyalty to the high standards of medical ethics is unflinching; it is unthinkable to betray professional secrets, still more to trade on that knowledge, as Mrs Gibson finds to her cost when her husband discovers that she does not share his view of his professional responsibilities. Such men do not carry out their life of service, deeply rewarding as it is, without cost to themselves. Even the self-controlled Mr Gibson admits to the need for 'peace and a decent quantity of cheerfulness when I come home', as an antidote to the scenes of physical and mental distress with which he is brought into constant contact. And, however wise they are professionally, they are, like all Elizabeth Gaskell's characters, ordinary fallible mortals where their personal life is concerned. One is not surprised that the young surgeon of Duncombe should make mistakes, all the more so as his love for the vicar's daughter gives him a dangerous indifference to the possible reactions of all the other females with whom he is surrounded. But even Mr Gibson, the acute physician and saturnine observer of the inconsistencies of others, proves incompetent to solve his domestic problems otherwise than by allowing himself to drift into a highly unsuitable marriage that creates problems compared with which the original ones appear trifling. Yet he never allows his foolish marriage to interfere with his professional competence; he remains the universally trusted and respected surgeon on whom all Hollingford relies.

The lawyer, like the doctor, has a less assured social position in the country town than the clergyman. But, unlike the doctor's, his position is a curiously ambiguous one, for he knows, through his profession, most of the family secrets, as well as the financial circumstances, of the county families who are his main clients, although he is never accepted as their social equal. As a rule, he accepts his anomalous status with a philosophy which is largely the result of habit. Mr Dudgeon, the attorney of Barford in 'The Squire's Story', is the head of a family firm which has managed the legal affairs of the neighbouring squires, as well as the commonalty, for generations, and his feeling towards them combines something of the old feudal allegiance with 'a kind of proud humility'. Edward Wilkins, the lawyer of Hamley in 'A Dark Night's Work', a man of outstanding talent and considerable wealth, is unable to accept his inferior status with as good a grace, and ultimately ruins himself by attempting to copy the way of life of his aristocratic clients in the hope of becoming accepted as their social equal.

If the small town attorney shares with the doctor a somewhat ill-defined social status, he is less likely than the doctor to find in his profession a passport to the liking and affection of the community in general. It is his doubtful privilege to become acquainted as often with the weaknesses of human nature as with its finer attributes, and the relations between himself and his clients are not as straightforward as those between the doctor and his patients. The country lawyers shown by Elizabeth Gaskell do not as a rule inspire much liking in those who consult them. They have no part in Cranford, that Utopian community where there is hardly any money and very little ill-will. In 'The Moorland Cottage', which dates from the same period, the legal profession appears, as it frequently does in Elizabeth Gaskell's work, in an unattractive light. There seem no grounds for supposing that she had, either at this early stage or later, any personal reason to dislike lawyers. Her attitude appears to have been motivated rather by a sense of the dangers inherent in the law's intervention in difficult and delicate situations, as 'The Moorland Cottage' suggests. Mr Buxton, a careless landlord, calls in an efficient lawyer, to put his affairs with his tenants in order. Mr Henry is 'scrupulously honest and honourable' but believes in driving hard bargains for his client. At the same time he offends Buxton by coolly exposing the full extent of his inefficiency as a landlord, and disgusts Buxton's young and idealistic son Frank by refusing to believe that the defaulting tenants might be induced to mend their ways if they were spared the publicity of a lawsuit. It is also owing to his implacable view of justice that the heroine's brother, who has been guilty of forgery, is threatened with trial and transportation and has to flee the country. At Hanbury Lady Ludlow's steward, Mr Horner, has not the same authority as a qualified attorney and never oversteps the bounds of his feudal allegiance, but his disapproval of the mortgage on her ladyship's hereditary estate in favour of her husband's Scottish property is an enduring source of latent animosity between them. The most sombre portrait of the country lawyer is in 'A Dark Night's Work'. Edward Wilkins' thwarted social ambitions undermine his character to such an extent that he is no longer able to manage his business without the help of a confidential clerk, later his partner. But Mr Dunster's dry efficiency and his meticulousness are a perpetual irritation to the lazy and self-indulgent attorney of Hamley and the concealed hostility between them culminates in a violent quarrel and a hasty blow from Wilkins, which is the accidental cause of the other's death.

The tragedy of Edward Wilkins is the consequence of his refusal to recognise the gulf between the middle classes and the county families. Even those who could normally aspire to bridge that gulf do not find it easy. The Honourable Mrs Jamieson, once she has become a resident of Cranford, finds that county families are reluctant to set foot in her drawing-room, which represents the social zenith to the Cranford gentility. Sir Peter Arley, of Arley Hall, used occasionally to visit his distant relatives, the Jenkyns, but Sir Peter's visits, like so much in Cranford, belong to the past. It is only at public functions that town and county normally come in contact and then only in a superficial way. Once a year Lady Cumnor entertains at the Towers the Hollingford ladies who help at her charity school, and they repay her with exhaustive and exhausting admiration of everything they see. A charity ball is another occasion when the great may be seen at close quarters, though they do not arrive till long after the 'punctual plebeians' and choose their partners, with rare exceptions, from their own party. They are, as Lady Harriet, the youngest of the Towers family, recognises, really 'a show and a spectacle', and their audience is justifiably disappointed when the duchess who is staying with the Cumnors arrives without her diamonds.

The life of the county families is none the less an integral part of rural England, and Elizabeth Gaskell does not neglect it in her painting of the provincial scene. Though fine old farm-houses like Sandlebridge, which had belonged to the same yeoman family for generations, were nearer to her heart than any stately manor, yet she knew the country house not only as a part of the landscape but from the inside also. Her wide circle of friends included more than one aristocratic household and she found much to interest her in such surroundings. On the eve of a visit to her friend Mrs Davenport at Capesthorne, she wrote to the artist Eliza Fox describing the house and its chatelaine as ideal subjects for her sketch-book: 'old hall, galleries, old paintings, etc., and such a *dame* of a lady to grace them.'[12] The past history of the houses which had sheltered the same family for generations made a powerful appeal to her historical sense. It inspired her early sketch 'Clopton House', and is the mainspring of the action in 'Morton Hall', where the dispossession of a Royalist landowner during the Commonwealth leads to subsequent tragedy. The history of their race lives on in the pictures, the furniture and the traditions of the old county families. The visitors to Hanbury Court are invited to accompany Lady Ludlow on 'a certain promenade around the hall, and through the drawing-rooms, with pauses before different pictures, the history or subject of each of which was invariably told by my lady to every new visitor— a sort of giving them the freedom of the old family seat, by describing the kind and nature of the great progenitors who had lived there before the narrator'.[13]

Pride of race is a characteristic of all the county families portrayed by Elizabeth Gaskell. It is formulated most categorically by Lady Ludlow, who is essentially a product of the eighteenth century, though she is seen in her old age in the first decade of the nineteenth. She believes that the old families of England, especially those who have not been contaminated by inter-marriage with city heiresses, are in fact a race apart, with 'gifts and powers of a different and higher class to what the other orders have'. Squire Hamley does not formulate his beliefs with the same precision, but he is very proud of belonging to the oldest family in the shire, one which dates from the Heptarchy, and despises his rich Whig neighbours, the Cumnors, as 'mere muck of yesterday'. The Countess of Cumnor, however, yields to none in pride of rank, pointedly ignoring the heresy once repeated by her youngest daughter that 'there is a tale that the first Cumnor began his fortune by selling tobacco in King James's reign'.

Pride of race is usually accompanied by a sense of noblesse oblige. Where this is lacking, mere arrogance is the result, as in the case of the far from admirable Bellinghams in *Ruth*. Normally, however, the great are very conscious of their social obligations. Again it is Lady Ludlow who exemplifies this to the fullest extent. Trained from a child by her father to fulfil her role as heiress of the Hanburys,

she is unremittingly active, even as an elderly widow, in super-
intending her steward and never allows him to take any steps
discordant to 'her hereditary sense of right and wrong between
landlord and tenant'. It is indeed her indulgence to her tenants
which partly accounts for her financial difficulties. No such stately
protocol as is observed at Hanbury Court surrounds Squire
Hamley's relations with his tenants, but he is keenly conscious of his
responsibility towards them. When a former gamekeeper is dying,
and wishes, out of feudal loyalty, to see him for the last time, the
master is as much aware as the old man himself of 'the claims of the
tie which existed between them'. Lord Cumnor is a genial landlord
when at home, and he and his much less approachable countess,
while accepting the worship of the townspeople as their right, do a
good deal for Hollingford and are 'generally condescending, and
often thoughtful and kind in their treatment of their vassals'.

This consideration for the welfare of their social inferiors, on the
part of the county families, does not, however, exceed certain
clearly defined limits. The lower orders are expected to keep to their
proper station in life. Lady Ludlow, who has been to Versailles in
her youth and counted close friends among the French noblesse, is
strongly influenced, like many of her class and generation, by the
anti-Jacobinism provoked by the excesses of the French Revolution.
She is firmly opposed to education for the lower orders, and refuses
to listen to the evangelical clergyman Mr Gray when he proposes a
school for the village children, even though charity and Sunday
schools had both been introduced during the eighteenth century
and names like that of Robert Raikes had spread even to Hanbury.
The unwelcome discovery that Harry Gregson, the poacher's son,
has been taught to read appears to her a social calamity: 'If our
lower orders have these edge-tools [reading and writing] given to
them, we shall have the terrible scenes of the French Revolution
acted over again in England!'[14] It is unfortunate that Lady
Ludlow's anti-Jacobinism should be further illustrated by an over-
long narrative of an episode during the Terror, even though it
involved a French friend of the Ludlows, for the narration
compromises by its length the artistic unity of the story as a whole.
But her horror at the idea of education for the lower orders is
genuine. It is only when Harry Gregson is crippled by an accident
and Mr Gray nearly loses his life in going to his rescue that she
forgives them both, and agrees to the building of a school, yielding
not to argument but to the appeal their misfortune makes to her

kind heart. She expresses, however, her strong wish that the boys should learn only reading, writing and the first four rules of arithmetic, and the girls reading only, the rest of their time being given to mending, knitting and spinning. The curriculum for girls is even more limited in the charity school set up by Lady Cumnor; they are taught to sew and cook, to be efficient housemaids and 'above all, to dress neatly in a kind of charity-uniform devised by the ladies of Cumnor Towers—white caps, white tippets, check aprons, blue gowns, and ready curtseys, and 'please, ma'ams', being *de rigueur*'.[15]

The great people of the county also set fixed limits to the consideration they show to those favoured members of the middle class with whom circumstances bring them into closer contact than is normally the case. Lady Ludlow cheers her solitude at Hanbury Court by entertaining there, at her own expense, six young girls, children of poor gentlefolk. They are treated almost as her daughters, but they are restricted 'in certain indulgences in dress and diet that might be befitting in young ladies of a higher rank, and of more probable wealth'. Lady Cumnor is kind to the widowed ex-governess of her family, Mrs Kirkpatrick, and sometimes 'Clare' is invited to stay at Cumnor Towers, but she is expected to fetch and carry for her ladyship and never to express an opinion except such as the countess approves. She is even expected to consider the entertainment of the Cumnor grandchildren during the Christmas holidays when arranging the date for her second marriage: 'It would amuse the children, going over to Ashcombe for the wedding; and if it's bad weather during the holidays I'm always afraid of their finding it dull at the Towers'.[16] This demand 'Clare' does manage to evade, but in general she considers any trouble well recompensed by the advantage of association with 'the Cumnors'.

Nevertheless, times are slowly changing. Molly Gibson has the courage to protest against the patronising way in which Lady Harriet speaks of her friends in Hollingford: 'Your ladyship keeps speaking of the sort of—the class of—people to which I belong, as if it were a kind of strange animal you were talking about . . .'[17] Neither Lady Ludlow nor Lady Harriet's mother, the countess, would have replied, as she does: 'Don't you see, little one, I talk after my kind, just as you talk after your kind. It's only on the surface with both of us.' This equation of rank with a distinction that operates at surface level, not affecting the common humanity shared by all, is again implicit in her further admission: 'I don't set myself up in solid things as any better than my neighbours.'[18] This does not mean that she encourages familiarity from those below her in rank, as Mr Preston, her father's land-agent, finds to his cost, but she equally dislikes the adulation lavished by the Hollingford ladies on everything to do with 'the Towers', and is surprised and delighted to find in 'Clare's' little stepdaughter such simplicity and truthfulness. She proves her genuine admiration of Molly's sterling qualities by defending her later against scandalmongers, and she finally creates a social precedent by inviting the doctor's daughter to stay as a welcome guest at the family mansion, where, on her only previous visit as a child, she had been either patronised or forgotten.

It is doubtful whether Lady Cumnor would have thought of giving such an invitation herself, though she is gracious to her daughter's guest. But she creates a social precedent by receiving at the Towers, without regard to their family background, the friends of her son, Lord Hollingford, who is a scientist of distinction. For his sake, she and the earl open their doors to 'all sorts of people', which means those who are distinguished for science and learning, without regard to rank. For Lady Ludlow such company would have appeared ominously reminiscent of the Encyclopédistes, but the widening of intellectual topics at the aristocratic dinner-table is highly congenial to Mr Gibson, who had responded to periodic invitations in the past only out of a sense of duty. In the eyes of Lord Hollingford, scientific ability is the highest possible recommendation, and it is for this reason alone that he is anxious to show honour to Squire Hamley's younger son, Roger, who is proving to be a brilliant scientist. It is as a scholar and traveller with an already established reputation, not as a scion of an ancient county family, that Roger Hamley is invited, on his return from his travels, to stay at Cumnor Towers.

It is during this visit that Roger realises that he loves Molly Gibson, and *Wives and Daughters* would have ended, had Elizabeth Gaskell lived to finish it, with their marriage. It is significant that, after showing various examples of the unhappiness caused by unequal marriages, she should have planned to conclude her latest work with one between the doctor's daughter and the Squire's son which holds out every promise of happiness. It is not a fairy-tale ending but a credible one. Molly has unconsciously absorbed from her upbringing a sterling sense of values which saves her from exaggerated deference to her social superiors. She has already learnt to be perfectly at ease as a guest at Hamley Hall where, in contrast to Cumnor Towers, refinement of taste is combined with a healthy rusticity closely akin to that of the yeomanry. Roger's allegiance is, in any case, primarily to science, not to his county background. It matters little to him, and it finally ceases to matter to the Squire, that the doctor's daughter should be 'of no family at all'.

Thanks to Elizabeth Gaskell's descriptive gifts, she can show not only the pattern of social life in provincial England in the first part of the nineteenth century but its material settling down to the smallest detail. We know how her people are dressed, what they eat, how their homes are furnished, as well as we know their place in the social hierarchy and the kind of lives they lead. Lady Ludlow, who is still faithful to the fashions of the eighteenth century, seems, as A. W. Ward says, to have stepped out of a portrait by Romney or Hoppner: 'She wore a great lace cap, nearly half her own height . . . a fine Indian muslin shawl folded over her shoulders and across her chest, and an apron of the same; a black silk mode gown . . . a quilted lavender satin petticoat.'[19] The ladies of Cranford ignore fashion in the interests of 'elegant economy', but they sometimes indulge in a new cap and, on special occasions, display a formidable array of brooches—Miss Pole is seen to be wearing no less than seven when she goes to the party at Mrs Jamieson's. Mrs Gibson has a very different attitude to dress, and appears at the Hollingford charity ball in a pearl grey satin gown 'with a profusion of lace and white and coloured lilacs', which attracts caustic comment from those who remember the days when she wore 'old black silks, and was thankful and civil as became her place as a schoolmistress'. Her sense of her increased social status extends to the introduction of a more aristocratic cuisine into the doctor's household, an innovation not welcomed by her husband, who 'had to satisfy his healthy English appetite on badly-made omelettes, vol-au-vents, croquettes, and timbales, never being exactly sure what he was eating'.

The furnishing of the house is similarly in tune with the status and character of the occupants. The vicarage parlour at Duncombe in 'Mr Harrison's Confessions' suggests a refined domesticity:

It was like a picture—at least, seen through the door-frame. A sort of mixture of crimson and sea-green in the room, and a sunny garden beyond . . . It looked so like a home that it at once made me know the full charm of the word. There were books and work about, and tokens of employment; there was a child's plaything on the floor, and against the sea-green walls there hung a likeness or two, one in water-colours . . . The chairs and sofa were covered with chintz, the same as the curtains—a little pretty red rose on a white ground. I don't know where the crimson came from, but I am sure there was crimson somewhere; perhaps in the carpet. There was a glass door besides the window, and you went up a step into the garden. (Ch. 3)

Most of the country town dwellers, however, live in houses less spacious than the vicarage or the doctor's house—which necessarily includes surgery and stable—and there is a certain sense of constriction about their small rooms, in spite of their comfort. Miss Matty, who had spent her youth in a rectory, unconsciously shows her awareness of her cramped surroundings in her preference for having her dining-room curtain drawn 'so as to exclude the dead brickwall of a neighbour's stables, and yet left so as to show every tender leaf of the poplar which was bursting into spring beauty'. Elizabeth Gaskell herself, while she delights in showing all the details of small town life, is usually more attracted, where the description of interiors is concerned, by the country house with its spacious rooms, set, like the farmstead, in a framework of woods and fields. The drawing-room at Hamley Hall in *Wives and Daughters* reflects the life-style of its owners, dignified but unpretentious and deriving its principal charm from its harmony with the Arcadian setting:

The room was forty feet long or so; fitted up with yellow satin of some distant period; high spindle-legged chairs and pembroke-tables abounded. The carpet was of the same date as the curtains, and was threadbare in many places, and in others was covered with drugget. Stands of plants, great jars of flowers, old Indian china and cabinets gave the room the pleasant aspect it certainly had. And to add to it there were five high, long windows on one side of the room, all opening to the prettiest bit of flower-garden in the grounds—or what was considered as such—brilliant-coloured, geometrically-shaped beds, converging to a sundial in the midst. (Ch. 6)

The country town society of Cranford and its many variants is to a large extent a closed one, with its own values. The great world of London is a long way away, though not so remote as in the pre-railway era. It is the distant sphere to which 'the county' gravitates during the season, but rarely does London society become a reality and not simply a topic of conversation in Elizabeth Gaskell's work. This is not because she herself was a stranger to it. Before her marriage, she stayed in the West End with her Holland relatives, Henry Holland, the well-known doctor, and Swinton Holland, the banker. After the publication of *Mary Barton* she became an honoured and highly popular guest in London drawing-rooms, and made frequent visits to the capital. But London society plays only a minor part in her portrayal of the social scene.

It features in the opening and closing chapters of *North and South*, for Margaret Hale's roots are not entirely in a Hampshire vicarage; she has been brought up partly by her wealthy aunt in Harley Street, and it is to Harley Street that she returns after the death of her parents. Her aunt belongs to the well-to-do upper middle class. She and her daughter Edith lead a pleasantly cushioned existence; the domestic wheels are well-oiled, and hospitality constantly dispensed to a circle of neighbours 'whom Mrs Shaw called friends, because she happened to dine with them more frequently than with any other people'. As a girl, Margaret accepts this way of life as a temporary necessity but, in spite of her aunt's kindness, she is thankful to return in the holidays to the shabby country vicarage, with its greater freedom.

When she finally goes back to Harley Street as an orphan, after her experience of Milton-Northern, the aimlessness of such an existence strikes her far more forcibly than before, and this in spite of the fact that the Shaw circle has widened since Edith married Captain Lennox and the young couple took up residence in the Harley Street house. Beauty and fashion distinguish the Lennox dinner-table, and it is further enlivened by the frequent presence of Edith's brother-in-law, Henry Lennox, a gifted barrister, and of his friends, who, like himself, are both well-informed and witty. Delightful as such dinners are, Margaret feels there is a hollowness about the brilliant conversation: 'Every talent, every feeling, every acquirement; nay, even every tendency towards virtue, was used up as materials for fireworks; the hidden, sacred fire exhausted itself in sparkle and crackle.'[20] These reflections are Margaret's, not Elizabeth Gaskell's, and Margaret lacks the gaiety and social flair of her creator, nor can it be supposed that the company in Harley Street ever rivalled in brilliance that to which the author of *Mary Barton* found herself introduced. Yet the deep seriousness which underlay her own vivacity and social grace prevented her from ever being unduly dazzled by London drawing-rooms, and after an evening of 'sparkling conversation' she could estimate such entertainment as a very evanescent pleasure: 'I keep smiling to myself and trying to remember things—all to no purpose,—the foam has faded from the Champagne'.[21]

There is a superficiality about the Londoners she portrays, not because they are necessarily superficial by nature but because worldly success is their goal. Henry Lennox is a gifted lawyer who loves Margaret Hale as much as he is capable of loving, but she instinctively senses the gulf between his ambition and her own very different scale of values. The Londoners who appear occasionally in other Gaskell works seem equally concerned with ambition and social eminence. Ralph Corbet of 'A Dark Night's Work' is an able lawyer, who graduates to a judgeship and Hyde Park Gardens, but he sacrifices Ellinor on 'the shrine of his ambition'. Mr Kirkpatrick, Mrs Gibson's barrister brother-in-law, is kind to his relations, but only when he has attained 'the comparative table-land of Q.C.-dom' and has time to remember them. It is at his house that his niece Cynthia meets Mr Henderson, the husband of her choice, a young barrister who promises to be as successful and as superficial as even Mrs Gibson could desire.

The glimpse of London which is all Mrs Gaskell gives of it in her work is very different from that given by her friend Charlotte Brontë in *Villette*, where a night spent at a 'respectable old-fashioned inn in the City', in the shadow of St Paul's, is an epoch-making event. It is informative to compare Lucy Snowe's account with Mrs Gaskell's actual description in her *Life of Charlotte Brontë* of the original of the inn in question—the Chapter Coffee House in Paternoster Row, where the Brontës stayed on their way to Brussels—which impressed her chiefly by its gloom and its isolated situation.[22] She understood what the first sight of the metropolis meant to her friend, and with what a mixture of excitement and apprehension Charlotte later reacted to her introduction into London society, but it is clear that she does not share the same attitude as the author of *Jane Eyre* when she writes: 'At the end of November she went up to the 'big Babylon', and was immediately plunged into what appeared to her a whirl; for changes, and scenes, and stimulus which would have been a trifle to others were much to her.'[23]

Perhaps Elizabeth Gaskell herself was more of the opinion of the forthright Mr Harrison, who became impatient when Miss Caroline

Tomkinson asked whether he could bear the change from 'the great metropolis' to a country village: 'In the first place, why could she not call it "London", or "town", and have done with it? And, in the next place, why should she not love the place that was her home well enough to fancy that every one would like it when they came to know it as well as she did?'[24] Certain it is that in her work in general London is firmly relegated to the background. It cannot, however, be completely ignored, even if it only acquires prominence in the Harley Street episodes in *North and South*. It is the place where county people like the Cumnors enjoy the gaieties that belong to their station, the mecca also of science and the law, as important for the career of a Roger Hamley as for that of a Henry Lennox. It is the limbo where Ruth is seduced and weak-willed provincials like Richard Bradshaw learn the arts of deception. For provincials of tougher calibre— in fact for most of the inhabitants of Cranford and its sister towns—it is, when all is said and done, a place not necessarily so very superior to everywhere else, where people speak with a curious accent and are rather too civil to be sincere, a place, moreover, which is by no means as self-sufficient as it pretends to be. In the opinion of the elder Miss Browning the metropolis owes a considerable debt to Hollingford:

'I ask you again, where does this fine society come from, and these wise men, and these distinguished travellers? Why, out of country parishes like this! London picks 'em all up, and decks herself with them, and then calls out to the folks she's robbed, and says, "Come and see how fine I am" "Fine", indeed! I've no patience with London . . .' (Ch. 41)

Miss Browning, though she has little use for London, is, rather unexpectedly, prepared to admit the advantages of foreign travel: '. . . there's a great opportunity for cultivation of the mind afforded by intercourse with foreign countries'. Elizabeth Gaskell herself enjoyed travel and, when she became an established writer, was able to make frequent visits abroad. Her knowledge of Germany is evident in 'Six Weeks at Heppenheim' and 'The Grey Woman', and her knowledge of Italy in the Roman episode in 'A Dark Night's Work', but in these cases the foreign setting serves chiefly as background for the action. In the essay 'French Life', which is in diary form and based on material gained in visits to

France, Mrs Gaskell uses her knowledge of the social scene to examine its variants across the Channel.

She was well equipped to do so. As a child she had learnt French from M. Rogier, the prototype of M. de Chalabre in her story 'My French Master', an émigré who taught dancing and his native language at Knutsford. Later she often visited France, especially Paris, and came to know French life at first hand. She was greatly helped in this by her friendship with Mme Mohl, whose salon was one of the most famous in Paris. They seem to have become close friends in 1854,[25] and from 1855 onwards she was a favourite guest at the Mohls' apartment in the Rue du Bac. Paris was not all she knew of France—her essay includes a visit to rural Brittany and later to Avignon—but it obviously provided the richest field for social observation. 'French Life' is a graphic and shrewd appraisal of a social scene which, to her trained eye, was interestingly different from the English one and yet not wholly dissimilar.

It is with evident sympathy that she describes the bourgeois households where she has been a guest. She admires the expert housekeeping and the careful organisation of the daily routine. In Cranford, too, such practical matters were of the first importance, and the way of life of the Parisian bourgeois was not without an affinity with Cranford standards. There is the same love of order, the same respect of tradition, the same homely dignity. Equally lively and perceptive is Mrs Gaskell's evocation of the Faubourg St Germain. As the guest of the Mohls she found most doors open to her, for the modest apartment in the Rue du Bac was the meeting ground for all that was most distinguished in Parisian society. Her account of being taken to see a reigning beauty, 'one of the *lionnes* of Paris', makes a striking contrast to the immediately preceding description of bourgeois neatness and economy. Proust would have recognised in the lady a kinswoman of the Guermantes. It is interesting to recall that part of *Wives and Daughters* was written during Mrs Gaskell's last visit to the Rue du Bac, the year after the publication of 'French Life', and one wonders if Molly Gibson's rather unusual type of good looks may have been suggested by those of the *lionne*, who is described as having 'a very peculiar style of beauty . . . black hair, long black curling eyelashes, long soft grey eyes, a smooth olive skin, a dimple, and most beautiful teeth'.[26] No one, however, could be more English than Molly, in spite of her appearance. The charming Cynthia, though both her looks and her guile can be sufficiently accounted for by her parentage, has more temperamental affinity with the Parisian beauty, whose manners were 'soft and caressing to the last degree'. Miss Browning, at least, sees a connection between her grace of manner and the fact of her having been at school in France, while Mr Preston is struck by the resemblance between Cynthia and the miniature of a famous beauty at the Court of Louis XV.

It is not, however, the reigning beauties of the Faubourg St Germain who interest Elizabeth Gaskell most but the women no longer young, like Mme Mohl and her friend, Mme de Circourt, who, as hostesses, maintained the great French tradition of the salon. Mme Mohl, who was English by birth but had lived in France from childhood, had, in her youth, thanks to the friendship of Mme Récamier, been present at the receptions at the Abbaye-aux-Bois in honour of the ageing Chateaubriand.[27] She had thus been in direct contact with a living tradition which went back to the seventeenth century and was associated with names like that of Mme de Rambouillet and Mme de Sévigné. These historical associations delighted Elizabeth Gaskell. She was particularly attracted by Mme de Sévigné, with whose letters she had long been familiar, and planned to write a book on her life and times. It was indeed to acquire material for this that she made the excursion to Brittany described in 'French Life' and saw the château of Les Rochers, once the country home of the marquise. It was, however, the art of the *salonnière* as still practised by hostesses like Mme Mohl that fascinated her above all. She was herself no novice in the art of hospitality, but she felt that in this field the French had acquired a mastery that deserved attention.

The essay 'Company Manners' contains her reflections on this subject and is at the same time one of the clearest statements of her own views on social behaviour. It was suggested by Victor Cousin's memoir on the marquise de Sablé published in 1854.[28] Her salon was the supreme achievement of the marquise's life, and Elizabeth Gaskell coins the expression 'the art of Sabléing' to sum up the qualities that make the perfect hostess. But Cousin was an habitué of the Mohl salon, and the wisdom of Mme Mohl is also perceptible in the views expressed, in 'Company Manners', by the author's French friends. It was the personality of the hostess that gave the great salons their distinctive quality, from the days of the Hôtel de Rambouillet onwards, but, as 'Company Manners' makes clear, the essential role of the hostess was not to shine herself but to ensure that her guests all received their due share of attention. Mme Mohl liked the conversation to remain general, so that anyone who wished could join in, and deplored the series of confidential chats into which it was apt to disintegrate in English society. The 'French lady' who, in the essay, gives advice on how to be successful in 'Sabléing' remarks on the need to be quick in perceiving those who have not had their share of attention and in leading the conversation away from any subject which might give pain to anyone present. Remembering the marquise de Sablé's known fondness for dainty things to eat, Mrs Gaskell appropriately compares her function as hostess to that of 'the silver saucepan in which they [her guests] were all to meet; the oil in which their several ingredients were to be softened of what was harsh or discordant'.[29] Such a truly courteous and kind conception of hospitality was in line with her own. Though naturally a brilliant talker, she was also an excellent listener and Susanna Winkworth remembered how 'she seemed always surrounded by an atmosphere of ease, leisure and playful geniality, that drew out the best side of everyone who was in her company. When you were with her, you felt as if you had twice the life in you that you had at ordinary times'.[30]

While she renders homage to the supreme social tact of a Mme Mohl or a Mme Récamier, Elizabeth Gaskell does not hesitate to add what she has learnt from her own experience of entertaining, for she is basically concerned not with the foreign but with the universally human. She draws on her reminiscences of evenings in an old country house in the depths of Wales as freely as on her recent memories of the Faubourg St Germain. She recognises the part played by material conditions in creating a friendly atmosphere, and the role of good eating as an adjunct to entertaining. Above all, she emphasises the need for naturalness in the social sphere as well as in any other. Conversation should develop naturally and flow as naturally 'into sense or nonsense as the case might be'. Elizabeth Gaskell has no admiration for conversational brilliance when it is deliberately contrived: '. . . there is but one thing more tiresome than an evening when everybody tries to be profound and sensible, and that is an evening when everybody tries to be witty. I have a disagreeable sense of effort and unnaturalness at both times; but the everlasting attempt, even when it succeeds, to be clever and amusing is the worst of the two.'[31]

She rounds off her argument in 'Company Manners' with a flourish by insisting that the good hostess must have a touch of the gypsy in her. This lively coda has a vital relationship with her main theme for, as she points out, only someone with this ingredient in their character, someone of quick impulse and ready wit, possesses the talent for improvisation that accompanies perfect naturalness and that gives a social gathering 'the flavour and zest of a picnic'. She recalls that impromptu entertainments were popular in the salons of the seventeenth century and were no doubt enjoyed by Mme de Sablé and Mme de Sévigné. She herself shared Mme de Sévigné's gift of ready adaptation, her love of adventure and her eager participation in the enjoyment of the moment. It may seem surprising that there should be this touch of the gypsy in the author of *Cranford*, but a moment's reflection will show that it would have been stranger had she lacked it. Only someone who was acutely aware of the artificiality of exaggerated decorum and rigid convention could have created the spinsters of Cranford and seen both the humour and the pathos of their over-regulated existence.

Elizabeth Gaskell had too much common sense not to realise the need for organisation in social life—and its place in life in general—but she never exaggerated its importance. Her letters show how much she depended also on the rapid improvisation of plans and expedients, and what refreshment she derived from the frequent variations which visits and travel introduced into the daily routine. On one of the rare occasions when she found herself alone for a few days she wrote to Eliza Fox: 'Nature intended me for a gypsy-bachelor, that *I* am sure of. Not an old maid, for they are particular and fidgetty, and tidy, and punctual,—but a gypsy-bachelor.'[32] She would no doubt have tired very soon of her solitude, but not of the freedom to introduce what variation she pleased into the timing of her activities. Her heroines often have something of the gypsy in them, even if they are unable to gratify their secret longing for an untrammelled existence. Margaret Hale, when she hears at night from her window in Helstone parsonage the stealthy movements of the poachers in the forest beyond the garden, is conscious of a kind of affinity with them: 'The wild, adventurous freedom of their life had taken her fancy; she felt inclined to wish them success; she had no fear of them.' Sylvia Robson is temperamentally more akin to her father, a man 'possessed by a spirit of adventure and love of change', than to her quiet mother. Molly Gibson 'breathes freely' when her stepmother's temporary absence leaves her at liberty to be natural, even if only for a week.

Naturalness is what Elizabeth Gaskell most admires, whether she finds it in an aristocratic drawing-room or in a farmhouse kitchen.

The hospitality of the great hostess, however spontaneous it may appear, has inevitably a degree of sophistication. 'It could not have been all art; it certainly was not all nature',[33] is her verdict on the outstanding social tact of Mme Récamier. She thoroughly admired 'the art of Sabléing' and felt that English hostesses might profit by emulating the charming marquise. But it is characteristic of her that, towards the close of 'Company Manners', she should cite, as an example of unflurried poise and perfect courtesy, an old Welsh herb-woman who belongs to that simpler world where hospitality is an instinct rather than an art:

I was once very much struck by the perfect breeding of an old Welsh herb-woman, with whom I drank tea—a tea which was not tea, after all—an infusion of balm and black-currant leaves, with a pinch of lime blossom to give it a Pekoe flavour. She had boasted of the delicacy of this beverage to me on the previous day, and I had begged to be allowed to come and drink a cup with her. The only drawback was that she had but one cup, but she immediately bethought her that she had two saucers, one of which would do just as well, indeed better, than any cup. I was anxious to be in time, and so I was too early. She had not done dusting and rubbing when I arrived, but she made no fuss; she was glad to see me, and quietly bade me welcome, though I had come before all was as she could have wished. She gave me a dusted chair, sat down herself with her kilted petticoats and working apron, and talked to me as if she had not a care or a thought on her mind but the enjoyment of the present time . . .[34]

4 The industrial scene

Elizabeth Gaskell loved the country, and she loved people. It was her innate sympathy with her kind which made her look with affection and interest on those who, as she says in the preface to *Mary Barton*, 'elbowed me daily in the busy streets of the town in which I resided'. But it is doubtful whether, had fate in the shape of her marriage to a city minister not decided her residence in Manchester, the industrial scene would ever have played a prominent part in her work though it was her handling of this theme that first brought her fame and still constitutes, in the opinion of some modern critics, her most lasting claim to remembrance.

From the start her attitude to life in the industrial city was strongly influenced by her 'deep relish and fond admiration for the country'. It is no coincidence that her first publication, in collaboration with her husband, a poetic sketch intended to be in the manner of Crabbe but 'in a more seeing-beauty spirit', should have for subject a life-long exile from the country, a woman destined to revisit her native fields only in thought and dream and finally, like old Alice in *Mary Barton*, in the second childhood which precedes death. Her first published story, 'Libbie Marsh's Three Eras', which is her earliest handling of the industrial theme, shows the fundamental stresses in her attitude when the working people, on their Whitsuntide excursion to Dunham Woods, look back on the motionless cloud of smoke on the horizon which indicates the position of what is described as 'ugly, smoky Manchester; dear busy, earnest, noble-working Manchester . . .' The attempt to compensate the instinctive recoil from the urban scene by an added weight of propitiatory adjectives is only partly successful. It may have been instinct rather than conscious design that decided the choice of a caged bird as the catalyst which sets the action of the story in motion, but when Elizabeth Gaskell countered Leigh Hunt's criticism of the important part given to the bird-cage with the argument that, though sympathising with his objection, she had drawn from the life, her defence had perhaps a deeper motivation than she realised.

But it was no part of her nature to make concessions grudgingly. Since her lot was cast in an industrial city, she entered as fully and sympathetically as she could into the lives of those with whom she was brought into contact. By the time she began to write *Mary Barton*, she had had at least thirteen years' experience of the milieu and the characters that were to be her theme, and that period had included the depression of 1836, 'the terrible years 1839, 1840 and 1841' and the resulting Chartist agitation. The years of its composition corresponded to the period when, after a short improvement, economic depression returned in 1845, worsening and causing a resurgence of Chartism in 1848. Conditions were still difficult for the working classes in the early fifties, the period of *North and South*, though there was some improvement. In the interval between *Mary Barton* and *North and South*, appeared *Ruth* and the stories 'Hand and Heart', 'Lizzie Leigh', 'The Heart of John Middleton' and 'Bessy's Troubles at Home', all concerned with an industrial society and its victims. After *North and South* Mrs Gaskell ceased to give a major place in her work to the problems of the victims of industrialisation. This did not mean she ceased to be concerned for the fate of the Manchester poor. When the American Civil War caused widespread unemployment among the cotton operatives of Manchester, she and her daughters were indefatigable in working for their relief. But the fact that she confined her treatment of the industrial scene to the first decade of her writing career contrasts strongly with her lasting preoccupation with pastoral and social themes.

As has already been said, the grief caused by a personal bereavement—the loss of her only son in 1845—had much to do with Elizabeth Gaskell's decision to undertake the writing of her first novel. It was undoubtedly the greatest sorrow of her life. '. . . hardly anyone knows how it has changed me', she wrote,[1] but it had not changed her compassionate nature, and with her the only palliative for grief was the one she advocates in *Mary Barton*, action which implies that 'there is yet hope of some good thing to be accomplished, or some additional evil that may be avoided'.[2] Her own child had died through illness, but children were dying not far from her home from hunger and squalid conditions—the mortality rate among workers' children below the age of five in the Ancoats area has been given as 35 to 40 per cent.[3] She did not write specifically to plead the cause of the children or to propose any social panacea—she disclaimed all knowledge of political economy—[4] but because the weight of the misery of the inarticulate multitude, of which children were the first and most helpless victims, pressed on her heart and because she believed, rightly, that it was in her power to give some utterance to their agony.

The sharpest sting of that agony was for many, as she knew, the feeling that their sufferings were unknown, or indifferent, to their more fortunate fellow creatures. She was not alone in realising that England had been divided by the Industrial Revolution into two worlds. Carlyle, whom she deeply admired, had condemned a 'society' which was no society, where the only link between masters and men was the cash nexus. Disraeli in *Sybil* had startled his contemporaries into a keener awareness of the existence of 'the two nations'. It was the sense of unmerited isolation which she found among the most thoughtful of the working men of Manchester that was the dominating idea in Elizabeth Gaskell's mind at the time when she was writing *Mary Barton*. Disraeli showed two worlds: she shows only one, immerses herself in it, becomes one of its inhabitants, speaks its language and so conveys, as no arguments could have done, the segregation in which its people exist. This sense of segregation is what distinguishes *Mary Barton*—and, in a less powerful register, the short stories with working-class backgrounds—from *Ruth* and *North and South* and gives Elizabeth Gaskell's first treatment of the industrial theme its peculiar force.

Her unerring powers of observation and description were never of more service to her than here, where she was dealing not with a milieu she loved but with one naturally uncongenial and so all the more oppressively, obtrusively present to her sensitive vision. The back-to-back houses, the dingy courts, the appalling cellar dwellings, the streets whose drabness is broken only by the meretricious splendour of the gin palace, this is the only world her people really know. If they venture beyond its borders, they seem to themselves to be in some exotic climate. When John Barton and his fellow delegates go to London to present the Chartist petition, they are as lost in the streets of the West End as the working-class wedding party in Zola's *L'Assommoir* when they venture into the galleries of the Louvre:

> . . . the grand streets we were in then! They're sadly puzzled how to build houses though in London; there'd be an opening for a good steady master builder there, as know'd his business. For yo see the houses are many on 'em built without any proper shape for

a body to live in; some on 'em they've after thought would fall down, so they've stuck great ugly pillars out before 'em. And some on 'em (we thought they must be th' tailors' sign) had getten stone men and women as wanted clothes stuck on 'em. I were like a child, I forgot a' my errand in looking about me. (Ch. 9)

The mill workers of Manchester are truly at home only in their own claustrophobic world, but Elizabeth Gaskell was too much of a realist to portray it as one of unrelieved misery. Her characters, like their prototypes, are doomed to pass their lives 'in strange alternations between work and want'. At the beginning of *Mary Barton* times are good and the Barton family are living in modest comfort. But the time inevitably comes when trade is slack and Barton and many others find themselves without work. The transition from relative comfort to grinding poverty is accompanied by the gradual disappearance of the treasured household possessions, dear for their associations as well as for their practical use, which have to be sold to buy food. Poetry and colour are drained from the Bartons' lives with the vanishing of the bright green japanned tea-tray and the crimson tea-caddy. Yet their cheerless, fireless home is a palace compared with the cellars not far away where families like the Davenports live. Elizabeth Gaskell felt that, in the terrible years of the trade recession, the poor of Manchester 'only wanted a Dante to record their sufferings' and that even his words would fall short of the 'awful truth'. Her picture of the Davenports' cellar is that of an inferno whose stench and squalor would have appalled the least sensitive observer. When Barton and his friend Wilson go to the help of the desperately ill Davenport and his family, they are greeted, on entering the cellar, by a smell so foetid as almost to knock the two men down. When they begin to penetrate the thick darkness of the place, they see 'three or four little children rolling on the damp, nay wet brick floor, through which the stagnant, filthy moisture of the street oozed up'.[5] The sick man himself lies on 'straw, so damp and mouldy, no dog would have chosen it in preference to flags'.

Barton does what he can to help, but the sight of such suffering activates his obsessive concern with the isolation of the poor and the failure of the rich to help them in their need, a situation associated in his mind with the parable of Dives and Lazarus: '. . . we pile up their fortunes with the sweat of our brows, and yet we are to live as separate as if we were in two worlds; ay, as separate as Dives and

Lazarus, with a great gulf betwixt us. . .' John Barton was chosen by Elizabeth Gaskell as her central character because, as she explained in a letter to the sister-in-law of her most trenchant critic, W. R. Greg, she had often encountered among the poor of Manchester men similarly obsessed with the inequalities of fortune: '. . . he was my hero, *the* person with whom all my sympathies went, with whom I tried to identify myself at the time, because I believed from personal observation that such men were not uncommon, and would well repay such sympathy and love as should throw light down upon their groping search after the causes of suffering, and the reason why suffering is sent, and what they can do to lighten it.'[6] The authenticity of the portrayal of John Barton was recognised by those who knew Manchester life. The Lancashire weaver and poet Samuel Bamford said: 'of John Bartons, I have known hundreds, his very self in all things except his fatal crime'.[7] He has seen his little son die, at a time when he had no work, when nourishing food would have saved the child, and to a friend who tries to convince him that the rich, too, know what it is to suffer, he replies with a question similar to one which had been put to Mrs Gaskell herself: 'Han they ever seen a child o' their'n die for want o' food?' But she is at pains to show that his concern is not only with his personal misfortunes: 'his class, his order, was what he stood by, not the rights of his own paltry self'.[8] The death of his own child has only heightened his concern for the fate of the other starving children 'who don't yet know what life is, and are afeared of death'. It is to further the people's cause that he becomes a Chartist delegate, and it is the rejection of their petition by Parliament that casts him into the despair which, combined with hunger, drives him to opium addiction. This is his condition when a strike breaks out. A meeting between the masters and the operatives' delegates, of whom he is one, ends in deadlock and the agony of these 'starved, irritated, despairing men' culminates in a desire for revenge embodied in Barton's 'Have at the masters!' Their fatal decision is taken, and it is he who draws the lot to kill Harry Carson, the son of his former employer, whose conduct at the meeting has done more than anything else to wound and alienate the despairing men.

   John Barton is the outstanding personality among the operatives. He is a man born and bred among the mills, whose natural intensity of character has been channelled by harsh environment and bitter experience into an obsessional brooding over the problem of rich and poor. But the figure of Job Legh must also be taken into account when considering Elizabeth Gaskell's presentation of the industrial scene. Legh has wider intellectual interests than Barton, and is an ardent amateur naturalist. He cannot escape the hard life of the Manchester weaver, but he is more philosophical in his attitude to hardship. During the strike he admits frankly that he would personally prefer to 'work for low wages rather than sit idle and starve', and that he became a trade-union member only for the sake of peace. But his deep attachment to his orphaned granddaughter shows that he is far from unfeeling and when, after committing the fatal crime, Barton disappears from the scene, returning eventually only to die, Legh emerges as counsellor and helper to those whom his friend's action has plunged into distress and danger. It is he who later puts the case for Barton, and for his class, to the father of the murdered man, the mill-owner Carson, with a moderation and a humanity which shows that he, of all the characters, has the truest understanding of the situation.

The world of Manchester is a man's world, but the women have an important part to play, far more important, John Barton feels, than their middle-class sisters. He is determined that his daughter shall never be 'a do-nothing lady, worrying shopmen all morning and screeching at her pianny all afternoon, and going to bed without having done a good turn to any one of God's creatures but herself'.[9] As a young girl, Mary Barton, flattered by the attentions of Harry Carson, indulges in 'Alnaschar-visions'—fortunately unknown to her father—of graduating into the comfortable company of mill-owners' wives, but she renounces such visions for ever when she comes to realise her love for Jem Wilson, her old playmate, a foundry worker. She is called upon, in the second half of the novel, to enact a heroine's part, which gives some foundation to her titular role, though Elizabeth Gaskell consulted her publishers' wishes in calling the novel *Mary Barton*, instead of giving it the name of her tragic hero.[10] Mary's efforts to shield her father and establish an alibi for her lover, wrongly accused of murdering Harry Carson, nearly shatter her health. That she survives is largely due to that indomitable spirit which she shares with so many Lancashire working women. It shows itself in a different way in Margaret, Job Legh's granddaughter, patient in her own troubles, even when threatened with blindness, but able to express her deep sympathy for the poor in her wonderful singing of such songs as 'The Oldham Weaver'. Not all the women have the power of endurance of Mary and Margaret. Mrs Wilson, the mother of Mary's lover, has been irritable in temper ever since her health was undermined by the accident from unfenced machinery which crippled her as a young factory worker. But she can still show her innate generosity at times of crisis. Sally Leadbitter, the dressmaker's apprentice, vulgar and a mischief-maker, is yet devoted to her bedridden mother. Even poor Esther, Barton's sister-in-law, who, with ambitions to become a fine lady, has allowed herself to be seduced and been driven to prostitution by the need for money to save her sick child, is still capable of making a supreme effort to warn her niece, when she thinks Mary is in danger of a similar fate.

In opposition to the spectrum of working-class life shown by Mrs Gaskell, her picture of the mill-owners is practically limited to the Carson family. Henry Carson is a self-made man, who has graduated from mill-hand to master. He had married a factory girl, but their children have been brought up in an atmosphere of wealth and ease. The first impression of the Carsons is an unfavourable one. When the weaver George Wilson trudges the distance between the Davenports' cellar and the Carsons' comfortable house, to ask for an Infirmary order for his desperately ill friend, he is shown into the room where father and son are sitting at their well-spread breakfast-table. The father gives Wilson an out-patient's order—obviously useless to a dangerously ill man—while disclaiming any personal knowledge of one who had worked in his factory for three years. The son gives Wilson five shillings for the 'poor fellow'—precisely the amount, as one critic has noted, that Barton had obtained from the pawnbroker when he pledged his coat and his one silk pocket handkerchief on Davenport's behalf.[11] The impact of this scene is comparable, in its sombre power, to the unforgettable pages in Zola's *Germinal* where the miner's wife comes to beg a five-franc piece from the family of wealthy shareholders, who never give money on principle but bestow on her some useless clothing and portions of the breakfast brioche for the underfed children. After this the outcome of the crucial meeting between the masters and the strikers' delegates is predictable. The Carsons and their fellow mill-owners refuse all but the most derisory concessions, and resentment and despair lead to crime. In the rich man, too, misery generates a passionate desire for revenge, but when he at last comes face to face with his son's murderer, he finds a dying man, to whom, at the last moment, he is unable to deny the longed-for assurance of his forgiveness. Unlike *Germinal*, which ends with the subterranean rumblings of future conflict, *Mary Barton*, in its closing pages, holds out a hope of future reconciliation.

Yet Elizabeth Gaskell is no sentimentalist. Before the novel ends, the scene at Barton's deathbed is followed by a discussion between Carson and Job Legh, in which the manufacturer's doctrine of utilitarian rationalism is opposed to the worker's belief that human relations are more important than economic theories. Neither convinces the other, but each listens, for the first time, to the other's viewpoint, and that Legh's argument has not been without effect is subsequently shown by Carson's increased considerateness as an employer. This moderation in his attitude comes, however, too late to save John Barton or to remove the impression left by the novel as a whole of the masters' intransigence. It was no part of Elizabeth Gaskell's design to stir up class conflict—'No one can feel more deeply than I how *wicked* it is to do anything to excite class against class'[12]—and she admitted that she had represented '*but one* side of the question', but it was the only one she then felt herself capable of treating with power, 'as I don't feel as strongly (and as it is impossible I ever should) on the other side . . .'[13]

Mary Barton was criticised not only for one-sidedness but for the prevailing sombreness of tone. The humour which was to irradiate every page of *Cranford* is rare by comparison in her novel of Manchester life. She herself felt that the sombreness was inherent in her subject: 'I acknowledge the fault of there being too heavy a shadow over the book; but I doubt if the story could have been deeply realized without these shadows'.[14] It is significant that what ultimately decides Harry Carson's death is not his refusal to listen to the weavers' deputation, but the fact that the appearance of these men, 'lank, ragged, dispirited, and famine-striken', is utilised by him as material for an admirably drawn caricature. In the circumstances, laughter was the deadliest insult to human dignity.

Yet if the laughter which comes so naturally to Elizabeth Gaskell is for the most part frozen at the source in *Mary Barton*, there are elements that lighten the shadows. Childhood exercises a conciliatory power: at the height of their misfortune Barton and his daughter can pause to help a child in distress, and it is the example of forgiveness unconsciously provided by a child which produces in the elder Carson the first impulse of mercy towards his son's murderer. The kindness of the poor towards each other—'the poor mun help the poor'—runs through the entire narrative. It is nowhere more movingly exemplified than in the character of old Alice Wilson, who finds time in a life of domestic drudgery to perform innumerable acts of kindness. Unconsciously, Alice exercises among her neighbours something of the priestly function, communicating an atmosphere of serenity which survives the decay of her bodily faculties.

It can hardly be a coincidence that old Alice, whose character had first been adumbrated in the early 'Sketches among the Poor', is not a native of Manchester, like most of the younger generation, but a countrywoman, drawn to the city in youth, at a time when work was scarce, by the hope of better wages. It has long been her most cherished wish to return to her country home. Her hope is never fulfilled, but in the second childhood which accompanies her last illness, she goes back in memory to the heather-covered hill-sides of her early youth.

It is easier to accept Alice's return in dreams to her native countryside than the emigration of Mary and her husband, at the end of the novel, to a rural home near a town in Canada. Elizabeth Gaskell gives a credible explanation in the difficulty of Jem Wilson's returning to his job after being on trial for murder, and in the engineering skill which makes it easy for him to obtain the Canadian post. Yet it is difficult to avoid the feeling that this is an escapist solution, in tune with the author's own 'deep relish and fond admiration for the country'. One wonders if even the glory of the Indian summer in Canada would really compensate Mary Barton, Manchester born and bred, for the absence of the factory chimneys and the smoke cloud towards which, on her one previous journey away from her native city, she had looked back 'with a feeling akin to the "Heimweh"'.

Of the shorter tales with working-class backgrounds which intervened between *Mary Barton* and *Ruth*, only one possesses to any degree the tragic force of the first novel, but all show the author's thorough knowledge of the milieu she is describing, including the two stories 'Hand and Heart' and 'Bessy's Troubles at Home', obviously didactic in purpose (they were first published in *The Sunday School Penny Magazine*), and no doubt resembling those she told her own scholars in the Sunday School at Lower Mosley Street. Conditions in these tales vary from modest comfort to squalor, but even the modest comfort is not maintained without unremitting effort; in 'Lizzie Leigh' only Susan Palmer's earnings support her usually tipsy father, and Bessy Lee is expected, at fifteen, to devote her entire time in her mother's absence to keeping house for a family of five. Bessy is fortunate in comparison with the motherless lad in 'Hand and Heart' who has to adjust to life in his uncle's unruly household in a dingy court. Destitution is the fate of Lizzie Leigh, when, like Esther of *Mary Barton*, she is seduced and abandoned, though, more fortunate than Esther, she is ultimately found by her family. Peculiar grimness attaches to the conditions described in 'The Heart of John Middleton', the most powerful of these stories. The scene is not Manchester but Sawley (identified by A. W. Ward as Whalley), in the vicinity of Pendle Hill, where John Middleton works, from childhood, in the recently built cotton factory, bullied as a child by his own father, who drags him to the factory to wind reels for him, and later victimised by the malicious son of the overseer. This deeply shadowed tale shows another aspect of industrialisation: the recently built factory attracts a throng of workers from the country, and these include rough and dangerous men, not agricultural labourers but poachers and vagrants, who combine factory life by day with poaching by night. 'By day, we all made a show of working in the factory. By night we feasted and drank.' In 'The Heart of John Middleton' even the countryside comes to share in the darkness of the industrial scene. Of the four tales, only 'Lizzie Leigh' offers at the end an escape to the undisturbed countryside dear to Elizabeth Gaskell, when the Leigh family, their search in Manchester at an end, return to the shelter of Upclose Farm. In all the stories, however, the motif of the child as an agent of conciliation persists. Children are themselves the main actors in 'Hand and Heart' and 'Bessy's Troubles at Home'; love of a child brings grief but also the resolution of conflict in 'Lizzie Leigh'; his meeting with the child who later becomes his wife revolutionises the life of John Middleton.

Ruth represents a transitional stage in the treatment of the industrial theme. Ruth's experiences in the first part of the novel seem to have been partly suggested by those of a girl of sixteen whom Mrs Gaskell visited in a Manchester prison. A dressmaker's apprentice, she had been seduced by a man socially her superior, forced by misery into prostitution and would have had nothing to hope for if Elizabeth Gaskell had not helped her to emigrate.[15] Ruth, like this girl, had not originally belonged to the working class; her father had been a small farmer and her mother a curate's daughter. But when left an orphan she is similarly apprenticed to a dressmaker and seduced by a young aristocrat attracted by her beauty. The life of a dressmaker's apprentice, as shown in *Ruth*, is one of unremitting drudgery. The dressmaking industry was not subject to the rules which limited factory hours and, when dresses were required for a coming ball, the girls slaved through most of the night, only to start again at eight in the morning. Mrs Mason is a respectable woman and does not, like the employer of Mrs Gaskell's unfortunate protégée, connive at her seduction, but she shows little sympathy or understanding in her treatment of her apprentices. On Sundays she conveniently assumes that they have friends who will entertain them to meals, and Ruth is usually left alone, cold and hungry, in the deserted workroom. Her plight is made worse by the fact that, unlike the other girls, she has come from a country home and feels stifled among the 'dismal, hateful, tumble-down old houses' in the decaying quarter of Fordham where Mrs Mason lives. The description of the Fordham environment is of crucial importance for the development of the novel, for it goes far to explain why Ruth, not yet sixteen, responds to offers of sympathy and protection from Bellingham.

When, however, Ruth, seduced and abandoned, is adopted into the Benson household, the situation changes. The Bensons, though poor, are people of education and refinement, and when Benson instructs Ruth, so that she in turn may teach her child, she becomes an educated woman, competent to act as visiting governess in a middle-class household. Her problem ceases to be that of a destitute seamstress and becomes that of the unmarried mother whose whole life is concentrated in her child, for whose sake Benson reluctantly condones the concealing of her true situation from her rigidly respectable employers.

But Eccleston, where the Bensons live, is an industrial town and Mr Bradshaw, Ruth's employer, is the head of its leading firm. *Ruth*, therefore, includes a study of a rich merchant and manufacturer, seen in his domestic life. Bradshaw has nothing like the status of Carson, a mill-owner in a vast industrial city, but he has worked hard to obtain his position and, without realising it, worships money and the power that money gives. He also has ambitions to become a public figure, and feels strong enough to oppose to the Tory candidate for Eccleston a Liberal of his own choosing. Ironically, the Liberal candidate turns out to be an aristocrat, the same man who had seduced Ruth. It is characteristic of Bradshaw that he dislikes the sense of inferiority which he feels in his presence, but can think of no way of relieving himself from it except by a display of wealth which makes not the slightest impression on a man so accustomed, like his ancestors before him, to everything that money can purchase that he only notices its absence, never its presence.

Ruth does not give the same painful sense of segregation as the dark world of the court dwellers in *Mary Barton*. Professional men, rarely mentioned in the first novel, here regain their normal importance in the community. Benson, the Dissenting minister, has both middle class and poor among his congregation. The doctor, who, in *Mary Barton*, appears only to confirm the fact of death or to announce its approach, regains here the stature he normally possesses as friend, helper and adviser in Elizabeth Gaskell's work. Mr Davis is a skilful doctor and a humane man who, even if all his efforts cannot save Ruth from succumbing to typhoid fever, does ensure the future of her son as his apprentice and eventual partner. Only the law, which, in *Mary Barton*, does not intervene to great purpose—it is Mary's own efforts which save an innocent man from being hanged—is even less effectively represented in *Ruth*, by the lawyer's apprentice who draws up old Sally's will but is transported before he can qualify, and, more seriously, by the briefless barrister Hickson, a friend of the Parliamentary agent for the Liberal candidate, who professes to wish to promote the return of Liberal members in the hope of effecting a reform in the law but in reality has no principle but expediency.

In *North and South*, serialised in Dickens' *Household Words* and subsequently published in book form in 1855, Elizabeth Gaskell returned, much more completely than in *Ruth*, to the industrial scene. The Milton-Northern of the novel is evidently suggested by Manchester. Yet the climate is not identical to that of the first novel. There had been some amelioration in the condition of the working classes by the early fifties. There had also been, after the continental upheaval of 1848, a more cautious attitude towards philanthropic interventionism. This may have affected Elizabeth Gaskell, always anxious to avoid in her work anything that could be misconstrued as an incitement to violence or class warfare. She had also been keenly sensitive to the accusations of bias against the employers directed at her after the publication of *Mary Barton*. At that time she had rejected suggestions that she should write another work showing the employers' side of the question. But she had not denied that they had problems, and that employers like the cotton-spinner Samuel Greg, the brother of *Mary Barton's* most trenchant critic, did endeavour to put into practice, at considerable cost to themselves, philanthropic schemes ridiculed by their colleagues as Utopian.[16] By the time she began to plan a successor to *Ruth*, she was able to consider the position of both masters and men with more detachment than in *Mary Barton*. It is significant that in *North and South* the industrial scene is viewed principally through the eyes of a newcomer to Milton-Northern, the parson's daughter from the South, Margaret Hale, for whom mill-owners and workers belong equally to an unknown world.

It is the mill-owner John Thornton who, with Margaret Hale, plays the principal part in the inner and outer action of the novel. Thornton belongs to a family originally moderately well-off, but his father had speculated rashly and committed suicide, leaving a burden of debts. He has in fact, like the elder Carson, risen to his present position as one of the leading manufacturers in Milton through his own efforts. He is, however, far more closely identified than Carson with the life of a great industrial city. He chooses to live in close proximity to his mill instead of almost in the country. Above all, he sees Milton, as Disraeli saw Manchester, as the symbol of a new age. The rapid development of the cotton industry is for him a matter of wonder and pride: 'Seventy years ago, what was it? And now what is it not?' And the machinery which has made this development possible is for him part of an immense and grandiose process, 'the war which compels, and shall compel, all material power to yield to science'. With this pride in the achievements of industry Thornton combines a strong sense of independence; he feels that he belongs to a new order, which should evolve its own laws. The pride of a new urban aristocracy is reflected in his attitude to his workers. He is no ruthless tyrant; he condemns the tyranny of the early cotton lords and welcomes the fact that need of manpower has made the position of masters and men more evenly balanced. But he is, on his own admission, at the time when Margaret Hale and her father first encounter him, the advocate of an autocratic system which denies the workers any opportunity to question the masters' decisions and actions. Yet this autocracy is based on an attitude more humane than the indifference displayed by Carson (until the closing chapters of *Mary Barton*) to the welfare of his 'hands'. Thornton does recognise that their interests are in fact identical. Moreover he shows a respect for his men, as individuals, which is totally different from Carson's ignorance of their very names or the still more wounding disdain of his son. He believes that it is within the power of any of his workers as individuals to graduate, by hard work and self-discipline, into positions of authority and even possibly to become masters in their turn. And he respects their independence absolutely, once business hours are over, and would consider it as much of an imposition, were he to interfere with the life they lead out of the mills, as if anyone were to interfere with his own freedom of action.

If Thornton is a more complex and finished study than Carson, the representative of the masters in *Mary Barton*, Higgins, the weaver, differs as much from John Barton, though he does not possess the unique importance that belonged to the earlier defendant of the workers. The character of Higgins is obviously based, like that of Barton, on Elizabeth Gaskell's personal knowledge of Manchester working men. Recognised by as competent a judge as Sir William Fairbairn as 'an excellent representative of a Lancashire operative',[17] the dogged and practical Higgins is as convincing in his own way as the intense and bewildered Barton. As forthright and independent as John Thornton himself, he resents anything that savours of patronage. Margaret Hale may visit his home, at his invitation, on equal terms, but not as lady bountiful. He does not think of the relations between employers and workers in terms of the parable of Dives and Lazarus but rather as a battle, in which he is on the side of his own class, a battle waged in less grim conditions than in *Mary Barton*. The Higgins live in a dingy court but not, until the strike breaks out, in conditions of actual privation. The elder daughter Bessy is a victim of the industrial system; she is dying, at nineteen, of tuberculosis, contracted when she was working among the cotton fluff in the carding room, but her father, though deeply attached to her, accepts the fact of her illness with philosophy. With similar philosophy he accepts the fact that all are not as competent to face hardship as himself. His neighbour John Boucher is, in his estimation, 'a poor good-for-naught as can only manage two looms at a time', but he is prepared to do his best for Boucher's ailing wife and small children. It is not help he asks for himself and his class but what he considers justice.

The strike which, in *Mary Barton*, brings disaster, clarifies the issues in *North and South*. An important factor in the struggle is the increased power of the trade unions. Although it is in irony that Thornton refers to the possibility of the masters finally having to go hat in hand to the Spinners' Union, to ask for labour at their own price, such a possibility would never have been mentioned, even ironically, in *Mary Barton*, where the unions have at best an almost conspiratorial role. His union is Nicholas Higgins' chief source of confidence; with its strength and resources behind them, he and his fellow unionists even welcome the prospect of a battle with the employers. It is not their intention to resort to physical violence, which they know would alienate public sympathy. It proves, however, less easy to direct the course of the strike than they had anticipated. Thornton's prompt action in sending for Irish workers is all that is needed to provoke a violent confrontation. It is the weak and irresponsible among the crowd, like the unfortunate Boucher, who incite the rest to violence. Only the desperate intervention of Margaret Hale averts disaster and ultimately leads, in conjunction with Thornton's courage, to the dispersal of the mob. The incident in turn leads to the collapse of the strike. The employers are now in a position to insist on their own terms, and responsible unionists are bitter towards those like Boucher who, through their misguided violence, ruined their cause. Higgins in particular does not spare the unfortunate man, and Boucher, scorned by the workers and unable, as former ringleader of the mob, to obtain from any employer the work which, as father of a large family, he desperately needs, is driven by fear and despair to suicide.

In her handling of the whole question of industrial strife Elizabeth Gaskell now does her utmost to be fair both to masters and men. Thornton, as he is when Margaret Hale first meets him, is a just employer but hardly a generous one, unyielding in his rigid application of the doctrines of economic fatalism. 'Margaret's whole soul rose up against him while he reasoned in this way . . .'[18] Higgins is admirable in his determination to make the best of difficult circumstances and to defend, in the interests of others as well as himself, the cause of what he and his fellow unionists consider to be justice. But Margaret Hale, when she learns of the ostracism to which those who do not wish to join the union are subjected, protests against a tyranny which appears to her quite as great as that of which the union accuses the masters.

Matters are not left in this state of deadlock, however. As in *Mary Barton*, the struggle eventually ends in a movement towards conciliation. Here, too, it is not economic doctrines but a better understanding between individuals which holds out most hope for greater harmony in the future. The economic theory which teaches that wages find their own level means nothing to Higgins, profoundly distrustful of theories: 'I'm not one who thinks truth can be shaped out in words, all neat and clean, as th' men at th' foundry cut out sheet-iron'.[19] It is the gradual establishment of more friendly relations between the worker and the mill-owner which causes each to see the other in a different perspective. Persuaded by Margaret Hale to apply to Thornton for a place in his factory, when he is workless after the strike, Higgins, known as a union leader, at first meets with a decided refusal, though he asks not on his own behalf but for the sake of Boucher's fatherless children, to whom he has given a home. Subsequently Thornton's sense of justice reproaches him for not having given the man a fair hearing. The interview in which the mill-owner comes in person to the weaver's home to offer him work marks a new stage in the development of both, and begins something in the nature of a friendship between them.

It is thanks to the better understanding that develops between the two that the first step is taken towards co-operation between master and employees. The scheme of a communal dining-room for the operatives, run by themselves, where Thornton's part is reduced to that of purveyor, appears less impressive than the mention of the reforms initiated by Carson in the closing stages of *Mary Barton*. But this one, modest in itself, is more convincing because it is actually put into practice and because, like the co-operative movement initiated by Robert Owen in whose spirit it appears to be conceived, it safeguards the independence of the workers. Anything else would have been unacceptable to Higgins' sturdy individualism, and it says much for the change in Thornton's attitude that he accepts the part of steward assigned to him with a good grace, and subsequently finds himself on occasion an invited guest. When business reverses lead to the failure of his mill and he has to look for a new position, he expresses his determination only to accept one where such experiments can still be carried out:

'My only wish is to have the opportunity of cultivating some intercourse with the hands beyond the mere "cash nexus" . . . I have arrived at the conviction that no mere institutions, however wise, and however much thought may have been required to organise and arrange them, can attach class to class as they should be attached, unless the working out of such institutions bring the individuals of the different classes into actual personal contact. Such intercourse is the very breath of life.' (Ch. 51)

The prevailing tensions in *North and South* go further than those between masters and men. It is two aspects of nineteenth-century civilisation which are contrasted. The distance between Thornton and his workmen is not so great as that which exists, on their first meeting, between Thornton and Margaret Hale. Thornton and Higgins are both North Country men, who speak the same language and share the same enjoyment of a fight. It is when the mill-owner meets the parson's daughter from the South that there is a clash between different languages and outlooks, which goes deeper than the clash between master and man. Higgins could conceivably have risen, in favourable circumstances, to be a 'master' himself. Margaret Hale feels certain, on first seeing Thornton, that he will never conceivably qualify as a 'gentleman'. One cannot but admire the skill with which Elizabeth Gaskell, through her use of Margaret as the focal point of the entire novel, relates the conflict of interests to the deeper conflict of values and makes of an industrial novel at the same time a far-sighted analysis of the problems of a new society in the process of evolution.

This wider purpose determines the particular use of the descriptive procedure, always an essential part of the Gaskell novel. In *Mary Barton*, the perspective was that of the cellar dweller. In *North and South* the cotton metropolis is seen chiefly through the eyes of Margaret, who has come from the rural beauty of a village in the New Forest. What strikes her at first is not so much the blackness of the 'Darkshire' milieu as its drabness: 'Quickly they were whirled over long, straight, hopeless streets of regularly-built houses, all small and of brick.' The only exception to this bleak uniformity is, here and there, 'a great oblong many-windowed factory'. The dimensions of these palaces of industry arouse no admiration in Margaret, who is repelled by the smoke and the noise and has no desire to penetrate inside their walls, even when told they contain 'every improvement of machinery . . . in its highest perfection'. The lack of fresh air is a source of dismay to the girl used to breezy commons and unused to fog and factory chimneys. Thornton's house beside the mill has a dismal outlook on to the yard and, when Margaret and her father first visit it, they are ushered into an opulent but unwelcoming apartment, which is in complete contrast to their own modest little drawing-room with its comfort and good taste:

> Everything reflected light, nothing absorbed it. The whole room had a painfully spotted, spangled, speckled look about it, which impressed Margaret so unpleasantly that she was hardly con-

scious of the peculiar cleanliness required to keep everything so white and pure in such an atmosphere, or of the trouble that must be willingly expended to secure that effect of icy, snowy discomfort. Wherever she looked there was evidence of care and labour, but not care and labour to procure ease, to help on habits of tranquil home employment; solely to ornament, and then to preserve ornament from dirt or destruction. (Ch. 15)

In the industrial milieu of Milton wealth, and the power wealth gives, are the standards by which success is judged, and the new social prestige of money clashes with the centuries-old prestige of class. Thornton, one of the most influential men in Milton, is immediately classified as a 'tradesman' by Margaret, on their first meeting, and relegated to a sphere inferior to her own, though her father now has to earn his living as a tutor. In the eyes of the redoubtable Mrs Thornton, the mill-owner's mother, however, Margaret herself is only 'a girl without a penny', who assumes unjustified airs, and her father 'appears a worthy kind of man enough; rather too simple for trade—so it's perhaps as well he should have been a clergyman first, and now a teacher'. The same clash of values is reflected at all levels. Dixon, the Hale's servant, who can never forget that her mistress had been a Beresford, considers, when another helper is needed, that any of the Milton girls should be proud to serve in such an aristocratic household. They, on the other hand, have doubts as to the solvency of a family who live in 'a house of thirty pounds a year' and have no connection with trade. Even Bessy Higgins, a devout admirer of Margaret, shows unflattering surprise when she hears that the Hales have actually been invited to dinner by the Thorntons, who entertain all the 'first folk' in Milton.

In Milton one does not require a classical education to be a successful business man. Culture is another traditional value which has depreciated in the industrial world: '. . . according to the prevalent, and apparently well-founded notions of Milton, to make a lad into a good tradesman he must be caught young, and acclimatised to the life of the mill, or office, or warehouse.'[20] Most manufacturers placed their sons in such situations at fourteen or fifteen, 'unsparingly cutting away all off-shoots in the direction of literature or high mental cultivation, in hopes of throwing the whole strength and vigour of the plant into commerce'.[21] Some, however, were more liberal and sometimes their children themselves expressed cultural aspirations. Elizabeth Gaskell had reason to know this; J. A. Froude was the much-respected tutor of the children of her friends the Darbishires, a Manchester family, and her husband counted among his own most gifted pupils the Winkworth sisters, daughters of a silk manufacturer. Thornton himself had learned Latin and Greek at school, in the days before his father's failure in business, and it is his desire to renew his knowledge of the classics in his spare time which first brings him into contact with the Hale family. This desire is, however, frowned on by his mother on the grounds that to have many interests 'does not suit the life of a Milton manufacturer'. And even her son, while he can now enjoy reading Homer, absolutely denies that the memory of the Homeric heroes was of the slightest help to him in his early struggles: 'I was too busy to think about any dead people, with the living pressing alongside of me, neck to neck, in the struggle for bread.'[22] Later, there is a confrontation between him and Margaret's godfather, Mr Bell, by birth a Milton man but an Oxford Fellow of many years' standing. In the discussion Bell stands by the priorities of Oxford 'with its beauty and its learning, and its proud old history'. His are the classic values, but Thornton rejects them in favour of what is almost a new romanticism: 'I belong to Teutonic blood; it is little mingled in this part of England to what it is in others; we retain much of their language; we retain more of their spirit . . . Our glory and our beauty arise out of our inward strength, which makes us victorious over material resistance, and over greater difficulties still.'[23]

Untraditional, noisy, smoky, dominated by the factory and the market, the industrial North is at first utterly uncongenial to Margaret Hale, parson's daughter from the South and a country-woman by birth. The fairness of Elizabeth Gaskell's treatment, evident in her attitude to masters and men, is equally evident in her dealing with two at first irreconcilable ways of life. Margaret naturally resents Thornton's blunt statement, made at an early stage of their acquaintance, of the superiority of his native town to the effete South: 'I would rather be a man toiling, suffering—may, failing and successless—here, than lead a dull prosperous life in the old worn grooves of what you call more aristocratic society down in the South, with their slow days of careless ease.'[24] Gradually, however, she comes to recognise that, if he does not understand the South, she is equally ignorant of the North. Listening to the conversation of the leading industrialists at the Thornton dinner-table, she is impressed by the sense of power they communicate and by their intense eagerness, which is in strong contrast with the superficiality she associates with her memory of London dinner-parties. By this time she and Thornton have arrived at a stage of 'antagonistic friendship'. Their discussion of the significance of the terms 'man' and 'gentleman' highlights their still persisting difference of outlook. She associates moral and social criteria as equally valid, indeed inseparable; he shows his individualism by attaching far more weight to the first than to the second: 'I take it that 'gentleman' is a term that only describes a person in his relation to others; but when we speak of him as 'a man', we consider him not merely with regard to his fellow-men, but in relation to himself—to life—to time—to eternity.'[25] Soon after he makes his declaration of love to Margaret, encouraged by her intervention during the strike, only to discover that, in her estimation, he still belongs to a different world. But the distance between them is by now far less great than she had imagined. The growing recognition that in reality she returns his love is accompanied by her increasing power to look with more objectivity at the differences between North and South.

The most open admission on her part that everything is not idyllic in the South is her vehement opposition when Higgins, the Milton operative, expresses his intention, after the strike, of going there in search of work as an agricultural labourer. The darkness of her picture of a labourer's life recalls the realism of Crabbe and can compare with the livid tones of Disraeli's painting of the same milieu in *Sybil* or of Kingsley's in *Yeast*: 'Those that have lived there all their lives are used to soaking in the stagnant waters. They labour on from day to day, in the great solitude of steaming fields—never speaking or lifting up their poor, bent, downcast heads . . . you of all men are not one to bear a life among such labourers.'[26] The unexpected harshness of this picture can be accounted for partly by the fact that Margaret is speaking here of the agricultural labourer, not of the farmer or the yeoman. Even so, the picture appears disproportionately dark by comparison with the glowing colours in which the pastoral setting of Helstone had been painted earlier in the novel. When Margaret subsequently returns on a brief visit, she finds, inevitably, minor changes which distress her chiefly because they are out of tune with her memories. She also finds startling evidence of the cruelty inflicted on an unfortunate animal by an old woman's ignorant belief in one of the most savage of the country superstitions. But the landscape is as beautiful as ever: 'Nature felt no change, and was ever young.' And life is still pursuing an even course for the villagers and for the men afield busy with the haymaking. 'The common sounds of life were more musical there than anywhere else in the whole world, the light more golden, the life more tranquil and full of dreamy delight.'[27]

It is clear that Helstone will always remain 'the prettiest spot in the world' for Margaret Hale. But, since the novel ends with her coming marriage to Thornton, it is evidently in the industrial North that her future life will be spent, among factory chimneys and the noise of machinery. Mrs Gaskell did consider, in a letter to Catherine Winkworth, the possibility of introducing a fire to burn down Thornton's mill and house, so that Margaret 'would rebuild them larger and better and need not go and live there when she's married',[28] but she rightly abandoned the idea. *North and South* does not end, like *Mary Barton*, with an escapist solution. Margaret will continue to live, out of love for Thornton, in the shadow of the mill, but it will always cast a shadow, and it is doubtful if she will ever fully share her husband's admiration for the new poetry of machinery. She might have said with truth, as Elizabeth Gaskell said of herself, that she was not naturally attracted by it. Like Elizabeth Gaskell, however, she had an intense sympathy for her fellows and would always join with enthusiasm in her husband's endeavours to establish closer contact with his work-people. It is this human sympathy, reflected in her friendship for Higgins and his daughter, which inspires what are probably the most moving episodes in *North and South*.

In this respect, however, it is less moving than *Mary Barton*. The first novel was the result of personal contact with the misery and squalor of the poorest districts of Manchester. The publication of *Mary Barton* revolutionised its author's life in a way she could not have foreseen, and made it impossible for her, as established writer as well as wife, mother and busy hostess, to maintain the same close contact with the Manchester work-people. For this reason the first work, which interprets the cry of a submerged population, is more absolutely original than the second, though the latter is wider in scope and far superior in construction. The critic W. R. Greg, though he personally preferred *North and South* and did not quarrel with the views expressed there, as he had done in the case of the earlier novel, was probably right in thinking that it was not 'as thorough a work of genius' as *Mary Barton*.

It was in Manchester that *Mary Barton* was planned and largely written. Yet a passage halfway through the narration suddenly opens a window on the country and shows that Elizabeth Gaskell, when engaged in creative writing, was already experiencing the relief of sometimes renewing contact with the beauty and the peace of rural surroundings. When Mary, sleepless through anxiety, goes out at night to fetch water from the pump in the court to quench her feverish thirst, the author suddenly intervenes to contrast the scene described with the surroundings in which she is then writing:

> The hard, square outlines of the houses cut sharply against the cold bright sky, from which myriads of stars were shining down in eternal repose. There was little sympathy in the outward scene, with the internal trouble. All was so still, so motionless, so hard! Very different to this lovely night in the country in which I am now writing, where the distant horizon is soft and undulating in the moonlight, and the nearer trees sway gently to and fro in the night-wind with something of almost human motion; and the rustling air makes music among their branches, as if speaking soothingly to the weary ones, who lie awake in heaviness of heart. The sights and sounds of such a night lull pain and grief to rest. (Ch. 22)

As her life in Manchester became increasingly busy, Elizabeth Gaskell found that her writing commitments could only be carried out with the help of recurrent periods of respite in country peace and fresh air. Her favourite retreat became Silverdale, where Lindeth Tower, with its top floor commanding extensive views landward and seaward reserved for her own use, provided the perfect refuge for a writer. *Ruth* owes much to the peace of Silverdale, and part of *North and South* was composed in surroundings equally beautiful, at Lea Hurst, the Nightingales' country home in Derbyshire, where the unrivalled view over the valley of the Derwent, seen from the windows of the room where she wrote, was in strong contrast to the industrial world she principally described, where 'the chimneys smoked, the ceaseless roar and mighty beat and dazzling whirl of machinery struggled and strove perpetually'.

Elizabeth Gaskell's own predicament was partly that of Margaret Hale. She was a country lover inescapably committed to making her home in Manchester. Like Margaret she came to understand that there were qualities to command admiration in her adopted city. When in 1859 her husband was offered the post of minister in the leading Unitarian Chapel in London and declined, she supported his decision on the grounds that 'he could never get in London the influence and good he has here . . .'[29] Part of that influence came from his evening lectures to audiences of working men at the Mechanics' Institutes and later to the students of Owens College. There was interest in literature as well as in science in some circles in Manchester, which had in fact wider horizons than those of Milton-Northern. The Gaskells' own home at Plymouth Grove became increasingly a focus of cultural life in the city. Yet there were aspects of Manchester to which Elizabeth Gaskell was never able to acclimatise herself. She was intensely susceptible to natural beauty, and the drabness of the city streets, the pall of smoke never ceased to oppress her with a sense of the unnatural. When inviting her friend Eliza Fox on a visit, she warned her to be prepared for 'a cold clammy atmosphere, a town with no grace or beauty in it . . .'[30]

The move to Plymouth Grove brought her nearer to the open country, and there was the pleasure of a more extensive garden, though it was a problem to decide 'what perennials will do in Manchester smoke',[31] but she still longed for wider prospects and more beauty than could be seen in 'dear old dull ugly smoky grim grey Manchester'.[32] The climate, especially during the winter, told on her health, and she often expressed the desire to be 'out of this misty foggy Manchester, which gives me a perpetual headache very hard to bear'.[33] To the lack of beauty and of fresh air was added, by the very circumstances of her life in Manchester, another major deprivation—lack of time. The Whitsun excursion to Dunham Woods in 'Libbie Marsh's Three Eras' is valued even more as a source of mental than of physical tranquillity:

> Depend upon it, this complete sylvan repose, this accessible quiet, this lapping the soul in green images of the country, forms the most complete contrast to a town's-person, and consequently has over such the greatest power of charm.[34]

After *North and South* Elizabeth Gaskell wrote no more novels of industrial life. The countryside and the country town became the principal settings of her tales, for she found them a more lasting because more congenial source of inspiration. Yet without Manchester her work would have lacked reverberations which give it a deeper resonance. It was Manchester that first taught her what human beings could endure and achieve in the most tragic conditions. It taught her, too, that the advance of science was an integral part of modern civilisation. Though she personally found the scientific spirit most congenial in its alliance with natural history, she believed with Job Legh that scientific inventions and industrial progress must be recognised and accepted. Yet it is significant that it is not in one of the Manchester novels but in *Cousin Phillis* that she introduces her warmest tribute to the genius of the northern engineers. Paul Manning's father, who has 'the same kind of genius for mechanical invention as George Stephenson', is admired and appreciated, when he visits Hope Farm, by Holman, minister and farmer. Manning, on his side, is keenly interested by what the other has to say about agriculture, and anxious to introduce improvements which will make his agricultural implements more effective. Both are united in the desire for practical achievement which will be to man's advantage. Neither is concerned with money-making as their principal aim. The scene in the firelit farm kitchen where Manning sketches his model for a new machine with a charred stick on the hard-wood dresser combines science with poetry and the stirring nineteenth century with the age-old past.

5 The family

Whether her characters live in country town or industrial city, Elizabeth Gaskell always considers their family relationships as a fundamental part of their lives. They were, of course, a fundamental part of her own. As when she wrote of Cranford or Milton-Northern, she was writing out of her own experience, as well as out of her observation. She could never have been happy without feeling herself to belong both to a community and to that smallest and most closely knit of all communities, the family. Experience of marriage and motherhood was, in her judgement, a valuable asset when she began her career as a novelist. To a young wife with literary ambitions, impatient of domesticity, she wrote: '. . . a good writer of fiction must have *lived* an active and sympathetic life . . . When you are forty, and if you have a gift for being an authoress you will write ten times as good a novel as you could do now, just because you will have gone through so much more of the interests of a wife and a mother.'[1] Her letters are full of evidence of her sympathetic understanding of her own four daughters: 'Are you prepared for four girls in and out continually . . .', she asked a prospective visitor. 'The girls *are* very nice ones, though I say it that should not say it, and I do think you will like them all in their separate ways . . . .'[2] She followed their development as they grew from childhood to adolescence, and her portrayal of her heroines, especially from *North and South* onwards, is clearly the more discerning because she could draw on this source. She did not, of course, limit her study of the family to her personal experience. Her wide observation and equally wide sympathies precluded any such exclusive viewpoint. There is, however, a particular richness and complexity in the study of Margaret Hale, Molly Gibson and Phillis Holman which suggests intimate personal knowledge, derived perhaps in the first two cases from memories of her own youth as much as from knowledge of her daughters. More evidently still, her own intense maternal feeling is reflected in her studies of mother-hood, especially in *Ruth*, which provides the most poignant and beautiful example of the devotion of the young mother.

Where husband and wife were concerned, Elizabeth Gaskell did not consider the reader should be allowed to intrude on the privacy of their personal relations, an attitude made clear at the close of her biography of Charlotte Brontë. The husbands and wives who feature in her tales are usually middle-aged and chiefly considered in their relationship to their children. But they are still as a rule united by deep affection, like the Hamleys and the Robsons. The only full-length study of a marriage that breaks down is *Sylvia's Lovers*, which is also, exceptionally, a study of the first years of a youthful marriage. It is entered into with passion on one side and apathy on the other, and even the birth of a child does not avert tragedy, though without it there could have been no final reconciliation. Nothing could have been less like Elizabeth Gaskell's own experience, as the affectionate dedication to her husband makes clear.

It is, however, the pattern of her own childhood and youth, rather than that of the Gaskell home, that seems to be most often reflected in the composition of the family units in her tales. Those where the children have both parents surviving by the time they reach maturity are in the minority, and death often intervenes in the course of the action to diminish the family. 'Hers is the very minimal family unit and subject to calamity . . .'[3] There was unfortunately nothing in the mortality rate in the first part of the Victorian age to make this situation unrealistic, but that it owed something to her own motherless condition as an infant, to the lack of close relations with her father and to the loss of her only son cannot be in doubt. The exposure of the family to the menace of illness and death is emphasised throughout her work. In her first published essay 'Clopton House' the deserted nursery is seen as being, of all the deserted rooms, the saddest, 'a nursery without children . . .' The wife of John Barton, the hero of her first novel, dies in childbirth while still a young woman, after he has already seen his only son die as a child, and in her last novel Molly Gibson's mother has died before the story opens. Of all the tales it is perhaps *My Lady Ludlow* which throws into darkest relief the inroads of mortality on the life of the family. Lady Ludlow, like Elizabeth Gaskell's mother, has lost most of her children in infancy; of those who lived longer the sailor son had been the first to go and the present head of the family, Earl Ludlow, is the last, dying without an heir.

Whether threatened or actually reduced to a memory, the family none the less counts for much in the lives of Elizabeth Gaskell's characters. More even than the physical or social environment, it is the home in which they live, or perhaps which they only remember, which helps to make them what they are. Elizabeth Gaskell aimed to paint ordinary people—*Wives and Daughters*, her masterpiece, is rightly called an 'every-day story'—but they are people of flesh and blood, with their particular circumstances and their personal background, as well as the wider environment they share with others. This insistence on the importance of the family is in tune with her natural liking for tradition and continuity, and with her acceptance of a social hierarchy. It was in tune, too, with the spirit of the times; the patriarchal pattern, deep-rooted in English tradition, was never more honoured than in the Victorian era. The family meant stability and peace. More significantly still, in Elizabeth Gaskell's eyes, as in those of many Victorians, it meant the transmission of moral principles and of high standards of conduct. Most of all, as far as she was concerned, it was the most natural medium for giving and receiving affection and consequently for satisfying the deepest need of the human heart. She was far too much of a realist, and far too keen an observer, to believe that this was in fact what all families achieved. The story of most of her novels and tales reveals what the individual characters give and receive, but also what they fail to give or receive, in their intercourse with their family.

The Victorians accepted the authority of the husband and father. Elizabeth Gaskell counted among her friends some pioneers of the Women's Rights Movement like Eliza Fox, at whose invitation she signed the Married Women's Property Bill, but her comment when she did so showed her lack of faith in the virtue of legislation in a predominantly masculine society: '. . . a husband can coax, wheedle, beat or tyrannize his wife out of something and no law whatever will help this that I see . . .'[4] As in her attitude to social problems, she recognised that the human factor could never be disregarded. She believed that there was an inherent dignity in the position of husband and father. She did not believe that feminine subservience in any way advanced that dignity. Her own husband was incapable of being an autocrat. Sometimes, when beset with problems, she even confessed to wishing that he were more of one: 'I long (weakly) for the old times where right and wrong did not seem such complicated matters; and I am sometimes coward enough to wish that we were back in the darkness when obedience was the only seen duty of women. Only even then I don't believe William would ever have *commanded* me.'[5] But she knows that such a state of affairs could never, in any case, have been a healthy one and that, too often, it reacted adversely on the well-being and even the unity of the family.

Her first sketch of such a situation is in the tale 'Lizzie Leigh'. James Leigh, Lizzie's father, is an impeccably honest but stern and inflexible man, whose wife has always accepted his judgement in everything as infallible: 'Milton's famous line might have been framed and hung up as the rule of their married life, for he was truly the interpreter who stood between God and her; she would have considered herself wicked if she had ever dared even to think him austere . . .'[6] It is he who decides that Lizzie is being made too much of by her mother and she is sent, at sixteen, to be a domestic servant in Manchester, where she is seduced and subsequently turned into the street by her employers. She dare not return home, for fear of her father, who, when he eventually hears the news, declares that she is no longer one of the family. There follow three years of silent estrangement between husband and wife. On his deathbed he expresses forgiveness of Lizzie and the mother ultimately finds her child again, but all hope of normal happiness is at an end for both mother and daughter.

The subject of paternal domination and wifely submission recurs in *Cranford*. The feminine society there has, paradoxically, been largely conditioned by the patriarchal régime of the former rector, the father of Deborah and Matty Jenkyns. Thanks to the softening influence of time, the gradual transformation—revealed in old family letters—of the ardent young husband into the proud but authoritative father, and of the light-hearted girl into the fond and anxious mother, appears almost a humorous process. Tragedy strikes when the son rebels against the exaggeratedly decorous régime enforced by his father, and welcomed by his elder sister, and leaves home after the humiliation of a public flogging. Miss Matty's own narration is substituted for letters as she recalls the disaster and its consequence, the death of her broken-hearted mother. Even here, time has softened tragedy into pathos, but a revealing light has been shed on Miss Jenkyns' rigid adherence to the standards dear to the rector and on the reason for Miss Matty's spinsterhood, due not to her incapacity for sexual love but to her docile yet heartbroken acceptance, typical of her mother's daughter, of the parental embargo on marriage with a yeoman farmer.

The most realistic and complex study of the autocratic husband and father, whose rule provokes disharmony in the family, is the portrait of the Bradshaw ménage in *Ruth*. Bradshaw's first appearance, when he arrives at the Dissenting chapel in Eccleston, accompanied by his wife, is the suitable prelude to his subsequent actions, and to her inaction: 'He was a tall, large-boned, iron man; stern, powerful, and authoritative in appearance . . . His wife was sweet and gentle-looking, but as if she was thoroughly broken into submission.'[7] The four children are, as might be expected, subjected to a strict discipline. The two youngest, 'well-behaved but unnaturally quiet' little girls, are not old enough to question their father's spartan rule. The only son, already grown-up, has always been apparently docile, but his pattern of behaviour was simply the result of intimidation. After the unnatural seclusion of his upbringing, he is unable to cope with the hazards of society and becomes an embezzler. The eldest daughter is a high-spirited girl who resents her father's autocracy but refrains from open protest till his domineering attitude over the question of her marriage has the opposite effect to that he intends, and produces a temporary estrangement between herself and the suitor whom she really loves but wrongly suspects of being chiefly concerned like her father, whose partner he is, with the material advantages of the match. Only the dismissal of Ruth, now the Bradshaws' governess, to whom her lover, repulsed by her, has transferred his attentions, saves the situation. It is no thanks to Bradshaw that she, after all, makes a happy marriage. His son, whom he has disowned on discovery of his embezzlement, is never mentioned by him till news comes of the boy's serious accident, causing an illness which shows that there is still feeling beneath the father's rigid exterior. The son survives, and a situation is found for him away from home, where it is hoped that he may do reasonably well in time, but any hopes for his future must remain modest ones: 'He will never be a hero of virtue, for his education has drained him of all moral courage . . .'[8]

The most disastrous lack in the Bradshaw household is the absence of any open expression of love or sympathy to accompany the paternal inculcation of principle. The younger children are obliged to take the existence of deeper feelings on trust: 'Just think how often papa lectures mamma; and yet, of course, they're in love with each other.' The grown-up son and daughter realise that their mother is affectionate by nature but has not the smallest influence on the actions of her husband. Just how much the woman's natural capacity for love and sympathy can achieve for the well-being of the family, when it is exercised freely, is evident from the different situation of the Hamley household in *Wives and Daughters*, where a man of naturally masterful temperament is influenced and in some things guided by the greater patience and the loving nature of his wife.

The first sketch of this situation is in the tale 'The Moorland Cottage', where the Buxton family anticipate the Hamleys. Buxton, a wealthy man of yeoman descent, is devoted to his delicate wife, whose unassuming sweetness of disposition is a source of strength both to him and to their son, as well as to all who come into contact with her. It is only after her death that the latent 'seeds of imperiousness' in her husband's nature develop and that there is for a time a danger of estrangement between him and his heir. The parallel with the Hamleys is evident, but not enough is seen of Mrs Buxton to justify the importance of the role ascribed to her. In the far wider canvas of *Wives and Daughters* a searching light is shed on the household at Hamley Hall, from the time when Molly Gibson is first brought there on a visit by her father, at the invitation of Mrs Hamley, the invalid wife of the bluff country squire. Like Buxton the Squire is devoted to his delicate wife, and the two sons, Osborne and Roger, have grown up in a happy and united home. Elizabeth Gaskell is too much of a realist to paint, even here, a picture of unclouded domestic bliss. The family does not see enough of outside society because the Squire, who has been imperfectly educated, feels ill at ease in it, even though he is inordinately proud of his long descent. Both parents exaggerate the gifts of the handsome elder son, the heir, and are insufficiently aware of the potentialities of the younger. Nevertheless Hamley Hall is a happy place when Molly comes to it, largely owing to the unobtrusive but pervasive influence of its mistress: 'Her children always knew where to find her; and to find her, was to find love and sympathy. Her husband, who was often restless and angry from one cause or another, always came to her to be smoothed down and put right.'[9]

Death intervenes, as so often in the Gaskell novels, to put an end to this happiness. Even before Mrs Hamley's death, the family horizon is darkened by Osborne's failure at Cambridge and by the debts he has incurred, and anxiety over him hastens the fatal termination of her illness. Had she lived, Osborne could have revealed to her the secret of his clandestine marriage to a French girl of humble origin and she might have succeeded in persuading her husband to accept the situation. As it is, the estrangement between the Squire and his elder son continues until Osborne himself dies suddenly, to the bitter grief of his father. Yet the family which has been deeply rooted in mutual love has power to survive. The younger son, Roger, becomes, on his mother's death, his father's support and companion while remaining, as he has always been, his brother's best friend and confidant. After Osborne's death he is the best friend also of the widow and of the infant son, the new heir, on whom the Squire is now able to lavish the passionate and proud affection formerly shown to Osborne.

The Hales of *North and South*, the Robsons of *Sylvia's Lovers*, the Holmans of *Cousin Phillis* are other examples of the basic unity of a family where parents and children are bound together in a bond of loving fellowship. Here, too, there is no suggestion of unrealistic perfection. Hale lacks the moral courage to tell his wife of his decision to resign his living till he has actually done so, and she deplores the move to the industrial North, but she accompanies him to Milton, where she bears increasing illness with fortitude for the sake of husband and daughter. Daniel Robson cannot control his recklessness, even for the sake of wife and child, but he loves them and they love him. Holman's wife cannot share her husband's intellectual interests, but they are devoted to each other and to Phillis, their child. Such families are not immune from calamity, but misfortune tightens the bonds between their members. Frederick Hale, a naval lieutenant living in exile since he was involved in a mutiny against an unjust captain, returns to England at the risk of discovery and death to see his mother before she dies. When Phillis falls ill, after her lover's defection, it is largely through the nursing of her parents that she recovers, and it is for their sake as much as for her own that she determines to fight her way back to cheerfulness. Bell Robson's frail health is shattered by the shock of her husband's arrest and imprisonment, but when she is called on to face the journey to York to see him in prison for the last time, her love gives her the strength to become her old self again, 'composed, strong and calm', and to communicate the same courage to Sylvia: 'Lass, bear up! we mun bear up, and be a-gait on our way to him: he'll be needing us now.'

Even when death removes both parents before the end of the action, as in *North and South* and *Sylvia's Lovers*, the family life remains part of the total experience of the children and exerts a stabilising influence. Margaret Hale and Sylvia Robson retain the unconscious assurance which comes from having been cradled in parental affection and the fundamental honesty they have absorbed from the atmosphere of their home. Margaret has had the example of higher ethical standards, but Sylvia, though by nature a creature of impulse like her father, has imbibed something of the un-compromising rectitude of her quiet mother. If she cannot forgive her husband for his deception, neither can she, in order to follow her lover, leave the home that contains their child. In the shorter tales also the memory of a beloved home can be a source of moral strength. The orphaned Lois Barclay of 'Lois the Witch' finds that the values acquired in the Warwickshire parsonage where she was reared, though not understood in her New England environment, are her chief resource in persecution and death.

In all such cases the children can remember a normal home life. Sometimes, however, one parent dies too soon to exert any real influence or even perhaps to be more than vaguely remembered. Exceptional importance then attaches to the relations of the remaining parent and the children. Elizabeth Gaskell returned more than once in her work to the study of such a situation. The absence of close relations with her own father, until near the end of his life, had been one of the least satisfactory features of her motherless though happy and sheltered childhood, and the stress she puts on the father–daughter relationship may be due, as has been suggested, to her own sense of deprivation in this respect.[10] It is often, in her work, a particularly close one. Sylvia Robson and Phyllis Holman are in some ways nearer to their father than the temperamentally more dissimilar wife. When the mother dies, the bond is exceptionally strong. John Barton tells Mary: 'Child, we must be all to one another, now *she* is gone.' In their case, the unnatural social conditions in which they live for a time exercise a divisive influence; he is increasingly involved in the plight of his fellow workers, she in the drudgery of a seamstress's life, and there ceases to be full confidence between them. But when Mary learns of her father's crime, the filial bond proves indestructible; she safeguards his secret and, when he returns home, a dying man, forgets his crime in her love and compassion, and sees in him only her father, 'in his sufferings, whatever their cause, more dearly loved than ever before'. In the tale 'A Dark Night's Work', published fifteen years later and set in a country town, a daughter has to live with the knowledge that her idolised father has been guilty of manslaughter, and does not love him the less, though the effort to conceal his crime costs her her lover and her youth. In Elizabeth Gaskell's final work, and masterpiece, *Wives and Daughters*, she gives her finest portrait of the relationship between father and daughter. The country surgeon's greatest interest in life is his motherless child and she instinctively recognises and responds to the affection which underlies his undemonstrative manner and his teasing: 'the two had the most delightful intercourse together—half banter, half seriousness, but altogether confidential friendship'.[11] In this 'everyday' story, the threat to their happiness appears in a not unusual form; Mr Gibson marries again, to give his daughter a better background as she grows up, but his choice of a second wife is an unwise one. Molly's first reaction to the news that he intends to remarry shows an uncharacteristic bitterness which is the measure of her acute misery and which produces a momentary estrangement between them. But she cannot bear the thought of any misunderstanding with her father, and her love for him gives her the power to accept the situation and endure patiently the difficulties consequent on the arrival of the second Mrs Gibson. She has her reward in the fact that, although they no longer enjoy the same freedom to be together, it is on her that her father's interests still principally centre.

Where it is the father who has been removed by death a particularly close relationship often exists between mother and son. The chief interest of 'The Moorland Cottage' lies in the study of the Browne family, to whom the wealthy Buxtons act as benevolent patrons. Mrs Browne, a curate's widow, is devoted to her son, but spoils him to such an extent that the boy, naturally selfish and unstable, is ruined by her indulgence. Her daughter, on the other hand, she neglects and she has no qualms about risking Maggie's happiness if it will help her worthless brother. By contrast Mrs Thornton of *North and South* is a sensible as well as devoted mother. She is not naturally a demonstrative woman and her manner to her daughter is more affectionate than to her son, but this is because she realises that the weaker Fanny is in more need of support and reassurance. Between her son and herself there is innate sympathy as well as deep affection. He is proud as well as fond of her, never forgetting what he owed to her example of power and resolve in adversity, and her love for him is none the less profound because she rarely puts it into words: '. . . her heart gave thanks for him day and night; and she walked proudly among women for his sake.'[12]

It seems that, where there is no father, the mother–son

relationship is sometimes closer than that between mother and daughter. Certainly the most salient example of the latter, that of Mrs Kirkpatrick and Cynthia, is a masterly study of the disharmony that can exist between parent and child, and is all the more effective because it contrasts with the concord between Mr Gibson and Molly. There are reasons why this relationship should have been at risk from a very early stage. Mrs Kirkpatrick had really loved her first husband as much as she could love anyone and had mourned his death, but she characteristically assumed that Cynthia was too young to realise her loss, thus denying her the consolation she needed. Forced to earn her living again as a governess, she sent the child to school at the age of four, and the régime once begun continued, Cynthia being frequently left there in the holidays as well, feeling that she was neither loved nor missed by her mother. Her envy of Molly's straightforward background and affectionate father is evidence of her sense of deprivation, and her desire to charm everyone in sight stems from the need to compensate for this, as well as from the awareness of her power to attract. In conversation with Molly she shows her consciousness of the blighting effect of an unnatural childhood:

'. . . a child should be brought up with its parents, if it is to think them infallible when it grows up.'
'But, though it may know that there must be faults,' replied Molly, 'it ought to cover them over and try to forget their existence.'
'It ought. But, don't you see, I have grown up outside the pale of duty and 'oughts'. Love me as I am, sweet one, for I shall never be better.' (Ch. 19)

The relationship between brothers and sisters is an essential part of the harmony of a united family. Elizabeth Gaskell's preference for the minimal family unit restricts her treatment of this aspect of family life, but she shows herself perfectly competent to deal with it, when opportunity offers. Her undying regret at the loss of her sailor brother is mirrored in the reappearance of the missing brother in *Cranford* and *North and South*. It is as an ageing man that 'Mr Peter' at last returns to Cranford, but Frederick Hale is still young when he makes a meteoric reappearance in the family home, and his sister feels 'an exquisite sense of relief' in his presence during the short time he is able to remain. In the powerful story 'Half a Lifetime

Ago', the only brother is, on the contrary, weak both in body and mind, but his sister renounces her lover in order to care for him. The relations between siblings are not, however, always so close. Maggie of 'The Moorland Cottage' is patronised and tyrannised over by her spoilt brother in a way which has been thought to have helped to suggest to George Eliot the position of Maggie Tulliver. The relationship between sisters is studied over a wider range of time than that of brother and sister. On one of the rare occasions when there seems to have been a hint of friction between Elizabeth Gaskell's own daughters, she wrote to the eldest, Marianne: 'I could not bear my life if you and Meta did not love each other most dearly . . . it is so dreary to see sisters grow old, (as one sometimes does,) not caring for each other, and forgetting all early home-times.'[13] In *Cranford*, near the beginning of her writing career, the Miss Jenkyns present a pattern of genuine sisterly affection and family loyalty, persisting over many years, which is reproduced in the Miss Brownings of her final masterpiece. *Wives and Daughters* also contains a rare study of fraternal affection. The two Hamley brothers are totally unlike in appearance and tastes and yet, as the editor of the *Cornhill* pointed out in his closing tribute to Mrs Gaskell, 'never did brotherly blood run more manifest than in the veins of those two' whose 'likeness in unlikeness' reproduces the affinity between the equally diverse father and mother.[14]

Of all family relationships, however, it was the maternal one which most deeply inspired Elizabeth Gaskell. In the diary she kept after her first child was born she recorded her belief that 'all a woman's life, at least so it seems to me now, ought to have a reference to the period when she will be fulfilling one of her greatest and highest duties, those of a mother',[15] and she continued to believe that the birth of the first child was the acme of a woman's life. The time when the child, young and helpless, belongs completely to the mother, is a halycon period in her novels and tales. It is most fully recreated in *Ruth*, where the young mother grudges even the time spent in sleep because it temporarily deprives her of the consciousness of her new-found happiness. The birth of Sylvia's child brings her the first real joy she has known since her irrevocable marriage. It is this time which recurs most vividly to the memory of the mother when, long years after, death is approaching: Mrs Hale remembers Frederick as a baby, and Mrs Hamley recalls her delight in her firstborn.

The loss of her only son, before he was a year old, introduced undertones of deep pathos into Elizabeth Gaskell's portrayal of the joys of maternity. In her work the young child's life is frequently menaced, and all too often claimed, by death. In her first writings this theme is intimately connected with the industrial setting. It is in industrial Manchester that the Bartons' son dies for lack of nourishing food and the delicate Wilson twins from fever, and in the same grim environment that Lizzie Leigh's two-year-old daughter falls to her death when her foster-mother's attention is momentarily distracted by the return of a drunken father. The death of Walter, the Vicar's little son, in 'Mr Harrison's Confessions', lacks such realistic motivation and, though not inherently improbable, strikes a discordant note in this tale of small town life whose humour, unlike that of *Cranford*, borders on the farcical. Yet in itself the episode is moving and serves as a poignant reminder of the 'never-ending sorrow' which was an ineradicable part of Elizabeth Gaskell's experience of motherhood. In the later works such scenes are rarer but it often happens that a family has suffered a similar loss in the past; Mrs Hamley's affection for Molly Gibson springs partly from the fact that she seems to fill the place that would have belonged to the daughter who had died in infancy.

The maternal instinct is at its strongest when the child is most helpless. It is not, however, only the infant who is peculiarly in need of love and care. Elizabeth Gaskell's maternal sympathy went out towards all those children whom she saw to be handicapped, through no fault of their own, in the struggle for life. Ruth's child is illegitimate, like the child of Lizzie Leigh, and of Esther in *Mary Barton*, and, as such, has no recognised place in Victorian society. All the care of Ruth and of the sympathetic Bensons cannot prevent Leonard from suffering as no child should have to suffer, when he learns the truth about his birth. *Ruth* is a plea for the illegitimate child as much as a demand for a more sympathetic understanding of the unmarried mother. It is not the rights of passion that Mrs Gaskell, who herself believed deeply in the sanctity of marriage, is defending in this book; it is the right of the human being, and most of all of the defenceless child, to a more humane treatment from a society which claims to be Christian and is too often merely conventional.

It may be a physical handicap which darkens what should be the natural happiness of childhood. 'Libbie Marsh's Three Eras', her first published tale, centres round a crippled boy, adored by his mother, and in 'The Manchester Marriage' a widow marries a man whose heart has been touched by the plight of her little crippled daughter. Both children welcome with touching delight any variation in their monotonous existence, while accepting it in general with pathetically unchildlike patience.

The suffering caused by mental illness also called forth the sympathy of Elizabeth Gaskell's maternal nature. In such cases the sufferer stood in danger of losing even the shelter of home. Treatment for this condition was then in its crude and often brutal infancy, and all were not as fortunate as Wordsworth's 'Idiot Boy', secure in his mother's love. When Susan Dixon's delicate young brother in 'Half a Lifetime Ago' becomes a half-wit as the result of an illness, only the sacrifice of the sister who has vowed to be as a mother to him saves him from being sent to an asylum. All that is finest in her nature responds to the inarticulate appeal of the poor child, intuitively conscious of the fate which awaits him: 'I will never let thee go, lad. Never! There's no knowing where they would take thee to, or what they would do with thee. As it says in the Bible, "Nought but death shall part thee and me!"' [16]

The ageing members of a family can be as helpless as children, and their plight too made a powerful appeal to Elizabeth Gaskell. The dying Alice in *Mary Barton* is carefully tended by her sister-in-law and her friends, who feel it a privilege rather than a duty to do so. Sylvia, when her personal happiness is at an end, can still nurse her prematurely aged mother with infinite patience and, after her death, has, for her sake, 'a stock of patient love ready in her heart for all the aged and infirm that fell in her way' and shows it in her filial care of Alice Rose.

It has been remarked that in the Gaskell works the function of the family sometimes extends beyond that of the actual family. In such cases it is often the presence of a child that provides the link between those not connected by blood. Such a situation is already present in 'Libbie Marsh's Three Eras', where Libbie's love of a crippled child causes her, after his death, to throw in her lot with the broken-hearted mother. It recurs in some form in almost all the major works: in *Ruth* the Bensons adopt the unmarried mother and her baby; in *North and South* Higgins assumes care of the orphaned Boucher children; in *My Lady Ludlow* the widowed countess becomes truly maternal in her attitude to the crippled Margaret Dawson; in *Sylvia's Lovers* Hester Rose and her mother provide a second family background for Sylvia and her child. In the shorter tales a similar situation is often found: Susan Dixon in later life takes into her own home the widow of the man she had once loved, and the children who might have been hers; Nest Gwynn in 'The Well of Pen-Morfa', crippled before her wedding-day, ultimately finds solace in the care not indeed of a child but of a half-witted woman who has less than a child's intelligence but all its helplessness and need of protection.

No consideration of the extended family, in the Gaskell works, can omit the important place of the family servant. Domestic service was the inevitable fate of working-class girls of the period, unless they aspired to what was considered the superior status of needlewomen or were employed in factories. Elizabeth Gaskell's opinion of the conditions under which seamstresses worked is shown in *Mary Barton* and still more forcibly in *Ruth*. Factory work for women was not, in her view, without grave drawbacks; she believed that it unfitted them for domestic duties—George Wilson's wife in *Mary Barton* is an example of the factory girl who has been in a mill since childhood and is completely undomesticated when she marries—and that the conditions could be physically harmful, as in the case of Bessy Higgins, while the greater independence conferred by their wage-earning capacity could have a demoralising effect, as in the case of John Barton's sister-in-law, the unhappy Esther. Yet she had too much understanding of human nature not to realise that domestic service also had its drawbacks. The lively and strong-willed Mary Barton is not prepared to 'submit to rules as to hours and associates, to regulate her dress by a mistress's ideas of propriety, to lose the dear feminine privileges of gossiping with a merry neighbour, and working night and day to help one who was sorrowful'. Her father, with his strong sense of social injustice, objects on more general grounds: 'he considered domestic servitude as a species of slavery; a pampering of artificial wants on the one side, a giving up of every right of leisure by day and quiet rest by night on the other.'[17] Mrs Gaskell's comments on the opinions of both father and daughter are informative for her own attitude: 'How far his strong exaggerated feelings had any foundation in truth, it is for you to judge. I am afraid that Mary's determination not to go to service arose from far less sensible thoughts on the subject than her father's.' Clearly she felt that there were cases where Barton's objections were valid; clearly she felt that Mary's objections were less serious, though she could understand them also. Her own attitude to the question was typical both of her humanity and of her common sense. Accepting as she did the social hierarchy of her time, it was natural that she should recognise the economic necessity for many girls to earn their living by domestic service which, like any other form of service, was bound to be subject to certain restrictions imposed by its very nature. But for her the domestic servant was also a friend, who played a valued and honourable part within the life of the family who employed her.

This was certainly the position in the Gaskell household. When Betsy, the girl who had devotedly looked after the two eldest children, was obliged to leave owing to home circumstances, Elizabeth Gaskell noted in her 'Diary': 'We have lost our dear servant Betsy . . . But we still keep her as a friend, and she has been to stay with us several weeks this autumn.'[18] Hearn, at first the children's nurse, was to stay with the Gaskells for more than forty years and was described by her mistress as being as much one of the family as any one of them. No other servant, naturally, could rival this record but others, too, remained in the household for years. Elizabeth Gaskell did not allow the many demands made upon her to prevent her from showing her interest in their personal lives: at the end of a letter giving an account of an exceptionally busy week is the news of the coming wedding of Mary, the cook, who is to be married 'from here of course'. It is characteristic of her outlook that she should praise in 'French Life' the Parisian system where families live in flats chiefly because it has 'the moral advantage of uniting mistresses and maids in a more complete family bond', and contrast it with the unnatural situation where young servants are segregated 'in the depths of a London kitchen'.[19]

Not surprisingly her most convincing studies of the place of the servant within the family circle are confined to cases where the household is a small one. It is not in the great house, with its numerous staff, that the servant naturally becomes a member of the family. Lady Ludlow moves in a sphere apart from her, preferably illiterate, domestics. The Cumnors and the Hamleys have advanced beyond this total aloofness, but a wide gulf still separates drawing-room from servants' hall. Even Lady Cumnor's 'own woman', Mrs Bradley, knows very well that complete subservience is expected by her formidable mistress. Hamley Hall is run on more modest lines than Cumnor Towers but here, too, a certain formality is observed in daily living and servants are expected to know their place and keep to it. After the death of Mrs Hamley, whose unobtrusive influence had kept the domestic wheels running smoothly, the unhappy Squire's irascibility is increasingly directed at his servants, though they like him well enough to endure it with a good deal of patience, and Robinson, the old butler, who is genuinely fond of his master, does his diplomatic best to placate and soothe him. Even he, however, only attempts to exert any influence in times of crisis, and his efforts meet with no more than partial success. It is noticeable that the distance between employer and staff in the large household appears to be just as great where master and mistress are themselves of working-class origin. 'The kitchen's free and keen remarks upon the parlour' are far from flattering in the Carson establishment, where only the nurse is treated by her employers with anything approaching friendliness.

The position is very different in the small household. Miss Betty Barker's Peggy or Miss Pole's Betty is on 'very familiar terms' with her mistress in their every-day intercourse and no one in Cranford is deceived when the latter tries to assume a more distant manner for the benefit of visitors. Miss Jenkyns, mindful of her dignity as rector's daughter, no doubt discouraged any intimacy with the servant but, after her death, Miss Matty, without losing any of her own unconscious and quiet dignity, finds her best friend in Martha, the blunt and honest country girl who becomes her maid of all work. Martha is the first of the memorable series of servants who, in the major works, play an essential role in the life of the family who employ them, though she has a precursor in Nancy of 'The Moorland Cottage'. The households principally studied in *Ruth*, *North and South* and *Cousin Phillis* would all be incomplete without them. They have their part also, though necessarily a more restricted one, in a number of the shorter tales. The status they are given in Elizabeth Gaskell's fiction is the one she feels they deserve; they exist not simply to provide comic relief or act as confidants but as human beings important in themselves and recognised to be so by the families they serve. In the interests of Martha Miss Matty finds the courage to contravene her sister's taboo, formerly accepted by herself, on 'followers'. The Benson's maid Sally is reminded by her first mistress—the mother of Faith and Thurstan—of the true dignity of the 'station of life' in which she is placed: '. . . your station is a servant, and it is as honourable as a king's, if you look at it right; you are to help and serve others in one way, just as a king is to help others in another.'[20] Such service is not an imposition in the Benson household because Thurstan and his sister are careful that, in all matters where an individual opinion is involved, Sally 'should be allowed that freedom which they claimed for themselves'. But they are glad when her wishes harmonise with theirs because 'they liked the feeling that all were of one household, and that the interests of one were the interests of all'.

This is the happy position in most cases. The servants receive material and moral advantages, and most of all—especially, it need hardly be said, in families where there are children—an outlet for the affections which might otherwise be denied them. In return they give their loyal service, a genuine interest in the affairs of the family and an affection which often amounts to devotion. They are not, any more than any other Gaskell characters, without their faults. Martha considers some of her mistress's little peculiarities as childish fancies unbecoming in an old lady (who can never have been young). Sally, as she later acknowledges with remorse, is harsh and unkind to Ruth on her first appearance in the Benson household because she suspects her of presenting a menace to the respectability of her master and mistress. But their faults cannot obscure the great value of the contribution they make to the family life and their unfailing help in times of crisis. When Miss Matty seems in danger of losing her home she finds another with Martha and her husband, and even after 'Mr. Peter's' return they remain together as one united household. Sally takes her money out of the bank to offer it to the Bensons when they are in financial difficulties, the money itself having come from an increase in her wages which she had never touched, intending to return it to them in her will. Perhaps the greatest contribution the servants make to the family life is the practical wisdom and good sense they have amassed through a long experience. Their employers have as much to learn from them as to teach them in this respect. Martha has less to contribute here than the older women, though she does achieve one memorable generalisation: 'Reason always means what some one else has got to say.' But it is Sally, rather than her employers, who does most to rouse Ruth from her despondency by pointing out, from her own experience, that tasks are always lighter when undertaken with cheerfulness. In *Cousin Phillis* it is the sharp-tongued and kindhearted Betty whose pointed admonition induces Phillis to make that effort to help herself without which the efforts of others are vain.

It is significant that Dixon in *North and South* lacks this practical wisdom. The reason is that, like Mr Mulliner in *Cranford*, she still thinks in terms of the servants' hall. Dixon has, in fact, never forgotten that she was once lady's maid to the beautiful ward of Sir John Beresford or ceased to regret her lady's marriage to a poor country clergyman, though she accompanied her to her new home. She is genuinely devoted to Mrs Hale, but persists in regarding Mr Hale as the author of all misfortune and, characteristically, likes Margaret Hale best when she shows a flash of the old Beresford haughtiness. It seems rather unfortunate that Mrs Gaskell, with the lack of care she sometimes showed in selecting names, should have given the same surname to the heroic old coachman in 'A Dark Night's Work' who faces hanging rather than reveal the secret of his master's guilt. Here the servant has to suffer for the errors of the master. The situation is not entirely dissimilar—in the comic, not the tragic, register—in *Wives and Daughters*. Old Betty, though not without her faults, has been a devoted nurse to Molly, and a more generous woman than the second Mrs Gibson would have retained her in her service, in spite of her grumblings at the new régime, but Mr Gibson's unwise choice of a wife has meant giving the old servants a difficult mistress and he is no doubt right in his wry surmise: '. . . the woman may be happier elsewhere'.

In any consideration of Elizabeth Gaskell's painting of family life, a peculiar interest attaches to her *Life of Charlotte Brontë*. It was the desire to 'make the world honour the woman as much as they had admired the writer' that made her wish to write a memoir of her friend, and this remained her motive when she agreed to undertake the official biography. When thanking Ellen Nussey for sending Charlotte's letters, she commented: 'I am sure that the more fully she—Charlotte Brontë—the *friend*, the *daughter*, the *sister*, the *wife*, is known, and known where need be in her own words, the more highly will she be appreciated.'[21] So well did she succeed in showing Charlotte Brontë in this light that to think of her became in future to think also of Haworth parsonage and the remarkable family who lived there.

Here Elizabeth Gaskell was faced with the task not of creating a fictional family but of reconstructing a real one. It was her declared intention to be true to the facts as she knew them. She relied primarily on careful selection from the material, chiefly letters, at her disposal, set in a framework of background information, commenting where she judged it necessary. Clearly, in the life of children so early left motherless, the part played by the father was of particular significance. What she heard of him from Lady Kay-Shuttleworth, and from Charlotte herself at their first meeting, suggested a wild eccentric character that appealed to her dramatic sense but was in startling opposition to her own ideal of fatherhood.

When she actually met him at the parsonage, she did to some extent modify this impression. She could not approve his reclusive habits, which, she felt, were largely responsible for the isolation in which his children grew up, and probably did not sufficiently consider how crushing must have been the accumulated weight of misfortune which changed an originally sociable nature into one so unnaturally dependent on solitude. She did, however, realise that he normally controlled his passionate temperament with 'resolute stoicism' and that he was a man of complete integrity and vigorous intellect, genuinely anxious to develop his children's abilities and far more concerned with their welfare and happiness than his stern exterior might suggest. Unfortunately some of the exaggerated accounts she had heard of his eccentricities found their way into her biography, though she withdrew them in the amended third edition. The patience and good temper he showed on this occasion finally opened her eyes to his real qualities and to the generosity of which he was capable.

Charlotte showed some of her finest qualities in her filial relationship and Elizabeth Gaskell was not wrong in affirming that to know her as a daughter was to appreciate her the more. 'Papa' was associated with the intellectual pleasures of her childhood, if he remained remote from the children's everyday life. As she grew up, she was quick to realise the problems he faced in supporting the family on his limited income and did her best to help him by attempts to earn her living as teacher or governess. As he grew older and his eyesight began to fail, she remained at home because she felt she was needed there. A letter to her friend Ellen Nussey, advising her to stay with her aged and infirm mother, rather than seek independence for herself, ends with the words: 'I recommend you to do what I am trying to do myself'. This letter is introduced in the biography with the comment: 'I call particular attention to the following letter of Charlotte's . . . the wholesome sense of duty in it—the sense of the supremacy of that duty which God, in placing us in families, has laid out for us—seems to deserve special regard in these days.'[22] With time there was an evident deepening of the relationship between Charlotte and her father, and the deaths of her brother and sisters, which followed each other with such tragic swiftness, further strengthened the bond between them: '. . . when anything ails papa I feel too keenly that he is the *last*—the only near and dear relative I have in the world.'[23] When she was absent from the parsonage on brief visits, the thought of him was constantly in her mind. Writing so soon after Charlotte's death, Elizabeth Gaskell could not give a full account of the period of tension when the discovery of his curate's desire to marry his famous daughter provoked Mr Brontë to the passionate opposition which, paradoxically, promoted Mr Nicholls's cause by moving Charlotte first to pity and then to a fuller understanding of her lover. She certainly approved Charlotte's final decision to marry Nicholls and rejoiced that 'by degrees Mr Brontë became reconciled to the idea of his daughter's marriage'. She stressed, however, that the daughter was still thinking of her father's happiness as well as her own: she and her future husband were to live at the parsonage and Mr Brontë was to have his help as curate as well as son-in-law.

In contrast to her relationship with her father, which became steadily closer with time, Charlotte's relationship with her sisters was extremely close from the beginning. The motherless children were, as Elizabeth Gaskell sympathetically noted, 'all in all to each other'. The portrait of Maria, the eldest, as Helen Burns in *Jane Eyre*, shows that she set an example of almost maternal tenderness which the nine-year-old Charlotte never forgot. When the depleted family was reunited after Cowan Bridge, she tried to become in her turn 'motherly friend and guardian' to Emily and Anne. As they grew up, she remained conscious of her responsibility, intervening when she feared their health was threatened and using her initiative in the interests of all. It was for the sake of her sisters even more than for her own that she did her utmost for years to promote the establishment of a school at the parsonage:

> She could bear much for herself; but she could not patiently bear the sorrows of others, especially of her sisters; and again, of the two sisters, the idea of the little, gentle, youngest suffering in lonely patience was insupportable to her . . . To have a school was to have some portion of daily leisure . . . it was for the three sisters, loving each other with so passionate an affection, to be together under one roof, and yet earning their own subsistence; above all, it was to have the power of watching over those two whose life and happiness were ever more to Charlotte than her own. (Ch. 10)

It was through Charlotte's initiative that their writings were sent to a publisher and they were still united in the beginning of their literary career. It was in this time of promise, not for herself only but for them all, that Charlotte wrote, of the affection of sisters for each other, 'there is nothing like it in this world, I believe, when they are nearly equal in age, and similar in education, tastes, and sentiments.'[24] Elizabeth Gaskell's method of allowing Charlotte to tell her story largely in her own words never had more poignant results than in the deeply moving accounts of the last illnesses and deaths of Emily and Anne. Only the bereaved sister could have found adequate expression for her ultimate loneliness: 'The great trial is when evening closes and night approaches, at that hour we used to assemble in the dining-room—we used to talk. Now I sit by myself—necessarily I am silent.'[25]

Where the bond between sisters was concerned, her biographer could let Charlotte speak for herself. On the subject of their brother Branwell she felt too strongly not to intervene with comments of her own. In 'The Moorland Cottage' she had shown how Maggie's happiness was almost wrecked by the conduct of her weak and spoilt brother, but in her fiction the sister is rescued from an intolerable situation by the timely intervention of fate. The reality at Haworth was different. Branwell was, in his childhood and early youth, a most gifted and engaging boy, Charlotte's special companion and her collaborator in the Angrian tales. Mrs Gaskell traces the influences that in her eyes combined to ruin his early promise, acting on his fatal weakness of will: his father's indulgence, the isolated life at the parsonage which drove a sociable and mercurial nature to find its only outlet in the society of the village inn, the family's belief in the supreme importance of the only son. Although she had herself passionately loved her own son, she saw all the danger of allowing the brother to feel superior to his sisters: 'There are always peculiar trials in the life of an only boy in a family of girls. He is expected to act a part in life; to *do*, while they are only to *be*; and the necessity of their giving way to him in some things is too often exaggerated into their giving way to him in all, and thus rendering him utterly selfish.'[26] The sisters' exaggerated belief in their brilliant brother, maintained to some extent in spite of his evident deterioration in character, was finally destroyed when, dismissed from his post as tutor, he returned home, a wreck in mind and body, dependent on drink and opium. What the sisters had to suffer during the last three years of his life Elizabeth Gaskell knew from what she had heard from Charlotte, as well as from her letters. That the unhappy brother had a right to the shelter of his home she does not dispute, but she realised what it must have cost them to see him in the grip of delirium tremens and to be the constant spectators of his morbid melancholy. Her intense sympathy with them moved her to denounce with uncharacteristic bitterness the woman whom the family believed, from his account, to be largely responsible for his downfall. So aware was she of the cost they must have paid in mind and body for their fortitude during those grim years, though they continued to write their novels, that she hardly did justice to the remarkable devotion of the father to his unhappy son.

It is probable that Elizabeth Gaskell's intense sympathy with the sisters arose partly from the fact that she was well aware how the daily spectacle of their brother's condition influenced the writings which were their chief means of escape from it, causing the sombre colouring critics were to complain of without realising that 'such words were wrung out of them by the living recollection of the long agony they suffered'. Certainly she, who had such high standards of family loyalty, never blamed Charlotte, as others have done later, with far less exact knowledge of the circumstances, for failing to show sufficient sympathy for Branwell. When he died, the sister who had once been closest to him could not feel she had lost a companion, but she did feel that she had lost a brother: 'Till the last hour comes we never know how much we can forgive, pity, regret a near relative. All his vices were and are nothing now. We remember only his woes.'[27]

Of Charlotte as wife, there was pitifully little to tell and that little Elizabeth Gaskell shrank from revealing in any detail, feeling that outsiders had no right to intrude on the privacy of husband and wife and knowing that Mr Nicholls was of all men the least likely to welcome such intrusion. It must none the less have rejoiced her heart, since she was aware of the very subdued expectations with which her friend had looked forward to her marriage, that, though of such brief duration, it was undeniably a happy one. She expresses her own feelings when she speaks of the friends who, standing outside 'the sacred doors of home' which closed upon her married life, were glad to catch occasional glimpses of the brightness within: '. . . we looked at each other and gently said, "After a hard and long struggle—after many cares and many bitter sorrows—she is tasting happiness now!" We thought of the slight astringencies of her character, and how they would turn to full ripe sweetness in that calm sunshine of domestic peace.'[28] Nothing is said of the achievement of the novels, though they had had their place in the biography. It is domestic peace that is to ripen Charlotte's

character, though that peace might be expected to react in turn on
the novels. The tragedy in the closing pages of the biography is not
that death claims the novelist with still undiminished powers but
that it claims the wife and unborn child.

Daughter, sister and wife, Charlotte Brontë lived all her life in the
orbit of the family. A rather shadowy figure in the background of
the life at the parsonage was her aunt, Elizabeth Branwell. Shadowy
at least she appears in the biography, though her role was by no
means a sinecure: she came from her native Cornwall to take charge
of the household after her sister's death and remained there till her
own death in 1842. According to Elizabeth Gaskell, 'the children
respected her, and had that sort of affection for her which is
generated by esteem; but I do not think they ever freely loved her.'[29]
The suggestion is of a rather unsatisfactory relationship, and, as far
as Charlotte was concerned, this was probably the case. Branwell,
her favourite, spoke of her at her death in much warmer terms. But
Elizabeth Gaskell recognised that the sisters did learn from their
aunt much that proved valuable later in the way of household skills
and organisation of their time: 'order, method, neatness in everything; a perfect knowledge of all kinds of household work; an exact
punctuality, and obedience to the laws of time and place, of which
none but themselves, I have heard Charlotte say, could tell the
value in after life.'[30]

The real centre of the house, during the childhood of the Brontës,
was not however their aunt's bedroom, where they received these
careful lessons, but the cheerful kitchen, presided over by Tabby,
the Yorkshire woman who possessed in real life the qualities that
made the Marthas and Sallys and Bettys of Elizabeth Gaskell's novels
into valued members of the family they served. Tabby brought love
and warmth into the children's lives. She spoke to them in the
unsentimental idiom they understood and they knew their interests
were safe with her. 'She abounded in strong practical sense and
shrewdness. Her words were far from flattery; but she would spare
no deeds in the cause of those whom she kindly regarded.'[31] As one
would expect, Elizabeth Gaskell does full justice to the part played
in the life of the family by the faithful servant who was to remain at
the parsonage for thirty years. She relates how when, as an elderly
woman, Tabby was temporarily incapacitated through illness,
Charlotte and her sisters showed they felt she was 'like one of the
family' by insisting on looking after her themselves, in addition to
doing the whole work of the house, rather than let her be removed to

be nursed in the village, as their aunt had suggested. Elizabeth
Gaskell does not forget to mention also the younger servant Martha,
at first Tabby's assistant, who became in her turn a loyal friend to
the family, remaining at the parsonage after Charlotte's death.

In the life of the Brontës Elizabeth Gaskell recognised that there
were elements beyond her comprehension: 'The family with whom
I have now to do shot their roots down deeper than I can
penetrate . . .'[32] In the closeness of their relationships with each
other, however—relationships so well understood and so admirably
recreated in her biography—they showed that even genius could
not dispense with the universal human need to belong to a family,
perhaps indeed felt it the more. Writing to Emily, then alone with
her father at the parsonage, out of the solitariness of the last part of
her stay in Brussels, Charlotte, in a letter quoted by her biographer,
expresses her longing for the sights and sounds of home:

> . . . I should like uncommonly to be in the dining-room at home,
> or in the kitchen, or in the back kitchen. I should like even to be
> cutting up the hash . . . and you standing by, watching that I put
> enough flour, and not too much pepper . . . To complete the
> picture, Tabby blowing the fire in order to boil the potatoes to a
> sort of vegetable glue! How divine are these recollections to me at
> this moment! . . . I pray, with heart and soul, that all may
> continue well at Haworth; above all in our grey, half-inhabited
> house. God bless the walls thereof! . . . (Ch. 12)

6 The individual

It has been said that Elizabeth Gaskell usually writes about ordinary people. The lives of her characters are interwoven with that of their family and of the community to which they belong. These ordinary people are none the less individuals, making their individual responses to the pressures of life. Elizabeth Gaskell was intensely aware of the dignity and importance of the human personality. Her novels of industrial life are not blueprints for the betterment of society nor her novels of country life a plea for a return to bucolic simplicity. They are each and all of them a plea for more understanding of the individual, more awareness that the most ordinary human society is composed of men and women each unique in their way and only to be fully understood in the light of that incontrovertible fact.

Believing as she did in the dignity of the individual, it was natural that she should be very conscious of the influence of education, the factor which can do so much to help the development of the personality but may also thwart or distort its growth. By education she meant something wider than simply the development of the intellect. In 'My Diary', speaking of her decision to send her four-year-old daughter to a day-school, she explains that her aim is 'not to advance her rapidly in any branch of learning, for William and I agree in not caring for this, but to perfect her habits of obedience, to give her an idea of conquering difficulties by perseverance'.[1] Her priorities never changed; in her eyes moral development was always more important than intellectual. Miss Matty is not equipped to teach the children of Cranford—she is not even completely mistress of the three Rs—but she has qualities which are in themselves infinitely more valuable than any book-learning: 'No! there was nothing she could teach to the rising generation of Cranford, unless they had been quick learners and ready imitators of her patience, her humility, her sweetness, her quiet contentment with all that she could not do.'[2] Miss Matty has to keep a shop instead of a school, when it becomes necessary for her to earn her living, but unconsciously she teaches her customers, adults as well as children, a good deal, as she hands tea or comfits across the table-counter: 'It was really very pleasant to see how her unselfishness and simple sense of justice called out the same good qualities in others.'[3] It is by example, not by precept, that moral truths are best communicated.

The value of such teaching is contrasted, in 'The Moorland Cottage', with the dubious value of formal instruction unaccompanied by any real sympathy on the part of the teacher. Maggie learns far more that is of lasting use from her visits to the invalid Mrs Buxton, who invites her from time to time to share in the occupations of her young niece, than she does from the routine tuition at home:

> While she was on these visits, she received no regular instruction; and yet all the knowledge, and most of the strength of her character, was derived from these occasional hours. It is true that her mother had given her daily lessons in reading, writing, and arithmetic; but both teacher and taught felt these more as painful duties to be gone through than understood them as means to an end. The "There, child! now that's done with," of relief, from Mrs Browne, was heartily echoed in Maggie's breast, as the dull routine was concluded.
>
> Mrs Buxton did not make a set labour of teaching. I suppose she felt that much was learned from her superintendence, but she never thought of doing or saying anything with a latent idea of its indirect effect upon the little girls, her companions. She was simply, herself; she even confessed (where the confession was called for) to shortcomings, to faults . . . Pure, simple, and truthful to the heart's core, her life, in its uneventful hours and days, spoke many homilies.[4]

This wider conception of education included none the less intellectual training in its scope. The evangelical clergyman Mr Gray who shocks Lady Ludlow, on his first arrival in Hanbury, by speaking of 'the right every child had to instruction', certainly has the approval of Elizabeth Gaskell. During the period of her writing career the need for education for all classes of society was beginning to be widely recognised, largely owing to the pioneer efforts of Sir James Kay-Shuttleworth, born in Rochdale and well known in Manchester, who in 1839 had been appointed Secretary to the new Committee of Council on Education set up by the Privy Council. By the time she wrote her last novel, *Wives and Daughters*, the Education Act was only five years distant, and she could contrast the charity school of the Cumnors with contemporary institutions where 'far better intellectual teaching is given to the boys and girls of labourers than often falls to the lot of their betters'. Usually, however, as in *Wives and Daughters* itself, she writes of the period of her own childhood and youth, when the children of the working classes were largely dependent on charity schools and Sunday schools for their acquaintance with the three Rs.

More than one of the leading characters in her novels and tales, coming from a working-class or rural ambience, suffers from lack of education. John Barton has had no intellectual training to help him to form a balanced judgment: 'No education had given him wisdom; and without wisdom, even love, with all its effects, too often works but harm.'[5] John Middleton, a factory hand, can neither read nor write at the age of seventeen. Sylvia, a tenant farmer's daughter, is almost equally illiterate at the same age. Ruth, also a small farmer's daughter, has only had a rudimentary education when her parents' death obliges her to become a dressmaker's apprentice. Circumstances usually force them to realise their lack and they try to compensate for it as best they can. John Middleton follows the girl he loves to school and for her sake learns to read and write in the company of the youngest children, to the disgust of his brutal father, who disapproves of literacy for simpler reasons than Lady Ludlow: 'My father hated the notion of folks learning to read, and said it took all the spirit out of them; besides, he thought he had a right to every penny of my wages . . . and grudged my twopence a week for schooling.'[6] Ruth determines, for her child's sake, to acquire the knowledge needed to direct his education: 'Her mind was un-cultivated, her reading scant . . . but she had a refined taste, and excellent sense and judgment to separate the true from the false. With these qualities, she set to work under Mr Benson's directions.'[7] Ruth, sensitive and artistic, proves to have a natural taste for 'book learning'. Sylvia, who has rejected her cousin's attempts to teach her, has no natural desire to learn but, for her child's sake, comes at last to regret her ignorance and is finally grateful to be taught to read.

For the middle and upper classes the education of their sons had long been an established necessity, given priority over that of the daughters. Those whose parents could afford it were sent to public schools, the others to the long established grammar schools or to private schools of varying degrees of efficiency. Squire Hamley has been deprived by circumstance of the normal education of his class but sends his sons to Rugby and Cambridge, determined they should not be handicapped as he had been. The effects of the best education, however, can be counteracted by the lack of a stable moral background. Edward Wilkins, sent to Eton by his ambitious attorney father, can never reconcile himself in afterlife to having a social status inferior to his former school companions. Maggie's brother in 'The Moorland Cottage' is given a place in a good school through the patronage of Mr Buxton, but he has been utterly spoilt at home and ruins his subsequent career through weakness and dishonesty. Benjamin Huntroyd in 'The Crooked Branch', the son of a small farmer, adored and spoilt by his elderly parents, is sent to a grammar school in a neighbouring town where 'to all appearance, he grew clever and gentlemanlike', but in this case the school itself is an agent of corruption: 'If it had not been so utterly bad a place of education, the simple farmer and his wife might have found it out sooner. But not only did the pupils there learn vice, they also learnt deceit.'[8] Benjamin becomes a scoundrel, even descending to an attempt to rob his parents of what little money they have left, after he has squandered most of it, and prepared to use violence, if necessary, to attain his end. Elizabeth Gaskell seems to have been very conscious of the sacrifices made by families for the education of their sons, and of the poor return they sometimes received for it, a situation most tragically exemplified in the case of Branwell Brontë.

The daughters' education was not usually considered a matter of so much moment. There was, however, a growing awareness of its importance in some circles. Elizabeth Gaskell herself had a Unitarian background, and the Unitarians believed in the culti-vation of the intellect. Her own schooldays were spent at the school of the Miss Byerleys, relations of the Wedgwoods, with whom her mother's family was also connected. Years later she remembered with pleasure the time spent in Warwickshire and declared herself unwilling to leave even in thought the scenes of such happy days as her schooldays were. Her own four daughters were educated partly by their parents and partly at school. In deciding where to send them, she was guided by her knowledge of their different characters. Marianne, the eldest, who was musically gifted, went to school in Hampstead; Meta, the second and most intellectual, made her own choice of Miss Martineau's school in Liverpool; Florence, the least intellectual, went to the Miss Greens' in Knutsford and Julia, the lively youngest, to a day-school in Manchester before finishing her education in turn at Knutsford.

The belief that education should allow the individuality to develop in its own direction was in line with Elizabeth Gaskell's belief in the natural. Mrs Buxton of 'The Moorland Cottage', though not a conscious theorist, understands this: 'She had no wish to make the two little girls into the same kind of pattern character. They were diverse as the lily and the rose.'[9] The futility of educational systems which seek to produce a type rather than to train an individual is exposed in the closing section of another early tale 'Morton Hall', which, though admittedly a digression from the main theme of the story, is interesting from this point of view. The three elderly Miss Mortons each have charge of their little niece for a week in turn, and the child has to adapt successively to their totally opposed systems. Miss Sophronia, the eldest, subjects her niece to the set eighteenth-century curriculum and standards of propriety, the same which had been current during the childhoods of the Miss Jenkyns (Miss Matty retains vague recollections of having read Mrs Chapone's *Letters on the Improvement of the Mind*) and of the narrator in 'My French Master'—another tale belonging to the 'Cranford' period—and which no doubt still commanded the allegiance of the young Elizabeth Stevenson's elderly aunts in Knutsford. Miss Annabella, slightly younger, has a different system, intended to 'develop the sensibilities and to cultivate the tastes', chiefly by the reading of sentimental novels. No clue is given to the system of Miss Dorothy, the youngest and most eccentric, except that, like the others, she insists on a refinement of language comparable to that of the French seventeenth-century *précieuses*, though the list of proscribed words varies with each sister. By the time she wrote the *Life of Charlotte Brontë* Elizabeth Gaskell had not lost any of her aversion to educational theorists. She suspects Mr Brontë of having been influenced in his children's education by Rousseau's *Emile* (not very justifiably, in view of his encouragement of their intellectual precocity) and recalls the trials of an aunt of her own, brought up by disciples of Thomas Day, author of *The History of Sandford and Merton*.

In the *Life of Charlotte Brontë*, the description of the period at Cowan Bridge School bears tragic witness to the permanent harm that can be done to the development of the individual by an unhappy educational experience. Charlotte Brontë is described as 'suffering her whole life long, both in heart and body, from the consequences of what happened there'. She suffered from seeing the harsh treatment meted out to Maria, and she suffered physically, like her two elder sisters, from the unhealthy material conditions, though, unlike them, she managed to survive. Much of the unforgettable chapter on Cowan Bridge School is taken up with the description of the unhygienic buildings, the badly cooked and tainted food, the bitter cold in winter. Elizabeth Gaskell, the mother of four children, was very much aware of the dangers of an education that ignores physical development. In 'My French Master' the father, a retired naval officer, intervenes to interrupt his daughters' lessons, when the weather is especially good, on the grounds that 'It was a shame to coop such young things up in a house, when every other young animal was frolicking in the air and sunshine'. The account of Cowan Bridge makes it very clear that 'book-learning' is only one part of education. Charlotte Brontë seems to have been interested enough in the lessons but her physical development suffered, and she also suffered morally from a régime which, in a highly-strung and impressionable nature, nurtured apprehension and a crippling sense of helplessness in 'the fell clutch of circumstance'.

Fortunately, Cowan Bridge was not the end of the story. Charlotte's education was continued at the parsonage in a manner which Mrs Gaskell found in some ways admirable. She could not approve the social seclusion in which a young family was growing up, but she did approve the lessons in household matters, the walks on the moors and the interest their father encouraged them to take in current affairs, through the medium of the newspapers and *Blackwood's*. When Charlotte went to school again at Roe Head, she received more formal instruction, and this was something Elizabeth Gaskell recognised as necessary to complement the wide range of miscellaneous information she had already acquired. Though she never considered learning as an end in itself, she believed that study had a necessary place in intellectual training. When her own eldest daughter, on her return from school, offered to give lessons to the two youngest, she accepted the offer primarily because of her admiration of Marianne's '*moral* management of them', but she added a condition: 'Only remember they must do *hard* and *correct* as well as interesting work—I mean such things as French verbs, and geography for Flossy; the dry bones of knowledge.'[10] Such knowledge did form part of the curriculum at Roe Head, but Miss Wooler was able to convert set lessons into a form of mental stimulus far more important than the lessons in themselves; her pupils were taught 'to think, to analyse, to reject, to appreciate'. Nor was their instruction entirely dependent on set lessons: during long walks through the countryside they were entertained by Miss Wooler with tales of its historic past. This was the sort of knowledge, minted from living experience, which Elizabeth Gaskell prized above what could be found in books.

Education for her was primarily education for life and through life, but a reasonable amount of knowledge was indispensable if one were not, like Squire Hamley, to be made uncomfortable for the lack of it. Marianne Gaskell is reproved for making a sweeping judgment about Free Trade, when she knows nothing about it, and her mother points out the advisability of their reading together Cobden's speeches and Adam Smith's *Wealth of Nations*: 'Have as many and as large and varied interests as you can; but do not again give a decided opinion on a subject on which you can at present know nothing.'[11] In 'A Dark Night's Work' Ellinor Wilkins, though naturally intelligent, is discouraged by her indolent father from any more serious intellectual effort than that entailed by 'a variety of desultory and miscellaneous reading'. He finds her a pleasant enough companion, but her fiancé Ralph Corbet, a clever young lawyer, becomes acutely conscious of her intellectual limitations, once his love for her begins to wane: 'It had become difficult for Ralph to contract his mind to her small domestic interests, and she had little else to talk to him about . . . The books she had been reading were old classics whose place in literature no longer admitted of keen discussion . . . There was no talking politics with her, because she was so ignorant that she always agreed with everything he said.'[12]

'Accomplishments' were an important part of middle-class education for girls in the first part of the nineteenth century. At the school where Elizabeth Stevenson was educated these included French, drawing, music and dancing. She was herself a good linguist, a lover of art and music and an excellent dancer. She believed in cultural and artistic activities, as she believed in everything that could enrich life, but in this sphere also she felt that individual aptitudes and tastes must be considered. Her two elder daughters, who were gifted for music and art respectively, received every encouragement to develop their talent. She saw no purpose, however, in 'accomplishments' simply cultivated for show by those with no real aptitude or interest. Fanny Thornton makes an appropriate entry into *North and South* when she is heard playing a 'morceau de salon' very badly, but with great satisfaction to herself. She is astonished that the Hales have no piano, but Margaret frankly admits that they sold it when they moved to Milton, as she herself cannot play well, though she is fond of hearing good music. Molly Gibson, on the other hand, has an excellent ear for music and practises regularly from inclination, though she is so far from wishing to impress others with her 'accomplishment' that she shrinks from playing in company.

Neither the acquirement of knowledge nor 'accomplishments' are, however, ends in themselves for any of the Gaskell heroines. When Margaret Hale is sharing her cousin's education in London, she returns to Helstone in the holidays with an assignment of work recommended by masters or governess and finds the summer's day 'all too short to get through the reading she had to do before her return to town'. When she comes home for good, however, there is no question of any systematic continuation of her studies, nor are they any apparent resource when she is transplanted to Milton-Northern. Molly Gibson fights hard in her childhood to get her father, who is always 'afraid of her becoming too much educated', to let her have French and drawing-lessons, and reads the books that come her way, but she is not really a scholar by inclination. Roger Hamley good-naturedly tries to interest her in his study of natural history when he sees her thoughts need diverting from her troubles, and she is intelligent enough to enjoy the books he lends her, but when her stepmother predicts, on the strength of this, that she will be 'quite a blue-stocking by-and-by', the term annoys her enough to make her say, with obvious sincerity: 'I'm afraid I'd rather be a dunce than a blue-stocking'. The only one of Mrs Gaskell's young girls who shows signs of a disinterested love of study is Phillis Holman, who has inherited something of her father's voracious intellectual appetite. It is a joy to her to read in the evenings with her father; she shares his love of Virgil, studies Greek and does her best to read Dante with the help of a dictionary. In Phillis, however, her intellectual interests appear to have outstripped her development in other ways. Her parents still see her as a child but her cousin Paul Manning, less intellectual than she but far shrewder, realises the anomaly of a seventeen-year-old girl who continues to wear a pinafore, and senses her remoteness from the normal interests of her age. But when Holdsworth, the sophisticated traveller who can help her with her Italian and who admires her beauty, appears upon the scene, she falls in love with him, suddenly and irrevocably. His departure leaves her desolate and she then proves to have less resources than Molly Gibson or Margaret Hale when they, too, face the prospect of life without the man they love. It is not to her Latin and Italian books that she turns for comfort; the blunt good sense of an old servant proves a more efficacious cure.

The role of instruction and study in the education of the Gaskell heroines is, indeed, not in doubt; it is to equip them for the business of living, but not to be a substitute for living. The same is true of its place in the Gaskell work in general. And always it is the moral education that matters most and that is received from the often unconscious influence of character and example, in the family life as well as in the schoolroom. When Ruth's son is old enough to be sent to a boy's school, a friend offers to pay for his education there, but Benson, when asked if he will try to persuade Ruth to accept the offer, is very dubious as to the wisdom of such a course: 'I doubt if the wisest and most thoughtful schoolmaster could teach half as much directly, as his mother does unconsciously and indirectly every hour that he is with her.'[13]

Once the formal education—or, it may be, simply the rudimentary instruction in the three Rs—is finished, the individual has to find an occupation or, more frequently, to accept the occupation that offers. As far as men are concerned, Elizabeth Gaskell usually shows them as engaged in occupations of which she knew something from her own experience. She had grown up in a country society where the landowner, the farmer and the professional man predominated and on moving to Manchester she had come to know mill-owners and factory workers. She drew very little on the intellectual and artistic society to which her fame as an author introduced her. Roger Hamley, the scientist, and Mr Bell, the Oxford Fellow, are exceptions in her work and are in fact seen predominantly as the Squire's son and as the friend of Mr Hale's youth. Inevitably her male characters frequently share the same profession or occupation and consequently to some extent the same interests and way of life. They remain none the less individuals with their own personal cares and ambitions, hopes and frustrations. Squire Hamley differs from the Earl of Cumnor not only as the small landowner differs from the great landowner but as a man of wholly dissimilar temperament, as irascible and impetuous as the Earl is amiable and prone to 'pottering'. No two priests could possibly be more unlike each other than those who hold in succession the living of Hanbury, as Lady Ludlow discovers when she expects from Mr Gray the same acquiescence in her wishes—even to the giving or not giving of a sermon—which she had unfailingly received from Mr Mountford.

In one respect, however, they are all alike: they are happier with an occupation than without it. There is of course no comparison between the suffering, in this condition, of the working man and the man with a comfortable home. The working man faces poverty, even starvation, both for himself and for his family. In such circumstances a John Barton, prone to extremes of love and hate, turns eventually to drink and opium, and finally to violence; a Davenport shows incredible patience as he hunts vainly for work before succumbing to the fever which kills him. Ironically, among the better off, it is the heirs of county families whom Elizabeth Gaskell sometimes shows as suffering for lack of occupation, though not of material comforts. Here, too, the individual temperament plays a decisive part. Osborne Hamley, who has failed to win a scholarship at Cambridge, has, unlike his younger brother, little interest in an outdoor life and longs vainly for an independence so that he can live away from home with the wife he has secretly married. Owen Griffiths, the heir of a Welsh squire, naturally indolent but violent when roused, like his father, leads an idle and purposeless life in a home made miserable for him by the enmity of his stepmother but has not the strength of mind to decide finally to leave it, in spite of his premonition of disaster.

But it is the woman's life that Elizabeth Gaskell studies in the greatest depth, and the answer to the question of occupation for her in the Victorian era admitted of no doubt: early marriage and maternity were her true sphere. Elizabeth Gaskell herself believed that woman's natural fulfilment lay in marriage and motherhood. She had married young, and she seems to have expected her daughters to do the same. It is noticeable that her young heroines never seem concerned by the prospect that they may not marry. Spinsterhood is as unthinkable for Mary Barton or Sylvia Robson as it is for their middle-class sisters. Molly Gibson has an ardent if not very eligible suitor at sixteen, and at nineteen Margaret Hale receives a proposal of marriage from an ambitious young lawyer in spite of her impecunious state. But they have no hesitation in rejecting suitors whom they do not love. Elizabeth Gaskell recognised all the importance of compatibility of temperament. Margaret Hale and Henry Lennox have different values and this would always have prevented a complete understanding between them. It may take time to discover where true compatibility exists. Mary Barton and Margaret Hale begin by refusing the man they eventually marry. In spite of their friendship Molly Gibson at first no more thinks of Roger Hamley as her ideal of a husband than he of her as his future wife: '. . . although they were drawn together in this very pleasant relationship, each was imagining some one very different for the future owner of their whole heart—their highest and completest love.'[14] It is only gradually and, it seems, unconsciously that she comes to love him so completely that, when he falls out of love with Cynthia, he is fortunate enough to find the wife who will appreciate him at his true value as Cynthia could not.

It would appear from the examples in her fiction that Elizabeth Gaskell rather distrusted the rapid courtship that gave little time for the acquirement of any true insight into character. In 'Morton Hall' Alice Carr's rash marriage to a man opposed in everything to the Puritan tradition in which she has been reared is a fatal mistake. Catherine Hearn of 'The Squire's Story', 'a romantic, sentimental girl', elopes with a lover who turns out to be a highwayman. Both these are relatively early tales, and it has been suggested that Mrs Gaskell became increasingly conscious of the dangers of such marriages. Certainly 'The Grey Woman', written in the period subsequent to her daughter Meta's broken engagement, is a grim example of the disasters that overtake a girl who is hurried into marriage by her family, proud of her making such a good match, and has not the courage to resist them. It may, however, be circumstance, not haste, that accounts for the union of two incompatible natures. Sylvia Robson marries her cousin Philip Hepburn, knowing his temperament is alien to hers, because of economic pressures and because she believes the man she loves is dead. Kinraid's return brings catastrophe, but the marriage could never have been a completely happy one because she and Philip are temperamentally unsuited to each other. But in spite of the hazards of matrimony Elizabeth Gaskell remains very much in favour of it, provided the partners are reasonably compatible. Miss Matty advises the young Mary Brown not to allow herself to be prejudiced against it by the warnings of the redoubtable Miss Pole and confesses to holding a very different opinion: '. . . she evidently looked upon a husband as a great protector against thieves, burglars, and ghosts; and said she did not think that she should dare to be always warning young people against matrimony . . . to be sure, marriage was a risk . . . but she remembered the time when she had looked forward to being married as much as anyone.'[15]

All women, however, did not marry and live happily ever after in the early Victorian era. In the light of her own experience Elizabeth Gaskell found it natural to portray youth as the season of love, and marriage as its culmination, but she was aware that for many the reality was different. She counted many unmarried women among her intimate friends, and she never saw the unmarried woman otherwise than as an individual or thought that her own married state entitled her to patronise those who were single. Mrs Robson, Sylvia's quiet mother, becomes quite scathing in her sarcasm at the airs and graces of Molly Corney when she secures a husband, and certainly Molly is patronising in the extreme when she comes home on a visit, giving directions to her younger sisters and rejecting any timid suggestions they venture to make 'with a toss of her married head'. Her work contains perceptive portraits of single women, not all of whom, of course, belong to the middle class. Some are single because they have devoted themselves to family ties, like Faith Benson or the 'stateswoman' Susan Dixon, some, like Miss Matty or Hester Rose, because they could not marry the man they loved, some, like Nest Gwynn, because they have been crippled by an accident and some, like Libbie Marsh, the seamstress, because, in spite of excellent qualities, they are so plain that—as their friends do not fail to point out—their fate is a foregone conclusion. According to the view of Mrs Gaskell's Parisian friends, as expressed in 'French Life', the English girl's matrimonial prospects were often unfairly compromised, even in wealthy circles, by the absence of a suitable dowry.[16] Mme Mohl, her greatest friend in France, felt strongly on this subject.[17] Elizabeth Gaskell herself was evidently dubious as to the wisdom of arranged marriages, but the plight of Ellinor Wilkins in 'A Dark Night's Work' does lend colour to the French criticism of the selfishness of some affluent English families towards their daughters. Ellinor fails to marry in youth partly because her spendthrift father can no longer honour the marriage settlement on which her ambitious suitor has counted. She does marry eventually, many years later, but she has lost both her youth and the man to whom, however unworthy he may have been, the love of her youth was irrevocably given.

Elizabeth Gaskell did not underestimate the dilemma of the single woman. Her first published tale was 'The Three Eras of Libbie Marsh' and Libbie states her position squarely as she sees it:

'. . . I know I'm never likely to have a home of my own, or a husband that would look to me to make all straight, or children to watch over or care for, all which I take to be woman's natural work . . .'[18] Libbie would evidently have mothered her husband as well as her children; it is not the married status nor the benefit of a husband to support her (considerations that weighed heavily with Molly Corney or Mrs Kirkpatrick) that she principally regrets: it is what she could have given, far more than what she could have gained. She does not stop at regrets, she goes on to consider what positive action is possible, and expresses the conviction that those in her position should not waste their time in 'fretting and fidgetting after marriage' but face facts and settle down to be old maids and, as such, look round for 'the odd jobs God leaves in the world for such as old maids to do'. She implements this by throwing in her lot with the mother of the crippled child she had helped to comfort. In *Mary Barton*, published the following year, there is no finer character than Alice, the selfless old countrywoman who has mothered her orphan nephew and is sick nurse to half the neighbourhood in the Manchester slum where she has to live.

Libbie and Alice have to work hard for their living, though they find time to help others as well. In the more leisured atmosphere of *Cranford* the problem of the unmarried woman presents psychological complications of a more complex nature. In his stimulating article 'Women without Men at Cranford'[19] Martin Dodsworth called attention to the real depth of a work which, in spite of its air of gentle nostalgia, is in reality a searching exploration of a feminine society, and others since, without necessarily endorsing his analysis, have agreed with him in this. Not all the ladies of Cranford are spinsters but it is Miss Jenkyns who at first is their leader, in virtue of her strong personality, though in theory she defers to the Honourable Mrs Jamieson, an aristocratic but inert widow. Unlike Libbie Marsh, Miss Jenkyns refuses to admit to any lack in her life, but her aggressive feminism is clearly not taken too seriously by Mary Smith, the young but percipient narrator. Miss Jenkyns, with her masculine bonnet, 'half helmet, half jockey-cap', is really doing her best to perpetuate the standards of her father, the late Rector, but she compensates for her unmarried state by refusing to accept the opinions of any younger man and finds Captain Brown's outspokenness as offensive to her notions of propriety as his literary taste is to her inherited admiration of Johnson. After the death of Miss Jenkyns feminism is represented, even less convincingly, by

Miss Pole, whose poor opinion of men is only equalled by her intense interest in all their doings. The women of Cranford in general do not really consider themselves superior to men, they are afraid of them, and this abnormal state of affairs is represented as both comic and pathetic. Any intrusion of the masculine element causes a state of near panic and when the turbanned Signor Brunoni visits the little town, his masculinity evidently adds to the awe-inspiring nature of his conjuring performance, watched by the ladies—with the exception of Miss Pole, who professes scepticism—with a deference suggestive of the harem. But the succeeding episodes of *Cranford* represent a gradual return to more normal conditions, at the centre of which is the unassuming figure of Miss Matty, Miss Jenkyns' younger sister.

The personality of Miss Matty is the most influential in *Cranford*. Its development had been prepared in the earlier chapters when she met again, after many years, the lover, of different social status from herself, whom she had refused in accordance with the dictates of Cranford 'propriety', voiced by her father and sister. Her growing doubts as to the wisdom of her decision had been increased by her sense of loss at his death. The first-fruits of her altered outlook are seen in her removal of the ban on 'followers', which permits her servant Martha to marry, and in her quiet criticism of Miss Pole's anti-matrimonial views. When Signor Brunoni turns out to be Samuel Brown, a penniless ex-soldier whose plight appeals to the kindness of the Cranford ladies in general, she shows all her hitherto thwarted maternal tenderness in her concern for his little daughter, who has never learnt to play, and later a very feminine interest in the engagement of Lady Glenmire, even if it is to the socially inferior Hoggins, the Cranford surgeon. The maturing of her personality is evident when she faces financial disaster with courage and braves the Cranford notions of 'propriety' by agreeing to sell tea to earn her living. When her brother returns, it is to a sister who welcomes his companionship but who can, on her side, offer him a home. Miss Matty is not feminist but feminine. Although she is a spinster and not a wife, it is in virtue of her womanly qualities that she finally triumphs over circumstances; her 'love of peace and kindliness' represents no longer weak subservience but a strength different but not inferior to that of her equally kind-hearted brother.

Realist as she was, Elizabeth Gaskell did not show all spinsters as achieving the same quiet triumph as Miss Matty. There are sour old maids like Miss Horniman, whose ill-natured innuendoes annoy Mr

Harrison, irritable old maids like Fraulein Müller, the inn-keeper's sister in 'Six Weeks at Heppenheim', formidable old maids like Miss Pratt in 'The Squire's Story', an almost Balzacian figure. But one cannot doubt that Miss Matty represents her conception of how an unmarried woman can best avoid a frustrated life and make it instead a satisfying one. 'I think an unmarried life may be to the full as happy, *in process of time*,' she wrote years later, when her own daughters had grown up, 'but I think there is a time of trial to be gone through with *women*, who naturally yearn after children.'[20] Into that sentence she compressed her own sense of the greatest deprivation of such a state (the deprivation most keenly felt by Miss Matty, softened but not effaced by time) and also implicitly suggests what was for her the only natural way of compensating for it. If maternity is denied, the exercise of maternal feeling is still possible. Miss Matty, it has been said, 'is a mother-figure to a larger and more important family—the Cranford community'.[21] It is interesting to notice how Elizabeth Gaskell's view to some extent corresponds to the accepted Victorian attitude and yet transcends it. The unmarried woman was generally expected to find her natural occupation in helping in the family home, or in those of her relations. Elizabeth Gaskell, while giving priority to the claims of the immediate family, extends the term to comprehend a wider circle as well.

Not every middle-class spinster, however, was a lady of leisure. For some the first necessity was to earn their living. But only a minority, in Mrs Gaskell's work, find themselves in this position. For those who do, there is normally only one obvious course, to teach in a school or to become a governess. Nursing was beginning to be accepted as a possible occupation, thanks to the example of Florence Nightingale, whom Elizabeth Gaskell knew and admired, but Ruth, it will be remembered, when she becomes a sick nurse, does so only when she has lost her post as governess and at the suggestion of the parish doctor, and no previous training is considered necessary. Teaching or governessing was generally recognised to be the most suitable employment for middle-class women. Neither occupation emerges in her fiction as particularly attractive. The Miss Tomkinsons in Duncombe and Mrs Kirkpatrick in Ashcombe keep a school, but from necessity, not choice, and in the case of Mrs Kirkpatrick, she is not even able to make it pay. The governess's fate depends very much on the family who employs her but is never an exciting one. Ruth fares best as she is naturally fond of children and the Bradshaws, till the secret of her past is discovered, highly approve of her. Mrs Kirkpatrick, when before her marriage she is a governess in the Cumnor family, is not unkindly treated but so much at the beck and call of the Countess that, even had she been a good teacher, she would have found it difficult to do much for her pupils' serious education. Miss Eyre, Molly Gibson's governess, has a loyal pupil in the doctor's daughter, but has much to endure from her former nurse, who resents her presence in the house. It speaks volumes for the kind of life formerly led by Miss Munro, Ellinor Wilkins' governess, that when she enters the Wilkins household, a modicum of comfort and leisure has come to represent her ideal of earthly bliss: 'Miss Munro had been tossed about and overworked quite enough in her life not to value the privilege and indulgence of her evenings to herself . . .'[22]

In her *Life of Charlotte Brontë* Elizabeth Gaskell had to deal with the considerable part teaching and governessing had played in her friend's youth. In her case, too, necessity had decided her choice of occupation: '. . . teaching seemed to her at this time, as it does to most women at all times, the only way of earning an independent livelihood.'[23] A natural fondness for children and understanding of them were obviously needed if, in spite of the often difficult conditions, such a life were to yield any real satisfaction. Elizabeth Gaskell knew that for a temperament like Charlotte Brontë's, in which these qualities—partly owing to a motherless childhood— had never been fully developed, there could not be a less congenial occupation. In her teaching post at Roe Head she had at least the advantage of Miss Wooler's friendship and some leisure in the evenings, but in her two posts as private governess there were, for her, few mitigating circumstances: 'No doubt all who enter upon the career of a governess have to relinquish much; no doubt it must ever be a life of sacrifice; but to Charlotte Brontë it was a perpetual attempt to force all her faculties into a direction for which the whole of her previous life had unfitted them.'[24] None the less, the whole force of Charlotte's powerful will was bent on the setting up, by herself and her sisters, of a school of their own. She crossed the Channel to study for further qualifications and it was not for lack of effort on her part that the projected school at the parsonage never materialised. Even though it did not materialise, the subject haunted her imagination. Schools, teachers and governesses feature far more prominently in her fiction than in that of Elizabeth Gaskell.

The difference is interesting, for it reflects the difference in their views on the position of the unmarried woman as an individual. It was not a total divergence; as far as legislation is concerned Charlotte Brontë was no more of a feminist than her friend; both agreed that the social system was not likely to be fundamentally altered by such methods; both believed that the 'emancipation of women' ought never to mean emancipation from the privilege of 'self-sacrificing love and disinterested devotion'. But Elizabeth Gaskell does not place the same emphasis on independence for unmarried women who are without immediate family duties to occupy them as does Charlotte Brontë. It is independence and the consequent development of the autonomous personality, not teaching in itself, that is the goal of Lucy Snowe or Frances Henri. Charlotte Brontë admired *Cranford*, but there is a vast difference between the old maids of Cranford and the 'old maids' in the eponymous chapter of *Shirley*. Miss Ainley is as kind as Miss Matty, and more actively philanthropic, and Caroline Helstone, when she faces a future without a husband, does her best to emulate her, but she gets no real satisfaction from her efforts. Instead she longs to leave her uncle's rectory and take a post as governess, even though there is no immediate financial necessity for her to do so. Margaret Hale, believing, like Caroline, that she will never be able to marry the man she loves, is also conscious of the triviality of her existence at her aunt's house in Harley Street and determines to make it more purposeful. But, in her case, the decision does not involve her leaving her relations' home to take up a career. She is able to achieve a purposeful existence where she is and, had Thornton never re-entered her life, she would never have forgotten him but neither would she have gone into a decline. The difference stems fundamentally from the fact that Elizabeth Gaskell's women are more maternal than Charlotte Brontë's and therefore less preoccupied with their position with regard to men than with their need to help the helpless of either sex and any age. Charlotte's heroines feel the need to affirm their personality, so that they can meet their lovers as equals or, if necessary, face the fact that they have no lovers. Shirley, the boldest of them, is proud of having 'a man's name' and of 'holding a man's position', even though she is no feminist at heart. Margaret Hale tries to shield Thornton from the mob not because she has a man's courage but because to do so is, in her view, the woman's prerogative.

In writing her biography of Charlotte Brontë Elizabeth Gaskell had to deal not only with her brief teaching career but with her much more significant career as novelist. The early Victorian era accepted the unmarried woman as teacher but was not so unanimous in accepting her as author. When Charlotte, at twenty-one, sent some of her poems to Southey for his opinion, she received little encouragement to cherish literary ambitions: 'Literature cannot be the business of a woman's life, and it ought not to be. The more she is engaged in her proper duties, the less leisure will she have for it, even as an accomplishment and as a recreation. To those duties you have not yet been called, and when you are you will be less eager for celebrity . . .'[25] Charlotte thought this letter 'stringent but kind' and wrote to thank Southey for it. It is significant that Elizabeth Gaskell, quoting it in her biography, still calls it 'admirable'. Southey's views were already partly outdated in 1837 and, when she wrote, names like those of Harriet Martineau and Charlotte Brontë herself were familiar, like her own, to the whole of the reading public. But it was her primary aim to show Charlotte as a woman to those who knew her only as an author, and as a woman faithfully performing her duty to her family. It was during a period when family loyalty kept her at the parsonage, with some time on her hands even when all domestic duties had been discharged, that she wrote *The Professor* and *Jane Eyre*. *Jane Eyre* proved conclusively that she possessed genius but the fact did not exempt her in Elizabeth Gaskell's opinion, any more than in her own, from continuing involvement with the life of the family. What it did mean, however, was that she had in future to acknowledge responsibility for the talent which had been given her and work to develop it, while at the same time remaining a devoted daughter and sister:

Henceforward Charlotte Brontë's existence becomes divided into two parallel currents—her life as Currer Bell, the author; her life as Charlotte Brontë, the woman. There were separate duties belonging to each character—not impossible, but difficult to be reconciled. When a man becomes an author, it is probably merely a change of employment to him. He takes a portion of that time which has hitherto been devoted to some other study or pursuit . . . and another merchant, or lawyer, or doctor, steps into his vacant place and probably does as well as he. But no other can take up the quiet regular duties of the daughter, the wife or the mother, as well as she whom God has appointed to fill that particular place: a woman's principal work in life is hardly left to her own choice; nor can she drop the domestic charges devolving on her as an individual, for the exercise of the most splendid talents that were ever bestowed. And yet she must not shrink from the extra responsibility implied by the very fact of her possessing such talents. She must not hide her gift in a napkin; it was meant for the use and service of others. In a humble and faithful spirit must she labour to do what is not impossible, or God would not have set her to do it. (Ch. 16)

In these words Elizabeth Gaskell expressed not only Charlotte Brontë's position but her own. In writing her friend's life she was obliged to consider the dilemma of the woman with exceptional gifts—a dilemma not confined to unmarried women alone, since the born writer or artist does not change her nature when she marries. It was a problem of which she had been conscious herself ever since *Mary Barton* made her famous. Writing in 1850 to the artist Eliza Fox, she showed her awareness of it: '. . . what follows in your letter about home duties and individual life . . . is just my puzzle . . .'[26] The 'individual life' in this context is the life of artistic creation. In theory she feels that a blending of domesticity and artistic creativity is desirable, but she acknowledges the difficulty of combining the two in practice: '. . . the difficulty is where and when to make one set of duties subserve and give place to the other.' The 'home duties' she refers to were of a more cheerful nature than those devolving on Charlotte Brontë, but the problem is essentially the same: the tension is not between self-abnegation and arrant individualism but between 'two sets of duties', each involving the response of the heart as well as the conscience.

Neither of the two friends would probably have claimed that they found a complete solution. Elizabeth Gaskell admits frankly to Eliza Fox: 'I don't think I can get nearer to a solution than you have done.' In the years that followed the need to meet the demands both of home duties and of a writing career did not cease to be a problem for her as it was for Charlotte Brontë. Both did their best to remain faithful to their dual commitment, though in ways as different as their temperament and circumstances, 'the one lonely, plain and intense, the other successful, healthy, graceful and beloved. . . .'[27] Neither the almost complete isolation of Haworth parsonage nor the ceaseless activity of Plymouth Grove were ideal settings for artistic creation. The second was, perhaps, from this point of view, even less propitious than the first, obliging Elizabeth Gaskell increasingly to take refuge elsewhere when she was writing, but she always returned to the busy home to watch over the interests of her family and indeed to be the dynamic centre of them. Charlotte Brontë, on her side, had leisure to write, but paid the price of too much isolation by suffering in health and nerves and occasionally had to seek change and stimulus away from home, though it was never out of her thoughts.

In her *Life of Charlotte Brontë* Elizabeth Gaskell was concerned not with an 'ordinary' character but with an exceptional one. 'I cannot measure or judge of such a character as hers,' she wrote in her conclusion. 'I cannot map out vices, and virtues, and debatable land.' Her strength lay indeed not in measuring and judging but in interpreting and sympathising. The fact that she was able to do this with considerable success in the case of Charlotte Brontë shows that there were depths in her own character unsuspected by those who are misled by the apparent tranquillity of *Cranford*. Not only the biography but her fiction in general indicates that, though her best loved characters tend to be the kind of people one meets in everyday life, she was, unlike Jane Austen (or at least Jane Austen as seen by Charlotte Brontë), well acquainted with the 'stormy sisterhood' of the passions, and could understand intensely emotive states as well as cheerful equilibrium and maladjustment as well as social normality.

Charlotte Brontë had a passionate temperament under a quiet exterior, like her heroines Jane Eyre and Lucy Snowe. Elizabeth Gaskell herself knew what passion was. Though she was as reticent on the subject of sexual passion as most Victorians, her reticence was not ignorance. The two of her heroines who are most remarkable for beauty and strong personality (and in this most like her own youthful self), Mary Barton and Margaret Hale, both have passionate temperaments and fall deeply in love. They are at first unaware of the nature of their feelings and unconsciously reject them, but once they realise their love, they accept it completely. Mary Barton declares her love for Jem Wilson in open court, at the trial scene, contravening Victorian conventions for womanly behaviour. Margaret Hale, by offering to help Thornton after his business failure, leaves neither him nor the reader in any doubt of her feelings. The sexual attraction between Thornton and Margaret is from the first as evident, though less emphasised, as that between Rochester and Jane Eyre. The difference is that their passion is presented in a social context, thereby losing something in intensity but gaining in realism, as Martin Dodsworth points out: '. . . Mrs Gaskell sees the extent to which our understanding of the role of passion in life is bound up with our understanding of other people and the social order within which, to a greater or less degree, they find their place.'[28] Even when they seem, to their own despair, to be moving further away from each other, Margaret and Thornton can still spare time and thought for an out-of-work weaver and his family. They love each other passionately, but neither is 'passion's slave'.

The passion which absorbs the individual to the point when it becomes the only reality in life was something which Elizabeth Gaskell could comprehend and pity, but which she never shows as other than destructive in its workings. Ruth, in her youthful immaturity and acute loneliness, becomes for a time the victim of such a passion. It is only when she is repudiated by society as represented first by the little holiday community in Wales, next by her lover's aristocratic mother and finally and most woundingly by her lover himself, that she realises the extent of her plight. There is an almost Hardyesque quality in the description of her futile attempt to overtake the carriage which is bearing her lover away, and her despairing collapse at the side of the mountain road: '. . . afterwards—long afterwards—she remembered the exact motion of a bright green beetle busily meandering among the wild thyme near her, and she recalled the musical, balanced, wavering drop of a skylark into her nest, near the heather-bed where she lay.'[29] In *Sylvia's Lovers*, the 'saddest story' she ever wrote, whose title she at one time thought of changing to 'Philip's Idol', it is Philip Hepburn who is the most tragic figure because Sylvia is his entire world. To possess her, he sacrifices his integrity; it is of her future happiness that he thinks when he prospers in business; it is of her he is still thinking when he leaves home and becomes a soldier in the hope of shortening his life, though he lives long enough for the final reconciliation at the moment of death. His is a corroding passion, hidden under a reserved exterior. Sylvia is also passionate by nature, but vehement and demonstrative; her apparent passivity during her brief married life is the measure of her unhappiness, and when Kinraid returns and she is obliged to send him away, all the force of her frustrated passion for him is channeled into the unforgiving anger which drives her husband into exile.

Elizabeth Gaskell, as a woman of strong vitality, was attracted by vital force in itself. She could admire the primeval vigour which she found in countryfolk, especially those living isolated lives, even while she realised it could have dangerous concomitants of harshness and brutality. Her biography of Charlotte Brontë begins with a memorable description not only of Haworth but of 'the rough population' of this corner of the West Riding, as she pictured them in the first quarter of the century, and, though she approves neither of 'arvills' nor riots, it is clear that she is at the same time attracted by the sheer vitality of a people 'so independent, wilful and full of grim humour'.[30] She credits them with being influenced by their 'rough Norse ancestry'[31] and, whether this is ethnographically correct or not, it shows, on her part, a natural appreciation of the strong and the primitive. She liked to think that her paternal ancestors, the Stevensons, were of Norse descent.[32] The characters of *Sylvia's Lovers* are capable at times of speech and action as fierce and vehement as the heroes of a saga. Daniel Robson, who has escaped from the press-gang in youth only by deliberately mutilating his right hand, cannot speak of them without his expression becoming one of 'settled and unrelenting indignation', and their renewed aggression in Monkshaven provokes him to violent action, for which he pays with his life. The same elemental force and the same harshness reappear in the country folk of some of the shorter tales. John Middleton, the poacher's son, who has been deeply wronged by an enemy, remembers 'our country proverb—"Keep a stone in thy pocket for seven years; turn it, and keep it seven years more; but have it ever ready to cast to thine enemy when the time comes" '.[33] The influence of his gentle wife and the eloquence of an itinerant preacher, though they make him change his way of life, cannot make him gave up his grim determination to have his revenge. Chance puts his enemy, now a broken man, in his power on a 'wild and terrible night', and there seems little disproportion between the fury of the elements and the struggle in his own heart before he at last yields to the entreaties of his dying wife and lets him go in peace.

This vital force and strength of will take, in the face of trouble and disaster, the form of a taciturn stoicism. Such stoicism may be outwardly repellent, but it often implies a remarkable courage. Susan Dixon, the owner of Yew Nook farm, seems unattractive enough on her first appearance in the story 'Half a Lifetime Ago', a 'tall, gaunt, hard-featured, angular woman—who never smiled, and hardly spoke an unnecessary word'.[34] But she had once been a high-spirited and handsome girl, who sent her lover away because he was not prepared to tolerate her feeble-minded brother. It was typical of her that, after they had parted in anger, she should turn immediately to 'one of the hardest and hottest domestic tasks of a Daleswoman', the making of clap-bread, much as the servant in Flaubert's *Un Coeur Simple* finds an outlet for grief in the vehemence with which she plies her washerwoman's beetle. The incident was prophetic of the vigour and efficiency with which she was to run the farm for the sake of the brother whose state worsened with the years and who finally died, leaving her alone. Many years later she rescues the body of a man from a snowdrift on a winter night and finds that it is her former lover, whose cry for help she had heard but who is dead before she can bring him into shelter. The farm labourers, when they arrive in the dawn of the next day, think he must somehow have managed to drag himself to the house. 'They could not have believed the superhuman exertion which had first sought him out, and then dragged him hither. Only Susan knew of that.'[35]

Elizabeth Gaskell admired and understood the qualities of such individuals, living in isolated country communities. She was not dismayed by harshness and bluntness, though she was repelled by deliberate cruelty and vice, but she recognised that such 'indomitable and independent energies' could, when misdirected, have terrible results. *Sylvia's Lovers*, in its wild, windswept setting, shows the primitive community of Monkshaven at the most tempestuous moments of its bleak existence: furious when the intervention of the press-gang turns the joyous return of the whalers into tragedy, grimly silent at the funeral of one of the victims, bent on retaliation when the clanging of the fire-bell on a bitter winter night proves to be a decoy to lure fresh victims into the clutches of the gang. The opening scene when the men whom the press-gang has snatched from their families, at the very moment of reunion, are marched through the streets of Monkshaven by their captors, who are armed to the teeth, has an elemental fierceness:

> . . . pressing round this nucleus of cruel wrong were women crying aloud, throwing up their arms in imprecation, showering down abuse as hearty and rapid as if they had been a Greek chorus . . . The stormy multitude swelled into the market-place and formed a solid crowd there, while the press-gang steadily forced their way on into High Street, and on to the rendez-vous. A low, deep growl went up from the dense mass, as some had to

wait for space to follow the others—now and then going up, as a lion's growl goes up, into a shriek of rage. (Ch. 3)

It is, however, not the corporate feeling of the crowd that is the primary interest of Elizabeth Gaskell on such occasions, but the reactions of the individuals. The seventeen-year-old Sylvia who, a short time before, had instinctively responded to the joyful excitement on the quayside, now shows that she is her father's daughter in her indignation against the gang: 'Let us go into t' thick of it and do a bit of help; I can't stand quiet and see't!' She is restrained from active intervention by her cousin Philip but, when she returns home, her father, on hearing her account of the riot, shows a violent anger prophetic of catastrophe to come: 'I've been whalin' mysel', and I've heard tell as whalers wear knives; and I'd ha' gi'en t' gang a taste o' my whittle, if I'd been cotched up just as I'd set my foot a-shore.'

In less isolated communities the primitive energies do not manifest themselves so directly, but Elizabeth Gaskell, herself a North Country woman, believed that they survived especially among the 'strong, self-reliant, racy and individual characters . . . still in existence in the North.'[36] It was to the impression of originality conveyed by the delineation of such figures that she attributed the success of Charlotte Brontë's first published novel: '. . . though "dark, and cold, and rugged is the North", the old strength of the Scandinavian races yet abides there, and glowed out in every character depicted in "Jane Eyre".'[37] A similar thesis is advanced by Thornton in *North and South* when he defends his Darkshire ethos. His values are not fundamentally very different from those of the Monkshaven whalers, activity, independence, will power, tenacity, the spirit of adventure which, in his case, leads him to harness the forces of nature in the new world of industry. Margaret Hale is aware of his 'rock-like power of character, his passion-strength' before she is aware of his passion for her, which is so intense that it finally awakes her own love for him. As in *Sylvia's Lovers* these vital characters are inevitably drawn into the upheavals that convulse their world. The mob scene when the strikers besiege the mill-owner's house is as menacing as the Monkshaven riots. In this case, however, the individual proves strong enough to dominate the crowd, Margaret by her dramatic intervention, Thornton by his courage and iron determination.

There is a similar basic strength and fire in Mrs Thornton, the mill-owner's mother, the 'firm, severe, dignified woman' who conceals her love for her idolised only son beneath an undemonstrative manner and does not hesitate to tell him 'unpalatable truths' when she considers they are called for. If she desires a daughter-in-law, it is certainly not Margaret Hale but, for her son's sake, she is prepared to accept her in spite of her Southern breeding. The incredible news that Margaret does not wish to marry him shatters her rigid control and reveals for a moment the force of passion which underlies it: ' "And she would not have you, my own lad, would not she?" She set her teeth; she showed them like a dog for the whole length of her mouth . . . And yet her heart leapt up light, to know he was her own again.'[38]

It may, at first sight, seem strange that, while admiring such strong and rugged personalities, Elizabeth Gaskell should at the same time be able to portray with such sympathy the gentle Miss Matty, the much enduring Alice of *Mary Barton*, the patient Mrs Hamley of *Wives and Daughters* and many similar figures. She could do so because she never confused gentleness with weakness, any more than she confused uncontrolled passion with true strength. Nothing, after all, is either stronger or more gentle than maternal love, the ruling force of her own nature. When portraying weakness, as distinct from gentleness, she shows a realistic awareness of the factors which have helped to produce it, and recognises that it can coexist with some very real virtues. Moreover, as an extremely acute observer of human nature, she knows well that it is a variable quality; those who are weak in some circumstances can be strong in others, and even the strongest have their moments of weakness. None the less, weakness in itself has the power to provoke her occasionally to an overt impatience. This is particularly noticeable when it causes prevarication, instead of the directness which she admired and which was a part of her own nature. The timid Miss Phoebe Browning, when called upon to act as adjudicator in an argument which has arisen between her elder sister and Molly Gibson, their guest—two frank and sturdy characters—receives, on the whole, rather less sympathy from Elizabeth Gaskell than she deserves in this, to her, very considerable dilemma:

> Molly was flaming with indignation; but she had appealed to the wrong person for justice. Miss Phoebe tried to make peace, after the fashion of weak-minded people, who would cover over the unpleasant sight of a sore, instead of trying to heal it.

'I'm sure I don't know anything about it, my dear. It seems to me that what Clarinda was saying was very true—very true indeed; and I think, love, you misunderstood her; or, perhaps, she misunderstood you; or I may be misunderstanding it altogether; so we'd better not talk any more about it. What price did you say you were going to give for the drugget in Mr. Gibson's dining-room, sister?' (*Wives and Daughters* ch. 13)

There is one form of weakness which Elizabeth Gaskell, as a realist, never minimises and that is bodily weakness. Difficulty in coping with the stresses of life may be due, in part at least, to a frail constitution. Mr Hale can never have been physically robust, and is ill-fitted to bear the strain caused by his son's wrecked career, the change to Milton and his wife's death. Osborne Hamley is blamed by his father for his laziness and for not succeeding at Cambridge like his brother Roger, but Mr Gibson, who has spoken with a man who knew Roger's tutor, has a doctor's view of the cause of one brother's success and the other's failure: '. . . the tutor said that only half of Roger's success was owing to his mental powers; the other half was owing to his perfect health, which enabled him to work harder and more continuously than most men without suffering . . . I, being a doctor, trace a good deal of his superiority to the material cause of a thoroughly good constitution, which Osborne hasn't got.'[39] Physical frailty does not preclude moral strength, as characters like the invalid Mrs Hamley or the crippled Margaret Dawson testify, but it puts grave strains on their powers of endurance and, in cases like Mrs Hamley's, shortens their life span.

The most salient example of Elizabeth Gaskell's recognition of the limitations imposed by a frail physique is, however, to be found in her treatment of this factor in *The Life of Charlotte Brontë*. It is the moral strength of Charlotte's character which she wishes above all to emphasise, and in this she triumphantly succeeds. But in this instance she perhaps overestimates the influence of the physical on the mental, insisting repeatedly on the 'permanent state of bodily weakness' against which Charlotte had to contend. Depression, nervous fears, etc., are usually ascribed to bodily causes, but this is hardly to make sufficient allowance for the influence of the mental on the physical, where an imagination of such extraordinary power is in question. She probably gives a more accurate statement of the position when she speaks of the importance to Charlotte Brontë, from early youth, of creating for herself 'long and deep histories of feeling and imagination', and concludes: 'This made it inevitable that—later on, in her too short career—the intensity of her feeling should wear out her physical health.'[40]

Elizabeth Gaskell's own heroines are usually characterised by the healthy balance of mind and body that she admired. Nevertheless that balance is temporarily threatened in each of the major works. There is always a physical cause: either they are utterly exhausted, like Mary Barton, by the weight of responsibility they have had to shoulder or they are particularly vulnerable through physical weakness, like Sylvia, reproached by Philip while she is recovering from childbirth. Always—with the exception of Ruth, a victim of typhoid fever—they possess the resilience to recover their health in the course of time, but exhaustion or illness temporarily gives a hallucinatory quality to their sensations, physical in origin but strangely disturbing while it lasts. Elizabeth Gaskell is never consciously a subjective novelist but here, perhaps, she was subconsciously influenced by her own experience. The pattern of overstrain, temporary exhaustion and returning resilience ran through her own life as well. The individuals she creates are not immune from illness, any more than she was, but none of them, not even Mrs Gibson, are ill from choice. There is nothing morbid about Elizabeth Gaskell's view of human nature. She admires sanity, health and vitality. She was essentially well-balanced, healthy and vital herself.

7 Mystery and the macabre

The stories in which Elizabeth Gaskell deals with the mysterious and the macabre are among her shorter works. These were not themes she considered suitable for development in full length works of fiction. It is noticeable that in what might appear at first sight an uncharacteristic field she retains her concern with the local setting, the family background and the personalities of those who play a leading part in the action. Nor do her basic values change: no mystery can obliterate the bounds between good and evil, health is always preferable to morbidity and evil itself always the ultimate horror. None the less, as a born storyteller she could not fail to recognise that such themes afforded exceptional opportunities for drama and suspense, both of which are important elements in her fiction in general. In her novels, however, as in life, they only acquire their full force at times of crisis. In some of her shorter tales mysterious and macabre elements are in the ascendant, and there is from the first an atmosphere of impending crisis.

They include two stories entirely centred round the supernatural, 'The Old Nurse's Story' and 'The Poor Clare'. It is an oral tradition that is behind storytelling of this kind, the tradition of the ballad. Elizabeth Gaskell, who loved and understood countryfolk, instinctively responded to the primitive force of the popular poems, 'abrupt, wild and dramatic',[1] which are handed down for generations by word of mouth. The qualities she appreciated can be seen in the Breton ballad, 'The Scholar's Story', which appeared in the 1853 Christmas issue of Dickens' *Household Words* and is believed to have been translated by her husband and introduced by herself.[2] This medieval tale of treachery and death is made more tragic by the innocence and helplessness of the victims, who reappear in the closing section as ghosts.

It was no coincidence that 'The Scholar's Story' should be published in a Christmas number of *Household Words*. The attraction of ghost stories told round the fire, an art closely akin to that of the ballad, had been firmly established for Victorian audiences by the author of *The Christmas Carol*. It was in Christmas issues of *Household Words* that both these tales of the supernatural first appeared.[3] Elizabeth Gaskell was herself a notable teller of ghost stories. Their attraction for her was not of that fearful kind felt by the ladies of Cranford, 'I SAW a ghost!'[4] she announces, in a letter to her London friend Eliza Fox, but adds she hardly expects to be believed by one who lives in such a prosaic place as Charlotte Street. It was in fact on a drive to an old house near Stratford on Avon, almost hidden by woods, that she claimed to have seen this apparition. It is a half-inhabited manor on the bleak Northumberland fells that is the scene of 'The Old Nurse's Story' and the isolated Trough of Bowland is the initial setting for 'The Poor Clare'. The strong, primitive passions felt by people living in such wild places are the cause of tragedy, as in the ballads, and are perpetuated, as often in the ballads, in spectral form.

But the realism of the setting, the authenticity of the period atmosphere, above all the convincing characterisation give credibility to these ghostly dramas. Though no rational explanation is given, the spectral element cannot be discounted as mere Gothic sensationalism. The narrator of 'The Old Nurse's Story' is a practical countrywoman and the narrator of 'The Poor Clare' a lawyer with a love of factual detail. And others see the phantoms, besides those directly involved. The dénouement of 'The Old Nurse's Story' was criticised by Dickens for this reason, but Elizabeth Gaskell refused to alter what was fundamental to her own treatment of the theme. For she is not concerned with the mystic or the visionary; she retains, even in this context, her distrust of them; she is concerned with the deadly consequences of such passions as jealousy, anger and hatred.

It was out of jealousy that, as a girl, the aged Miss Furnivall of 'The Old Nurse's Story' had revealed to her father Lord Furnivall the secret of her sister's clandestine marriage to a foreign musician, and the existence of their child. As a result he had driven both mother and little daughter—supposed to be a cottager's child to whom she had taken a fancy—out of the manor house in which they were living to their deaths on the snowy fells. The force of hatred thus released causes the haunting. The devoted nurse gradually realises that a ghost child is trying to lure her own charge, Rosamund, the living descendant of the Furnivalls, to a similar fate. The theme builds up, through mounting tension, to a terrifying climax when the initial tragedy is re-enacted in the great hall on a snowy winter night. The power behind the spectral apparitions exercises its full destructive force against its potential victim, protected only by the nurse:

> . . . I held her tighter and tighter, till I feared I should do her a hurt; but rather that than let her go towards those terrible phantoms. They passed along towards the great hall-door, where the winds howled and ravened for their prey . . . And Miss Rosamund was torn as by a power stronger than mine, and writhed in my arms, and sobbed (for by this time the poor darling was growing faint).
>
> 'They want me to go with them on to the Fells—they are drawing me to them. Oh, my little girl! I would come, but cruel, wicked Hester holds me very tight.'[5]

The child is saved by the strength of the nurse's love. But old Miss Furnivall, who has spent the years in sterile remorse, dies paralysed as the result of being obliged to watch the part played, in the terrible scene, by the wraith of her youthful self.

In 'The Poor Clare', which is set in the first part of the eighteenth century, it is again the hatred aroused in a passionate nature which is at the origin of the haunting. The Irish countrywoman Bridget Fitzgerald is herself conscious of the force of her nature: '. . . my heart's will is fearful and strong'.[6] When her faithful spaniel, the one thing left to her to cherish in memory of her vanished daughter, is callously shot by Squire Gisborne, whose path it happens to cross, she utters the curse which results in his young daughter's being haunted by a demoniac double. Elizabeth Gaskell's treatment of the 'doppelgänger' motif is characteristic. Instead of being, as in Poe's *William Wilson*, evidence of a divided personality, this 'ghastly resemblance' is totally alien to the real character of the innocent victim. Like the phantoms in 'The Old Nurse's Story' this emanation of hatred can only be dispelled by the force of a stronger power. Bridget Fitzgerald, on discovering that Lucy Gisborne is in reality the child of her passionately loved daughter, now dead, exerts all her strength to free her granddaughter from the demoniac apparition. She becomes a member of the Order of the Poor Clares in expiation, entering a convent in Antwerp, and finally gives her life for her enemy Gisborne, whom the chances of a military career have involved in quelling a riot of the Antwerp mob. But she dies in the assurance that by her sacrifice Lucy has been freed from the curse.

In these tales of the supernatural the poetic atmosphere inherited from the world of ballad and legend interposes a sort of screen between the reader and the violence of the passions involved. There is no such mitigation of stark tragedy in 'Lois the Witch'. If *Sylvia's Lovers* is the saddest story Elizabeth Gaskell ever wrote, this episode of the Salem witch-hunts in seventeenth-century New England is undoubtedly the grimmest. She wrote out of evident knowledge of the period concerned. The pseudonym 'Cotton Mather Mills', which she used in her early writings, was borrowed from Cotton Mather, author of *Memorable Providences relating to Witchcraft and Possessions*, published in 1685—who appears in the course of the story—and she was obviously acquainted with the historical records of the witch trials at Salem in 1692 and followed them in several respects.[7] The terrible delusion which sent nineteen victims to the gallows in that fatal year is the agent which determines the death of the unfortunate Lois. Though her personal history is probably invented, it is unfortunately all too certain that others as innocent as she suffered as cruelly.[8]

In 'Lois the Witch' a macabre theme is treated with the same essential sanity as the spectral theme in the ghost stories. Elizabeth Gaskell does not lose her sense of proportion in relating the tragedy of Lois Barclay. It is not only in New England that dangerous superstitions are rife. As a child in her nurse's arms, in her father's Warwickshire parish of Barford, Lois Barclay had witnessed the drowning of a witch, and the old woman had cursed the parson's daughter whose father had not intervened to save her. But in the town of Salem, as Elizabeth Gaskell shows it, influences abound which are peculiarly favourable to fostering the germs of superstition until they develop into a contagion. When in May 1691 Lois, now orphaned and obliged to seek a home with her only living relatives in New England, lands at Boston, she finds that Puritan austerity can be tempered by a kindly hospitality, but the journey to Salem is a journey away from sanity. The road is through forests reported to be full of 'dreaded and mysterious beasts and still more to be dreaded Indians'. The town itself, within its double circle of stockades, seems to be beleaguered by the forest in its dangerous and frightening isolation.

The relatives of Lois, the Hickson family, leading citizens of Salem, all bear the marks of their grim environment. Her uncle is an invalid who has lost the will to live and does not long survive. Grace Hickson, his wife, New England born and bred, is a stern matriarch who does not welcome the arrival of her niece and dismisses with harsh intolerance her initial attempts to defend the values of her dead parents and their loyalty to Church and State. Her children all reveal, in different ways, the effects of a repressive milieu where the expression of natural feeling is discouraged, laughter and beauty are absent, and there is all too much opportunity for the obsessive brooding which Elizabeth Gaskell believed to be among the most potent causes of maladjustment. Manasseh, the son, is unbalanced in mind; Faith, the elder daughter, nurses in sombre silence an unrequited love for one of the pastors; Prudence, the younger, is a malicious child. Even the old Indian servant, Nattee, who sometimes relates weird tales in her broken English over the kitchen fire for the benefit of the young girls, is, unlike most servants in the Gaskell works, no source of comfort; she speaks of the wizards of her race, herself believing and shuddering as she narrates, yet unconsciously taking pleasure in her power over her hearers, members of the oppressing race which had chased her people from the hunting-grounds which had belonged to her fathers. In this unhealthy atmosphere it seems inevitable that Manasseh should fall hopelessly in love with Lois, already 'troth-plight', as she tells him, to a lover in England, and that in his confused mind, where religion and superstition are inextricably mixed, there should form the conviction that his cousin is foreordained to marry him, or else to encounter a violent death. Such is the convincing prelude to tragedy in the winter of 1691-2 when, in the long, dark evenings, whispered tales of 'temptations and hauntings, and devilish terrors' gain an increasing hold on the Puritan imagination. 'Salem was, as it were, snowed up, and left to prey upon itself'.[9]

The mounting tension builds up to a climax when the two young daughters of the stern Pastor Tappau are seized with a hysteria thought to be demoniac possession caused by witchcraft, which acts like a deadly contagion, almost every household being found to contain supposed victims. The first person to be convicted of witchcraft is predictably the Tappau's Indian servant Hota, whom one of the children has named in her delirium, before the assembled community. The second is Lois herself who, in a similar assembly called after the hanging of Hota, is accused by her cousin Prudence, who has been seized by convulsions. The real cause of the child's condition is made clear to the reader. It has been self-induced out of an exhibitionist desire to attract as much notice as the Tappau children. But the malicious Prudence chooses to consider Lois responsible, partly because of tales of English Hallowe'en customs innocently told by her cousin but far more from instinctive jealousy of a nature so different from her own. Lois is condemned as a witch although, by a supreme irony, hers is the most innocent, the most healthy and the most loving personality in Salem.

In the painful closing scenes, Elizabeth Gaskell as narrator retains her balanced outlook. While recognising that such motives as personal malice played their part in the mass hysteria, she also recognises that many were sincere in their deluded belief in the guilt of those accused of witchcraft. Grace Hickson, a proud woman, humbles herself to the point of begging Lois to release her son Manasseh from her evil spells, and does not believe her niece when she protests that she cannot undo what she has never done. Most movingly, Lois herself, in her prison cell, is tempted to wonder if she is indeed a witch, but is roughly recalled to reality by a physical circumstance, the consciousness of the weight of her iron fetters when she makes an impatient movement. Even in such conditions lucidity is estimated by Elizabeth Gaskell as preferable to 'the wild, illimitable desert in which her imagination was wandering'. Subsequently Lois refuses to confess to an imaginary crime, even to save her life. She retains, in the face of fanaticism and dark superstitions, her religious faith and spends her last night in her prison cell comforting the old Indian servant Nattee, who has also been condemned to be hanged as a witch.

The grim tale has an epilogue. The concluding paragraphs incorporate the published statement made twenty-one years later by those who had acted as jurors during the Salem witch trials and who now admitted and regretted their terrible delusion. They also record the recantation of Justice Sewall, who had participated in the trials. But the last word belongs to the English lover of Lois who, still unaware of her cruel death, had crossed the sea in the autumn of 1692 to fetch her back to Warwickshire. For him such belated attempts at justice are small consolation: 'All their repentance will avail nothing to my Lois, nor will it bring back her life.'[10] None the less, for her sake, he vows to join his prayers to those of Justice Sewall each year on the day which the repentant judge has set aside to pray for forgiveness: 'She would have willed it so.'

In 'Lois the Witch', as in 'The Old Nurse's Story' and (though with a less perfect art) in 'The Poor Clare', the use of the supernatural and the macabre is symptomatic of the underlying conflict between good and evil. There is not the same sense of spiritual conflict in the other tales where Elizabeth Gaskell allows mystery and horror to predominate, though the bounds between good and evil remain firmly fixed. It is noticeable that horror rather than mystery usually predominates, and the mystery in itself usually proves to have more mundane causes than the haunted atmosphere of seventeenth-century Salem or the sinister legacy left by the force of hatred in passionate natures.

This is evident in the essay 'Disappearances'. Her interest in the subject can evidently be traced to a personal source, the mysterious disappearance of her own brother on his voyage to India. The essay contains an account of several such mysterious happenings, in general well authenticated and narrated with her usual skill, but in the majority there proves to be a rational explanation. Even in cases where no explanation is ever found she does not suggest that there was no material cause to account for it. On the contrary, she refers to the greatly increased possibilities for investigating such cases of disappearance which now exist, thanks to the 'Detective Police'. Indeed the essay begins with an eulogy of recent police detective work, of which she gives a practical illustration.[11]

'The Squire's Story', first published in a Christmas number of *Household Words*,[12] is really an early version of the detective story, centred around the figure of the eighteenth-century highwayman Higgins who lived for years in Knutsford, accepted by town and county, both alike ignorant of the real nature of his activities when he was absent 'visiting his estates in the South, and collecting his rents'.[13] Knutsford, thinly disguised as Barford, is the scene of the action and local society is well portrayed, especially in the hunting scenes, where Higgins is in his element. But the sinister impression which the handsome stranger makes on his first appearance, when a latent sadism is suggested by his behaviour to the urchins who crowd too inquisitively round the newcomer, is to some extent contradicted later by his convivial qualities and his not unhappy marriage to a local squire's daughter, who remains in ignorance of the real source of her husband's affluence. Even when he becomes housebreaker as well as highwayman, one is hardly prepared for the macabre conclusion. Impelled by a guilt-ridden conscience, Higgins insists on narrating to an unwilling listener all the chilling details of the murder at Bath, two days before, of an old woman reputed to be wealthy, details which could not possibly have been known so soon to any newspaper, though he appeared to think it possible. Suspicions thus aroused are soon confirmed by further evidence, and Higgins is convicted of the murder and hanged. Unfortunately, the central figure of the story remains unconvincing, and even the trusting wife and the old father-in-law are too lightly sketched to inspire much sympathy, though their plight does indicate, as often in Elizabeth Gaskell's work, the inevitable involvement of a whole family in the misfortune or the guilt of one of its members.

In 'The Crooked Branch', on the contrary, the decline of a family through the perverse selfishness of a much loved only son is made all the more convincing by the unerring skill of the characterisation, and builds up to a powerful climax of suspense and horror. The story was first published under the title 'The Ghost in the Garden Room' in a Christmas issue of Dickens' *All the Year Round*[14] as part of a collective series 'The Haunted House', and supposed to be told by the ghost of the judge who presides at the final trial scene. The link was established by means of a prologue.[15] But the supernatural element was not an integral part of the tale, which Elizabeth Gaskell later reprinted without the prologue and under the more appropriate title.

She never painted a more realistic picture of countryfolk than when she showed Nathan Huntroyd, his wife, Hester and their niece Bessy, content to give their toil and their time to the running of the small dairy farm of Nab-End, in the North Riding, and asking no reward beyond its modest prosperity. The seeds of decline are sown when Benjamin, the idolised only son, is given an education which encourages him to despise their way of life. He goes off to London on the pretext that a year or two will establish him as a lawyer. He becomes instead a wastrel, whose visits home are always made with the intention of obtaining money. The old farmer's savings are reduced, by these insatiable demands, to a few pounds, and it is to obtain this pitiable little sum, hidden in an old stocking, that he reappears one night, under cover of darkness, accompanied by two fellow thieves, when the family have lost trace of him and fear that he is dead.

The climactic scene of the robbery is developed with great power. The suspense is heightened by the fact that it is related chiefly from the point of view of Bessy, the farmer's niece, who, when she realises housebreakers have entered, is able to summon neighbours to their aid but is obliged to listen in the darkness to the sound of the ensuing struggle. Two of the robbers are disabled but, unknown to the others, Bessy allows a third to escape when she recognises, to her horror, in the darkness, the voice of her cousin begging her aid. She does so not because she had once loved him but for the sake of the aged parents, who, she hopes, will never know of his villainy. But when his accomplices are brought to trial, the old farmer and his wife are called as witnesses, and the testimony they are obliged to give, under oath, reveals that they had always known the truth. Nathan had opened the door to the robbers because they had both recognised their son's voice, and his wife had heard him calling to his accomplices to throttle her if she persisted in crying for help. The ordeal of bearing witness against her son proves too much for the strength of the old mother, who dies as a result, and her husband bitterly blames the judge for having forced them to reveal, in open court, the callous cruelty of their only child.

'The Doom of the Griffiths' depends ostensibly for its plot on the supernatural, the effects of a curse. In this case, however, the curse is not linked directly with the action; it was a Griffiths of nine generations back who had earned the malediction through his treachery. Elizabeth Gaskell described this story as 'per se, an old rubbishy one',[16] begun originally when her daughter Marianne was a baby, whose only merit was to be founded on fact. The supernatural element is not important in itself. What force it has is really given to it by Squire Griffiths and his son Owen who, by brooding on the old prophecy that the last male of the race, nine generations later, would slay his father, increase the possibility of its fulfilment. The enmity which grows up between father and son is sufficiently accounted for by the Squire's second marriage to a selfish and designing woman, with a young son as malicious as herself. The situation is made the more dangerous because both are men of fiery temper when roused. The heir, neglected at home, finds consolation in a secret marriage to a village beauty and in the birth of their child. But the secret is discovered by his father, thanks to the malice of his stepmother, and there are violent scenes between father and son. The result is the accidental death of the infant, and of the Squire himself, while the unfortunate Owen and his wife, forced to flee, are drowned in the stormy waters of Tremadoc Bay. In spite of explicit references to the curse, this accumulation of fatal accidents within the space of half a day, though vividly narrated, is more suggestive of melodrama than of any supernatural agency. There is none the less an authentically tragic note in 'The Doom of the Griffiths', due less to the horror of what appear to be infanticide and parricide than to the sudden shattering of the precarious happiness of the unfortunate Owen, deeply in love with his young wife and devoted, like her, to their happy and healthy child. The poignancy with which the beauty of this brief idyll is evoked reminds one, as in *Ruth*, that it was in similar surroundings that Elizabeth Gaskell had sustained the loss of her infant son.

In 'The Grey Woman' spectacular action predominates. The story of the beautiful miller's daughter from Heidelberg who marries the elegant M. de la Tourelle, supposedly a French nobleman, only to discover that he is in reality a leader of the notorious 'Chauffeurs', brigands who terrorised the left bank of the Rhine during the first years of the French Revolution, is obviously in the Gothic tradition. Elizabeth Gaskell probably heard tales of their exploits during her first visit to Germany in 1841, which may well have provided the starting-point for this story.[17] Certainly the description of the inn at Heidelberg where she sees the picture of the unfortunate Anna Scherer is the most convincingly realistic in the tale. From the moment when Anna arrives at the robber castle in the Vosges, suspense and horror provide the main interest. Three murders and all the terrors of the chase, during which Anna and her faithful maid Amante flee from her pursuing husband, fill up the rest of a narrative full of suspense. So terrible is the nightmare through which she lives that she loses all her beauty and becomes 'an old grey woman'. The contrast between the robber chief's elegant and even effeminate appearance and his cold-blooded cruelty accentuates the horror of the situation. He remains 'young, gay, elegant as ever' till he is finally hunted down by the husband of one of his victims and pays the penalty of his many crimes. 'The Grey Woman' is absorbing as a tale of horror, but it lacks the tragic quality possessed by 'The Doom of the Griffiths' because the timid and weak-willed heroine never entirely gains the reader's sympathy. The only completely sympathetic character is the courageous maid Amante, who is killed by the 'Chauffeurs'.

The fantasy 'Curious if True' was the first of Elizabeth Gaskell's contributions to the newly established *Cornhill Magazine*, edited by Thackeray.[18] Perhaps not surprisingly it is different in tone to any of the previous tales. The title fits the deliberately mystifying approach. The narrator, Richard Whittingham, begins by announcing his descent from 'that sister of Calvin's who married a Whittingham, Dean of Durham'. The effort to trace collateral descendants of Calvin takes him to France, and he makes Tours his headquarters. Such is the sober prelude to what proves unexpectedly to be a tale or perhaps a dream of the supernatural. Losing himself in a forest, Whittingham comes across a château where a reception is in progress, and finds, to his surprise, that the mention of his name procures him an immediate welcome. But it is soon evident to the reader that the benevolent shades of Charles Perrault and Madame d'Aulnoy preside over this strange gathering; the characters have all stepped out of fairy-tales, but they wear the costumes and have the courtly manners of the 'Grand Siècle'.[19] There is mystery here, but nothing macabre; instead, the play of Elizabeth Gaskell's humour, necessarily largely banished from the previous tales, is allowed full scope. These fairies are habitués of the salons, with the social compulsion to gloss over anything discreditable in their past history. Bluebeard's widow (now remarried) defends her much misunderstood former husband: 'The best of husbands will sometimes be displeased . . .' But the link with the popular origin of the fairy-tales remains: the characters sometimes use patois and, significantly, the most lovable of them is Red Riding-Hood, the peasant child, whose phantom haunts the forest on this night of all the year and to see whom traditionally brings good fortune. Mystery and humour are increased by the fact that Richard Whittingham himself remains unaware of the reason of his enthusiastic welcome and of the tender enquiries for his cat. But there are deeper elements in this highly original fantasy, which perhaps it is not too much to call surreal.[20] This mysterious castle is coeval with the life of folklore and legend:

I could almost have fancied that I heard a mighty rushing murmur (like the ceaseless sound of a distant sea, ebbing and flowing for ever and for ever), coming forth from the great vacant galleries that opened out on each side of the broad staircase and were to be dimly perceived in the darkness above us. It was as if the voices of generations of men yet echoed and eddied in the silent air.[21]

8 Religion

The world of every true artist implies a conception of life in virtue of which all its parts cohere and from which they derive their deepest significance. In the case of Elizabeth Gaskell there can be no doubt that hers was a religious conception, and that her religious faith, while it did not make her a novelist, determined her interpretation of those areas of life with which she dealt. She was born into a Unitarian family and she married a Unitarian minister. Unitarianism had historically a Socinian basis, but questions of doctrine are not discussed in Elizabeth Gaskell's work, which is impregnated with the spirit of New Testament Christianity. The memory of the Brook Street Unitarian Chapel at Knutsford was dear to her, but what matters is the moral and spiritual atmosphere in which she grew up and which was essentially a Christian one.

It was one of religious tolerance. The Unitarians were liberal in outlook. They themselves enjoyed, in the nineteenth century, an assured status, especially in the northern and midland counties where they had most adherents, but this had not always been the case. Elizabeth Gaskell's awareness of the dangers of religious fanaticism was certainly made keener by her nonconformist inheritance. It is typical, however, of the breadth of her outlook that, in her most sombre study of this tragic subject, it is the Puritans, who had been involved in a common condemnation with the ancestors of her own faith, who are the persecutors. The treatment accorded to the innocent Lois and her fellow victims is just as cruel as that received by the Huguenots at the hands of their Catholic brothers under Richelieu and after the Revocation of the Edict of Nantes, which she records in the essay 'Traits and Stories of the Huguenots', or that endured by the unfortunate 'Cagots', from the Middle Ages till almost the end of the eighteenth century, which is the subject of another essay, 'An Accursed Race'. Bridget Fitzgerald, the leading character in the story 'The Poor Clare', would not have been so much feared and detested by the countryfolk as 'the Coldholme witch' if she had not been at the same time 'the Irish Papist'.

Elizabeth Gaskell's own position, however, was one where her Unitarianism involved neither oppression nor social inferiority. Through her mother, a Holland, she was connected with some of the leading Unitarian families, cultured, influential and sometimes wealthy, the Wedgwoods, Darwins, Turners. Her husband's congregation at the Cross Street Unitarian Chapel in Manchester included many of the leading members of the city's industrial, philanthropic and intellectual life. She had no heritage of animus against Anglicanism to overcome in her advocacy of tolerance. During her schooldays at Stratford she habitually worshipped at Holy Trinity, where the Miss Byerleys, though of Unitarian family, themselves attended, and she counted many Anglicans among her close friends.

Her works include numerous examples both of Anglicans and Dissenters, and in no case does their church or chapel affiliation prejudice her treatment of them. In the novels and tales with industrial settings, church-goers are few among the submerged population, though religion is of vital importance to the development of the characters. In *Mary Barton* the selfless Alice Wilson is 'Church o' England' and Davenport, heroic in his patience, is a Methodist, but Job Legh seems to have no religious affiliation, though his integrity is based on religion. Ruth, who comes of an Anglican family, is saved from suicide by the intervention of Benson, the Dissenting minister, and finds peace in the Benson household, but the most prominent member of his congregation is the self-righteous Bradshaw. In *North and South*, the workers' chief representative, Higgins, considers his daughter's 'Methodee fancies' as illusions, but Margaret Hale is a Churchwoman who cannot sympathise with her father's doctrinal doubts, though she can and does sympathise with him. A similar lack of sectarian bias is evident in the shorter tales. John Middleton finds the eloquence of a hillside preacher more congenial than the church services that mean so much to his wife, but it is under her influence that he eventually finds the power to forgive the enemy on whom he has sworn revenge. In the novels and tales which are centred on country town or village, Elizabeth Gaskell seems to have felt that Dissent was less in place than Anglicanism. It is to the outskirts of manufacturing Eccleston that she transports the Brook Street Unitarian Chapel at Knutsford in her fullest description of it. The rector or the vicar, not the minister, is the leading spiritual authority in Cranford or Hollingford, and the lives of the inhabitants are not the less influenced by their religious belief on that account, though there may be less allusion to it. Differences in religious outlook cause some controversy, however, in the Hanbury of *My Lady Ludlow*, where my lady's conservative Anglicanism clashes with the Evangelicanism of Mr Gray. It has even been suggested that 'the character of Mr Gray is that of a Nonconformist minister in the guise of a Church of England clergyman'.[1] Here, too, Elizabeth Gaskell presents both points of view with discerning sympathy. In the Monkshaven of *Sylvia's Lovers*, the church represents spiritual authority to the majority, including Sylvia's parents, but Philip Hepburn has been brought up amongst Quakers. The Haworth of the Brontës had strong Methodist traditions, and Elizabeth Gaskell pays tribute in the *Life* to the tolerance of Mr Brontë who 'with all his warm regard for Church and State, had a great respect for mental freedom'[2] and could, on occasion, as Charlotte recorded, firmly curb the impatience of High Church curates with Dissenters.

With her usual realism Elizabeth Gaskell, though herself without sectarian bias, shows that this is by no means always the case with her characters. Her humour comes into play as she makes it clear that prejudice, ignorance and such mundane considerations as a sense of social superiority are sometimes involved. Mr Peter, having startled Mrs Jamieson by his absurd tales, asks her to remember, in extenuation, that 'he had been living for a long time among savages—all of whom were heathens—some of them, he was afraid, were downright Dissenters'. Lady Ludlow disapproves of the coming marriage of her agent, Captain James, a retired naval man, with the daughter of a Dissenting tradesman from Birmingham on grounds that have little to do with theology: 'I could not—I cannot believe it. He must be aware that she is a schismatic; a baker's daughter; and he is a gentleman by virtue and feeling, as well as by his profession, though his manners may be at times a little rough . . . what will this world come to?'[3]

Such prejudice Elizabeth Gaskell could show as ridiculous, but her tolerance never reached the lengths where religion itself is not taken seriously. She was deeply religious and religion for her meant Christianity, founded on the Bible and especially on the New Testament. She never discussed questions of doctrine, but she did believe that Christianity, with its central doctrine of love, is dangerously misinterpreted when it is turned into a religion of fear and retribution, so that it becomes, as her husband said in a phrase in one of his sermons, quoted by Edgar Wright; 'a thing of gloom and terror, not of light and love'.[4] She is not concerned to question the order of the universe, nor the existence of evil, nor, in her own sphere and time, the economical problems of the industrial era. What she does question is conduct which, either deliberately or unconsciously, contravenes the spirit of Christianity.

The emphasis on conduct is vital to her religious outlook. She gives importance to thought in as far as thought must always precede and influence action. She is no mystic or quietist, in love with the virtues of contemplation, and her characterisation is noticeably less convincing when it touches on mystic or visionary states of mind. When Maggie Browne, as a child, indulges in visions of heaven and angels in her moorland retreat, this is recognised as harmless and even beneficial, up to a point, but her mentor, Mrs Buxton, considers that it is not a tendency to be unduly encouraged: '. . . there was danger of the child becoming dreamy, and finding her pleasure in reverie, not in action, or endurance, or the holy rest which comes after both, and prepares for further striving or bearing.'[5] One suspects, from the *Life of Charlotte Brontë*, that Elizabeth Gaskell had similar reservations as to the virtues not of moorland walks but of moorland reveries where the young Brontës were concerned. It is noticeable that, in such of the juvenilia as she examined, she much preferred Charlotte's graphic account of real occurrences to the 'wild, weird' character of her purely imaginative writing. Her distrust of the visionary in religious experience is evident in her treatment of Bessy Higgins in *North and South*. Bessy, dying at nineteen, finds solace in the visions of the 'book o' Revelations', but there is a hysterical quality in her longings and raptures and Margaret Hale, though she does not, like Bessy's father, dismiss them as 'Methodee fancies', advises her not to 'dwell so much on the prophecies but read the clearer parts of the Bible'.

If she believed there was danger in over-absorption in apocalyptic visions, Elizabeth Gaskell believed there was danger also, in religious practice, in giving too much thought to self-examination and probings of the individual conscience. Too much introspection was in any case uncongenial to her temperament. She deplored the growth, in her own generation, of the 'vivid self-consciousness that more than anything else deprives characters of freshness and originality'.[6] So much the more did she deprecate the undue analysis of their own virtues and failings on the part of those who allowed it to degenerate into self-absorption, neglecting in consequence the practical duties which they conveniently dismissed as distractions. Sally, the Bensons' servant, as a young girl, goes through a phase of neglecting such mundane duties as making eatable puddings in order to reflect on her spiritual condition, remarking darkly: 'I wish folks would be content with locusts and wild honey, and leave other folks in peace to work out their salvation'. Her gentle mistress, the mother of Faith and Thurstan, though prepared to make the pudding herself, is anxious that Sally should get her priorities right and asks: 'Sally, do you think God has put us into the world just to be selfish, and do nothing but see after our own souls? or to help one another with heart and hand, as Christ did to all who wanted help?'[7]

Far more important than any amount of thinking in itself is the simple faith that trusts the promises of the Bible and acts on them. Because Elizabeth Gaskell is concerned with human beings, none of them succeed in doing this to perfection all the time. She is not unrealistic in discerning the most saintly qualities in those who have the most to endure. For Alice Wilson, Ruth, Lois and, in the shorter tales, characters like Libbie Marsh, Nest Gwynn and Nelly Middleton, circumstances are, in different ways, as unpropitious as they can well be, but they triumph over them in virtue of their faith. The same can be said of the crippled Thurstan Benson, of Captain Brown, of Mr Gray and of Gilbert Dawson in 'The Sexton's Hero'. Such Christian heroism is not attained by all, but others, with a more mixed lot, succeed in enduring periods of adversity with courage in virtue of their trust. It is this which makes possible the fortitude of Margaret Hale, the patient sweetness of Miss Matty and the continuing benevolence of Lady Ludlow when early happiness is overshadowed by personal sorrows. Those who are not so assured in their faith often turn instinctively to those who are when their own life becomes difficult. Mary Barton derives obvious strength and comfort from the society of old Alice, and of the quiet Margaret Jennings, and Sylvia, in her misery, is thankful to be taught to read from the Bible by Alice Rose, who points to it as the source of consolation and tells her: 'It's religion as must comfort thee, child, as it's done many a one afore thee.'[8]

But Christian faith and conduct are of value only when they are felt and seen to be sincere. Sincerity in itself made an irresistible appeal to Elizabeth Gaskell. Her deep love for her family and for a wide circle of intimate friends came from the heart and constantly found expression in actions as well as in words. She distrusted fine words that did not lead to practical results. Hearing in 1859 that an American lady was to lecture in Manchester on anti-slavery, she made the incisive comment: 'All the Anti Slavery people will attend her lectures to *be* convinced of what they are already convinced, and to have their feelings stirred up without the natural and right outlet of stirred up feelings, the power of simple and energetic *action* . . . I don't call the use of words *action*: unless there is some definite, distinct, practical *course of action* logically proposed by those words.'[9] Valuing sincerity as she did, it is not surprising that she should have been keenly aware of the harm frequently done by lack of consistency between principles and practice in a professedly Christian society.

This is made very clear in her first novel. John Barton might have drawn from his knowledge of the Gospel, limited as it was, power to endure his life of hardship, had he seen others trying to put its precepts into practice also. At the moment of death, he puts his own consciousness of this into words: '. . . I can say this, I would fain have gone after the Bible rules if I'd seen folk credit it; they all spoke up for it, and went and did clean contrary . . . At last I gave it up in despair, trying to make folks' actions square wi' th' Bible; and I thought I'd no longer labour at following th' Bible mysel.'[10] In contrast to John Barton, Mr Bradshaw, the leading member of Thurstan Benson's Dissenting congregation, is, in his own eyes, a model of all the virtues and constitutes himself the censor of the actions of others: 'every moral error or delinquency came under his unsparing comment'. When however ambition draws him into local politics and he sponsors a candidate for Eccleston in the Dissenting interest, he finds himself expected to sanction bribery and agrees, though at the expense of an uneasy conscience. But the knowledge that he has been guilty on this occasion of transgressing the moral code he respects only has the effect of making him determined to quench any possible slander by being 'stricter and sterner than ever'. His Pharisaism is seen in its full force in his denunciation of Ruth and his unforgiving attitude to the son who has been found to have committed forgery, and whose prosecution he himself urges.

By making Ruth the central character of her second novel, Elizabeth Gaskell showed the difference, in their attitudes to the seduced girl, between those who, in Victorian society, genuinely tried to put their Christianity into practice and those who, consciously or not, were far more concerned with social convention.

The importance of the role of Esther in *Mary Barton* had already shown her concern with the fate of the prostitute, and the same theme had recurred in the tale 'Lizzie Leigh'. In both cases the harshness of a parent or relative had precipitated tragedy, and the need to support a child had been a determining factor. Ruth is not a prostitute—she would have committed suicide on being abandoned by her lover without the intervention of Thurstan Benson—but a very young and friendless girl who is seduced by the man she genuinely loves. She lives in a world of illusion until abandoned by him, and her subsequent grief and despair is alleviated only by the understanding kindness and generosity of the Bensons. Theirs is authentically Christian conduct, but the Pharisaism of society is directly responsible for much of Ruth's suffering. Her employer treats her with unjustifiable harshness at a crucial moment; the mother of her seducer, a lady bountiful in her own sphere, blames her for having entrapped her son into vice and considers that a bank note for £50 and the offer to produce her admission to a penitentiary are all that is called for; her seducer, on recovering from his illness, resumes his life as an affluent and respected member of society and becomes eventually the Liberal member for Eccleston, whom Mr Bradshaw considers worthy of every attention.

If hypocrisy, even though unconscious, is none the less unchristian, truthfulness is a positive sense is a necessary part of the Christian ethos. The value Elizabeth Gaskell attached to it is reflected by the part it plays in her fiction, where the cost of speaking the truth is frequently a major issue. It is the one which faces Thurstan Benson when his sister suggests that, if Ruth were said to be a widow, her unborn child would be spared all the trials that accompanied the stigma of illegitimacy. Accustomed to rely on her practical sense, he yields to the argument for the sake of the helpless child: 'It was the decision—the pivot, on which the fate of years moved; and he turned it the wrong way.'[11] For a time the concealment of the true situation does seem to guarantee peace for Ruth and happiness for her child, but Benson feels that, in yielding to sophistry, he has compromised his former power of acting as he believed to be right without undue fear of the consequences. Inevitably the deception is finally discovered and Ruth has to undergo intense suffering, of which the worst part is to see her child suffer also. Benson naturally comes in for his share of Mr Bradshaw's violent denunciation, since he has concealed her true position, but ·he finds it easier to accept this, and even to see Bradshaw temporarily leave his congregation, than he has done to live with the consciousness of his deception. Margaret Hale, like the Bensons, finds herself suddenly faced with a situation in which, by lying, she can shield another. Since it is her own brother who is in danger, her dilemma is more acute than that of the Bensons. For his sake she tells a falsehood which, as it turns out, was not needed to shield her brother, already in fact beyond the range of pursuit. In *North and South*, however, the love interest is an important part of the whole, and Margaret's remorse at having told a lie derives a good deal of its sting from the fact that Thornton knows she has done so, and that she has consequently sunk in his esteem. Thornton, who does not know she has a brother, is really much more concerned with the possibility that she may have been shielding a man she loves. But Margaret is too proud to admit that her conduct could ever be touched by the breath of scandal. All the more significant is the humility with which she acknowledges that, in lying, she has been guilty of a fault which he would be right to censor. It is in *Sylvia's Lovers* that the deliberate concealment of truth is accompanied with the fewest mitigating circumstances and leads to the most tragic consequences. Philip Hepburn has no true motivation other than his own passionate and unreciprocated love for Sylvia when he deliberately withholds the fact of Kinraid's seizure by the press-gang, of which he has been the only witness. He attempts to justify his silence to himself by his belief that his rival is incapable of constancy to any woman, but his own marriage to Sylvia is based on a lie and is shattered by Kinraid's eventual return to claim her promise.

Untruthfulness, however, does not always take such definite forms. There is a deviousness sometimes to be encountered in social conduct which is far more difficult to detect and whose effects are more insidious. Elizabeth Gaskell could smile with kindly tolerance at the evasions and pretences of the Cranford feminine community, intended to avert exposure of the hard facts of poverty or spinsterhood, just because they really deceive nobody and nobody expects that they should. Cranford convention demands that Mrs Forrester's guests should assume that their hostess has had no share in the preliminary baking operations in the kitchen, but has left them all to her one small maid, 'though she knew, and we knew, and she knew that we knew, and we knew that she knew that we knew, she had been busy all the morning making tea-bread and sponge-cakes'. The evasions and pretences of Mrs Gibson in *Wives and*

Daughters are a different matter. The portrait of Mrs Gibson is not drawn in a spirit of harsh indictment. Elizabeth Gaskell gives full weight to the circumstances that have helped to make her what she is, the natural temptation to a woman neither brave nor active by nature, with no money and no family behind her, to try to avoid strenuous effort by relying on her social graces. Unfortunately this has come to mean sacrificing the strict truth whenever she deems it expedient. Mr Gibson, misled by her grace and amiability, believes he has found the right stepmother for Molly, but discovers in course of time that she has 'a very different standard of conduct from that which he had upheld all his life, and had hoped to have seen inculcated in his daughter'. Mrs Gibson's account of people and events is always decided by her own interest, and she manipulates facts accordingly, without even realising how she distorts the truth. According to herself, she would have died of self-reproach, had she done so to the slightest extent: ' "The truth, the whole truth, and nothing but the truth" has always seemed to me such a fine passage. But then I have so much that is unbending in my nature . . .'[12] Her daughter Cynthia is more clear-sighted and, though certainly 'not remarkable for unflinching morality', recognises that her standards are not those of Mr Gibson's household, and regrets it. The duplicity, conscious or unconscious, of both mother and daughter, is in striking contrast to the straightforward honesty of Molly, accustomed to her father's standards and a life without concealment.

It is not to be expected that Molly should remain blind to her stepmother's 'perpetual lapses from truth' or that, with a young girl's lack of toleration, she should not often feel tempted to tell her 'some forcible home-truths'. But she manages to hold her tongue and, as time passes, she does more: she genuinely pities Mrs Gibson when she forfeits her husband's esteem through her lack of honesty and frequently becomes the target for his irony, without understanding the reason for his annoyance. Molly exemplifies unconsciously the spirit of charity which is the essence of Christianity as Elizabeth Gaskell understands it. Without it, sincerity becomes austerity and good deeds lose the greater part of their value. It could be said that, for her, the quality of kindness is the seed of the divine which she believed to exist, however hidden, in every human being. She detects it, in *Mary Barton*, even in the unprincipled Sally Leadbitter, who almost brings about Mary's ruin by acting as go-between for Harry Carson: 'Sally's seed of the future soul was her love for her mother, an aged bedridden woman . . . for her, her good-nature rose into tenderness . . .'[13] But human kindness needs to be guided and controlled by religion if it is to become the divine agent of healing and comfort it was meant to be. Ruth's natural tenderness for her child develops through the influence of religion into the love which, while still cherishing him as the being nearest to her heart, sends her to nurse the helpless victims of typhoid and, at last, the former lover whose selfishness had blighted her youth. When Nest Gwynn, in 'The Well of Pen-Morfa', is left alone without lover or mother, she is roused from bitterness and despair by the counsel of an itinerant Wesleyan preacher: 'Henceforward, you must love like Christ, without thought of self, or wish for return. You must take the sick and the weary to your heart, and love them. That love will lift you above the storms of the world into God's own peace.'[14]

The charity which 'suffereth long and is kind' does not judge others. The allocation of guilt and punishment is one of the most perilous activities in which faulty human nature can engage. In Elizabeth Gaskell's fiction the belief in retribution as something justifiable and even desirable on moral grounds is frequently the cause of suffering and misunderstanding far more serious than the original fault. It destroys the peace of families, as in *Cranford* or *Ruth* or 'Lizzie Leigh', causing division between parent and child and between husband and wife. It threatens the efforts of those who are trying to build up a new life: after Bradshaw's denunciation, Ruth and her child feel like pariahs in Eccleston, except in the sanctuary of the Benson household. Even when wrongdoing becomes crime, the intervention of the law cannot obscure the fallibility of human attempts to apportion guilt and punishment. The introduction in some of the novels and tales of the court room and the prison has its own significance. Obviously the plight of the fugitive from justice or the prisoner on trial has dramatic possibilities which were attractive to a born storyteller like Mrs Gaskell, but it involves deeper issues as well. The most painful trial scene is that in 'Lois the Witch', where the pathological condition induced in a whole community by superstition and fanaticism at their worst makes both trial and sentence a shameful travesty. But human justice is fallible in nine-teenth-century England as well as seventeenth-century Salem. Jem Wilson in *Mary Barton* and the old servant Dixon in 'A Dark Night's Work' are both innocent, but the circumstantial evidence against them is such that both would have been hanged, without the desperate efforts of their friends to produce at the last moment the further evidence that saves them. Wilson's acquittal is a shattering blow for Carson, the murdered man's father, whose violent determination to be avenged elicits from Elizabeth Gaskell the revealing comment: 'Oh, Orestes! you would have made a very tolerable Christian of the nineteenth century!' But when Carson finally sees the real murderer, he sees not a hardened criminal but a dying man, as unable to survive his crime as the master whose memory the old servant Dixon is shielding.

The harshness of human attempts at justice and the difference between the laws of men and the mercy of Christ are seen at their starkest in *Sylvia's Lovers*. Daniel Robson is guilty of inciting the rioters against the press-gang, who in a time of national emergency—the Napoleonic Wars—have the support of the government. Prospects are bleak for Robson, but the hopes of his friends are raised for the first time when, in the customary sermon preached to the judges before the opening of the York assizes, 'the clergyman said so much . . . about mercy and forgiveness'. Their hopes are fallacious. Robson is sentenced and hanged, and his death reduces his family to poverty, shortens his wife's life and fosters in his young daughter a bitterness which has its share in her later unwillingness to forgive her husband. Even those who manage to escape the extreme rigours of the law suffer from having incurred its condemnation, or even its suspicion. Frederick Hale, who has been involved in a mutiny against a tyrannous captain, dare not revisit his native land except at the risk of his life. Jem Wilson, though acquitted, is discredited in the eyes of his fellow workers and feels that he has no choice but to emigrate, if he wishes a normal life for himself and Mary. Elizabeth Gaskell does not deny the existence of crime but she shows that it is possible to suspect the innocent, and that there may have been much to tempt a man to a disastrous action. She does not romanticise the criminal; Barton is a tragic figure, but the brutal thief and unnatural son in 'The Crooked Branch' is a thoroughly despicable one. What she does is to show that human attempts at judgment are always fallible and that they should always be tempered with mercy.

A religion which is based on love and forgiveness, and which believes they should be shown in action, inevitably involves concern with social conditions. Elizabeth Gaskell was, all her life, actively involved in helping her family, her friends and the community in which she found herself. Her concern is necessarily reflected in her novels, whether the location is urban and industrial or rural and agricultural. Cranford and Drumble are not two worlds but one, as far as the ultimate spiritual reality is concerned, and it is possible to be Christian or unchristian in either. But material suffering is much more evident in Drumble than in Cranford, and the note of social concern is far stronger in *Mary Barton* than in *Wives and Daughters*. It was indeed the feeling that there was 'something to be done' that roused her from her grief at her child's death to show the agony of the Manchester poor.

But *Mary Barton*, when first published in 1848, aroused the indignation of the Manchester mill-owners not only because it showed them as hard to their employees but because some of them at least felt that it was an indictment of their religion. The millocracy of Manchester had a number of representatives among William Gaskell's congregation at Cross Street Unitarian Chapel, a fact which, as Valentine Cunningham points out, makes the exceptional courage of Elizabeth Gaskell in writing as she did the more evident.[15] The neutrality and detachment of classical economics were generally approved by employers who prided themselves on their integrity and considered it perfectly justifiable to pursue a course that satisfied their rational judgment, whatever the result might be for the worker. Men who were in no danger of seeing their own families suffer hunger, whatever the state of the market, could argue that if workers would only be provident, they could save enough out of their wages to keep themselves from want in times of recession, an argument that showed little knowledge of the average worker's kind of existence. In the opinion of Elizabeth Gaskell, common sense was more important in such circumstances than logic, and the charity that should accompany religion more important still. Nothing could alter the economic condition of trade in 1839, but Job Legh, the working man, opposes the non-interventionism of the employer Carson, who believes in laissez-faire, with arguments of a different order:

'. . . I'm clear about this, when God gives a blessing to be enjoyed, He gives with it a duty to be done, and the duty of the happy is to help the suffering to bear their woe . . . You can never work facts as you would fixed quantities, and say, given two facts, and the product is so and so. God has given men feelings and passions which cannot be worked into the problem, because they are for ever changing and uncertain . . . Now, to my thinking,

them that is.strong in any of God's gifts is meant to help the
weak,—be hanged to the facts!' (Ch. 37)

In *North and South* the initial attitude of the mill-owner Thornton is
autocratic like that of Carson. He is considered by his workpeople
as 'what the Bible calls a "hard man",—not so much unjust as
unfeeling . . .' To Margaret Hale's suggestion that he might
explain to his employees the economic reasons for their low wages,
he replies proudly: 'We, the owners of capital, have a right to choose
what we will do with it.' Margaret, like Job Legh, lifts the argument
on to another plane by replying 'A human right' and, when
questioned further, explains: 'I said you had a human right. I meant
that there seemed no reason but religious ones, why you should not
do what you liked with your own.' Thornton takes up the
implication that his is a secular morality, saying: 'I know we differ in
our religious opinions; but don't you give me credit for having some,
though not the same as yours?' She evades the challenge to a
theoretical discussion, but makes her own standpoint perfectly
clear:

'. . . All I meant to say is, that there is no human law to prevent
the employers from utterly wasting or throwing away all their
money, if they choose; but that there are passages in the Bible
which would rather imply—to me at least—that they neglected
their duty as stewards if they did so.' (Ch. 15)

In both the industrial novels religion rather than economics is
seen to be the true solvent of the social dilemma. Not change in
legislation but change in the personal relationship between masters
and men is the first necessity. The workers are individuals, as
different from each other as Legh from Barton or Boucher from
Higgins. They need to be understood individually as well as
collectively, and that can only be done if the employers make the
effort, an effort which, to be successful, requires the aid not only of
reason but a sincere and charitable religious faith. Carson and
Thornton both live to make a radical change in their attitudes to the
men who work for them. The wish that is described as lying closest
to Carson's heart, in his later years, expresses the only viable
solution to industrial conflict, as Elizabeth Gaskell saw it:

. . . that the truth might be recognised that the interests of one

were the interests of all, and, as such, required the consideration
and deliberation of all; that hence it was most desirable to have
educated workers, capable of judging, not mere machines of
ignorant men; and to have them bound to their employers by the
ties of respect and affection, not by mere money bargains alone; in
short, to acknowledge the Spirit of Christ as the regulating law
between both parties. (Ch. 37)

Mary Barton, though it aroused indignation among the
Manchester mill-owners, was applauded by the leaders of liberal
thought; it brought her letters from Ruskin and Carlyle, Kingsley
and F. D. Maurice, Dickens and Cobden. Her circle of friends
extended to include most of the progressives of the period. She
shared, like them, the awakened social conscience of Victorian
England, but had most in common with those who gave most
importance to Christianity as the surest agent of moral and
consequently social regeneration. She referred to Kingsley as 'my
hero', and was anxious that the *Tracts on Christian Socialism* which he
published in conjunction with the other pioneers of the movement
should be circulated among working men. She recognised that
Kingsley and his friends believed, like herself, that it was religious
feeling that could best heal the ills of the present society.
    But she was less didactic and less militant in her attitude than the
pioneers of Christian socialism. Kingsley, though not a revol-
utionary, was attacked as one, and *Alton Locke* attracted sterner
reviews than *Mary Barton*. Though *Mary Barton* gives voice to the
agony of the factory workers and their families in times of industrial
depression, it is made evident that the solution does not lie in violent
action, which leads in turn to further violence and ultimately to
greater misery: 'It is a great truth that you cannot extinguish
violence by violence'.[16] By a tragic irony, the very men who, acting
as they believe in the interests of their oppressed comrades, have
been the instigators of violence, subsequently feel impelled to try to
mitigate its effects, but their efforts are useless as long as they remain
committed to such a course. John Barton is appalled by the frightful
suffering of the weaver who, because he is a knob-stick, has had
vitriol flung at him by one of the strikers, but his indignation only
inflames his hatred of the masters and leads to further violence and
to the shooting of Harry Carson. Daniel Robson, having incited the
townspeople of Monkshaven to attack the inn which was the
headquarters of the press-gang, and to burn it down, hears the

moans of the terrified cow in the shippen, and leads it to safety, and subsequently gives all the money he has with him to the equally wretched man of all work of the inn, who has lost his livelihood. Neither of these actions can prevent him from being hanged for felony, while the weak and feckless inn servant, whose evidence had been material against Robson at the trial, dies miserably in dire poverty, ostracised by the townspeople and tortured by remorse.

By exposing the danger and the ultimate futility of violence, Elizabeth Gaskell inevitably showed herself an advocate and indeed a promoter of social stability. It was not social stability that was her primary aim, it was Christian charity, but, since she was the fortunate possessor of strong and lucid common sense, she knew that a policy of reconciliation was ultimately to the advantage of all. She did not advocate Christianity as a social panacea, but she believed that Christianity, by influencing the individual conscience, must eventually produce changes in social attitudes and consequently reforms in legislation—which she did not herself attempt to define in detail, knowing that they must be subject to change with changing social conditions. A Christianity which did not show itself in action was suspect in her eyes. She believed in the silent action of the leaven, but not in the salt that had lost its savour.

The ultimate responsibility remains with the individual. It is the way in which the individual reacts to the pressures of life, in the circumstances in which he or she is placed, which matters most, though those circumstances necessarily involve others as well, since none of us lives in isolation. There is no essential difference between Elizabeth Gaskell's attitude in her social novels and in her chronicles of small town or country life. The human condition, as she saw it, was always a precarious and never for very long an easy one, and religious faith the only ultimate security. Material conditions are hardest in the Manchester slums, and there also are found the most dramatic contrasts between despair and faith: 'The evil and the good of our nature came out strongly then. There were desperate fathers; there were bitter-tongued mothers (O God! what wonder!); there were reckless children; the very closest bonds of nature were snapt in that time of trial and distress. There was Faith such as the rich can never imagine on earth; there was "Love strong as death". . .'[17] Trial and distress come to Cranford or Hollingford in different and less dramatic form, but they come none the less surely and there too human nature is put to the test. Molly Gibson faces no material privation when her father decides to remarry, but her quiet, happy life is totally disrupted by the news: 'It was as if the piece of solid ground on which she stood had broken from the shore, and she was drifting out into the infinite sea alone'.[18] When Roger Hamley advises her to welcome the future stepmother for her father's sake, his advice is in tune with the Christian ethos, though he does not explicitly invoke its authority for his 'sermon'. Molly makes up her mind to follow his counsel but, for the girl of seventeen, what might appear to some as trifling matters are acute trials, as when her father expects her to address her uncongenial stepmother as 'Mamma'. The request is put by him at a moment when he has just returned from seeing a patient die, and Molly first makes an impetuous protest and then agrees to do as he wishes. His response shows that he understands the sacrifice of personal feeling that is involved, and also in what perspective he views it: 'You won't be sorry for it, Molly, when you come to lie as poor Craven Smith did tonight.'[19]

As a doctor Mr Gibson was familiar with death, and his daughter with the mention of it. Mrs Gibson predictably shies away from the unpleasant topic, saying irritably to her stepdaughter: 'What dreary knowledge of death you have learned, for a girl of your age!' There was in fact, as has often been remarked, in contrast to twentieth-century attitudes, no Victorian taboo on death corresponding to the taboo on sex. In view of the mortality rate, to which many churchyards still bear witness, it would not have been easy to impose one, and Elizabeth Gaskell would not have been the realist she was had she attempted to ignore or to minimise the part played by mortality in human existence. She often treated the subject of death, not because it held any morbid attraction for her but because she had seen its action in her own family and in those of many others, and knew it must ultimately be experienced by all. She brought to her treatment of it her close and accurate observation, her great compassion and, underlying all, her religious faith.

Personally she had little fear of death. It is typical of her that the most explicit reference to the subject, in her letters, occurs in connection with her concern for her children: 'As for death I have I think remarkably little constitutional dread of it—I often fear I do not look forward to it with sufficient awe, considering the futurity which *must* follow—and I do often pray for trust in God, complete trust in him—with regard to what becomes of my children.'[20] Her attitude was, as she recognised, different from that of Charlotte

Brontë. With a sure instinct for perspective, she chose as fitting introduction to her *Life* of her friend a description of Haworth which rapidly narrows down to the churchyard, the church, and the crowded mural tablets commemorating the deaths of the Brontë family. She realised how familiar to the inhabitants of the parsonage must have been 'the passing and funeral bells so frequently tolling . . . and, when they were still, the "chip, chip" of the mason, as he cut the grave-stones in a shed close by'.[21] Yet to a woman of her resilience, it seemed not impossible to live even in such a milieu without being unduly affected by it: 'In many, living, as it were, in a churchyard, and with all the sights and sounds connected with the last offices to the dead things of everyday occurrence, the very familiarity would have bred indifference. But it was otherwise with Charlotte Brontë.'[22] Her friend's apprehension of death she realised but did not personally share. Neither mystic nor visionary by temperament, she was not, as she recognised, strongly conscious of experiencing that awe at the idea of futurity which is so movingly expressed by the Brontë heroines from the child Jane Eyre to the mature Lucy Snowe; she believed firmly in the future life, but made no attempt to probe its mysteries. Young Mary Smith of *Cranford*, as practical and unsentimental as her name, reflects for a moment on the question of mutual recognition in another sphere, and then answers it with a settled faith in the persistence of the most human and divine of the virtues, love: 'I thought of Miss Jenkyns, grey, withered and wrinkled, and I wondered if her mother had known her in the courts of heaven: and then I knew that she had, and that they stood there in angelic guise.'[23]

Elizabeth Gaskell's attitude to the fact of death is neither mystical nor speculative. She accepts it as the closing act of life on this earth. As a Christian she does not envisage it as tragic in itself, but she recognises there is far more occasion for mourning, on the part of the bereaved, in some circumstances than in others. In old age, death is natural; the decline of the bodily faculties is, for her, not senility with its humiliating connotations but the natural preliminary to a new state of being. Old Alice Wilson is happy and at peace in her second childhood—'that blessing clouded by a name'—and the doctor who pays a perfunctory call to confirm the fact of approaching death is represented as mistaken when he gloomily shakes his head over her 'as if it was a mournful thing for one so pure and good, so true, although so humble a Christian, to be nearing her desired haven'.[24]

It is far harder for a bereaved family to accept the loss of a child. Sometimes it may be material conditions caused, in the last analysis, by man's selfishness, which are responsible, as in the case of little Tom Barton. But death may claim the child who is surrounded by every care, like the Vicar's son Walter in 'Mr Harrison's Confessions'. Elizabeth Gaskell knew from her own experience the grief of the mother who, in this world, can never see again except in dreams the 'sweet looks' of her dear child. Death may also suddenly remove the adult with, apparently, a long life still before him. Osborne Hamley succumbs prematurely to heart disease and his father is at first inconsolable, though the discovery that his son has left an heir gives him some comfort. Accidental death is not infrequent in the Gaskell fiction, but it is often the result of heroic intervention to save another's life. The best known instance of such heroism is that of Captain Brown in *Cranford*, but Gilbert Dawson in 'The Sexton's Hero' also sacrifices his life in rescuing others, trapped by the tide on the sands of Morecambe Bay, and young Gregory in 'The Half-Brothers' perishes in rescuing his stepbrother in a snowstorm on the Cumbrian fells. None of them ignore the danger and probable consequences of what they are doing, but Elizabeth Gaskell makes it clear that they are acting in the strength of a religious faith which, in the older men, has already become second nature, and that it is in that light that their sacrifices should be understood.

The most unnatural of deaths is death by violence. As might be expected, it is unknown in Cranford or Hollingford, but not in those places where a bitter sense of grievance and mutual hatred distorts the normal relationship between members of a community. The actual murder of Harry Carson, the mill-owner's son, is not described, but its immediate consequences are realistically shown, the violent anger of the father at the sight of the dead, the pitiful attempt of the distraught mother to interpret the final calm of death as the transient repose of sleep. Similarly the suicide of the weaver Boucher, rejected both by the employers and by his fellow workers as one of the leaders of the riot, is not actually seen, but the physical appearance of the drowned man is mutely eloquent of what he has suffered. Margaret Hale's indignant protest against Higgins' harsh condemnation of the unfortunate man's folly, made while both are still in ignorance of his fate, acquires a grim significance when, almost in the same moment, the men bearing the body arrive in the squalid street: 'You have made him what he is!'

Violence is also responsible for the death of the sailor Darley in *Sylvia's Lovers*. Darley is killed when the press-gang from the man-of-war *Aurora*, lying off the Yorkshire coast, board a whaling ship just as she is nearing Monkshaven after her months at sea and her crew make an attempt at resistance. In *Sylvia's Lovers*, however, the whole question of death through the violence of man is placed in the context of the Christian religion. The chapter 'The Sailor's Funeral', as the title suggests, is not concerned with the dead man in himself; it hinges on the dilemma of the vicar, who has to preach a funeral sermon in a very difficult situation: 'Dr Wilson had had a very difficult part to play, and a still more difficult sermon to write, during this last week. The Darley who had been killed was the son of the vicar's gardener, and Dr Wilson's sympathies as a man had been all on the bereaved father's side. But then he had received, as the oldest magistrate in the neighbourhood, a letter from the Captain of the *Aurora*, explanatory and exculpatory. Darley had been resisting the orders of an officer in his Majesty's service . . .'[25] Painfully aware of 'the discord between the laws of man and the laws of Christ', the old vicar preaches a sermon on the text 'In the midst of life we are in death' which evades, as he well knows, the problem posed by the circumstances of Darley's death. But his conscience reproaches him for the inadequacy of his words: 'Had he nothing to say that should calm anger and revenge with spiritual power? no breath of the Comforter to soothe repining into resignation?' The sermon is a failure, yet the preacher himself has not wholly failed in his mission as a peace-bringer; the congregation are still angry as they go away, but not with their vicar; he remains the priest who, for forty years, has been loved for his practical kindness and respected for his office. And the man who, of all the congregation, most needs consolation, the bereaved father, does not leave in the end uncomforted, not by the sermon but by the contact with a higher reality:

> He had come to church that afternoon . . . for he felt in his sore, perplexed heart, full of indignation and dumb anger, as if he must go and hear something which should exorcise the unwonted longing for revenge that disturbed his grief, and made him conscious of that great blank of consolation which faithlessness produces. And for the time he was faithless. How came God to permit such cruel injustice of man? Permitting it, He could not be good. Then what was life, and what was death, but woe and

despair? The beautiful solemn words of the ritual had done him good, and restored much of his faith. Though he could not understand why such sorrow had befallen him any more than before, he had come back to something of his childlike trust . . . (Ch. 6)

Death is always seen, in the world of Elizabeth Gaskell's fiction, as part of life. Darley's funeral brings a whole community together, like that of Ruth at Eccleston, in a common grief and a common hope. But the simplest funeral can be a source of consolation and strength to a bereaved family. The weaver Davenport has a pauper's burial, but his wife follows the coffin with her two elder children, accompanied by the two neighbours, Barton and Wilson, who had done so much to help her. Elizabeth Gaskell makes no secret of the fact that such simplicity seems to her far more in tune with the occasion than the display considered necessary, at that period, by the better off: 'It was a simple walking funeral, with nothing to grate on the feelings of any; far more in accordance with its purpose, to my mind, than the gorgeous hearses, and nodding plumes, which form the grotesque funeral pomp of respectable people.'[26] The hollowness of an outward display which corresponds to no real depth of feeling in the mourners is made evident in *My Lady Ludlow*. When the last remaining son of the countess dies and is buried in distant Vienna, the whole village and estate assume every outward sign of mourning, though Lord Ludlow was practically unknown in either and no one really mourns for him except his heartbroken mother. The artificiality of the situation emerges clearly from the description: 'The church bells tolled morning and evening. The church itself was draped in black inside. Hatchments were placed everywhere, where hatchments could be put. All the tenantry spoke in hushed voices for more than a week, scarcely daring to observe that all flesh, even that of an Earl Ludlow, and the last of the Hanburys, was but grass after all.'[27]

Death is, inevitably, a more frequent visitor in the great industrial city than elsewhere. Elizabeth Gaskell wrote of *North and South* to Dickens, in whose *Household Words* it first appeared as a serial: 'I think a better title than N. & S. would have been "Death and Variations". There are 5 deaths, each beautifully suited to the character of the individual.'[28] The ironic comment shows that she was well aware of the criticisms, including probably those of Dickens himself, of the place given to mortality in her work, but not unduly disturbed by them. She had no need to be, for it is never a love of sensationalism or morbidity which dictates her choice of the subject. She had, after all, lived in Manchester; Dickens had not. She was being realistic in recognising the frequent brevity of life both in *North and South* and in *Mary Barton*. Deathbeds in themselves certainly did not possess for her the morbid attraction they had for the mother of Jem Wilson, who reproached her son for profiting so little from witnessing the last hours of John Barton: '.`. . thou mightst just as well never be at a death-bed again, if thou cannot bring off more news about it; here have I been by mysel all day . . . but, thinks I, when Jem comes he'll be sure to be good company, seeing he was in the house at the very time of the death . . .'[29]

In the Gaskell work death is in fact more frequently reported than actually witnessed. And the dead are usually more eloquent than the dying. The instinctive shrinking of the young Margaret Hale from her first sight of mortality is natural, as natural as it is for the weaver's daughter, Mary Higgins, to invite her in all simplicity to come and see her dead sister. But Margaret finds that death looks more peaceful than life. With the same simplicity the country-bred Sally invites Mr Donne, the former Bellingham, to see the dead Ruth. He is awed into admiration by the ineffable repose of her peaceful beauty but, with him, the impression is only a temporary one. Mr Benson's rebuke is enough to turn his passing remorse into irritability, and he leaves the house with the characteristic reflection: 'I wish my last remembrance of my beautiful Ruth was not mixed up with all these people.' What matters most for Elizabeth Gaskell is always the reaction of the living. And, even in these circumstances, she is careful to avoid any sentimentality or lack of realism in portraying it. Bellingham cannot learn anything from the mute eloquence of the dead because he has made it impossible for himself to understand it. But the stern Bradshaw, to whom, in spite of his self-righteousness, religion has always been important, and who has returned to Benson's church on learning of his son's effort at reform, and finally even come to acknowledge Ruth's true worth, is moved by her death to become the comforter of her son. Higgins, who has scorned his daughter's 'Methodee fancies', is impelled by his sorrow at her death to accept the comfort offered by Hale, the parson, and to affirm his own belief that there was a purpose behind her life, even if, like John Barton, he cannot reconcile what men say about religion with the place they give it habitually in their actions.

In *Wives and Daughters* the attitude of Squire Hamley, when his elder
son is found dead, is a masterly study of remorse mingled with
persisting pride. The old man now regrets the estrangement which
had latterly existed between him and his heir with all the force of a
passionate nature. It is this which embitters his sorrow and
interferes with his efforts to derive consolation from his religious
faith: ' "I do try to say, God's will be done . . . but it's harder to be
resigned than happy people think . . . of late years we weren't"—
his voice broke down, but he controlled himself—"we weren't quite
as good friends as could be wished; and now I'm not sure—not sure
that he knew how I loved him." ' [30] The discovery that Osborne has
left a son acts as a powerful source of consolation, and he transfers to
the child much of his love of the father. Yet for long he refuses to give
the mother—French, Catholic and 'of no family'—the place that is
her due, though such recognition, on his part, would certainly have
meant more to the dead Osborne than anything else.

It is rare in Elizabeth Gaskell's work for the dying themselves to
be fully conscious or articulate, but in two of the novels, *Mary Barton*
and *Sylvia's Lovers,* they are directly involved in the final resolution
of the action. The material cause of the conflict in *Mary Barton* lies in
industrial conditions, but the dying John Barton thinks in terms of
good and evil: '. . . now he knew that he had killed a man, and a
brother—now he knew that no good thing could come out of this
evil, even to the sufferers whose cause he had so blindly espoused.' [31]
His plea, 'I did not know what I was doing', is at first rejected by the
employer whose son he has murdered. But Carson finds an echo of
the same words in the Gospel, in Christ's own extenuation of human
guilt, and returns in time to convey to the dying man the assurance
of the forgiveness for which he so desperately craves. Barton lives
only long enough for the reconciliation, but Carson's changed
attitude is implemented in the reforms which he subsequently
undertakes.

The ending of *Sylvia's Lovers*, like that of *Mary Barton*, presents a
deathbed reconciliation which marks the culmination of the whole
of the previous action. Here, however, it is not between two
individuals whom social conditions have separated to the extent
that they are literally strangers to each other, but between husband
and wife. The final scene of *Sylvia's Lovers* is more deeply moving, for
in it culminate the emotional tensions as well as the moral conflicts
that run through the book as a whole. Elizabeth Gaskell consciously
had this dénouement in view from the start. She has been criticised

for extending the action, in the last part of her story, to include the siege of Acre, where Philip saves the life of Kinraid, and his temporary halt, on his return to England as a wounded and disfigured ex-soldier, at the hospice of St Sepulchre. But the wider stage links remote Monkshaven more closely with the war which has disrupted the lives of Philip and Sylvia and makes the compulsive nature of the return of Philip, incapable of finding rest in any other place, the more evident. For a solemn moment, the whole action seems to halt, as he does, looking down from the hilltop at the town which contains his wife and child, before it moves on to the final crisis, the last meeting between himself and Sylvia, when, after saving his child from the waves, he lies dying in the poor cottage within sound of the sea. Here, for the first time in the Gaskell work, the central consciousness is that of the dying man himself, who is fully aware of his condition: 'He had been often near death as a soldier . . . but yet he had had a chance. But now there was the new feeling—the last new feeling which we shall, any of us, experience in this world—that death was not only inevitable, but close at hand.'[32]

The deep seriousness of Philip's religion, an integral part of his life since childhood, was never more evident than now. Looking back to his early years, which seem almost as if they were the very present, he recalls 'the strong resolve of an ardent boyhood, with all a life before it to show the world "what a Christian might be"'. The temptations that had defeated him rise clearly before him, 'the thoughts, the arguments that Satan had urged on behalf of sin, were reproduced with the vividness of a present time. And he knew that the thoughts were illusions, the arguments false and hollow; for in that hour came the perfect vision of the perfect truth'.[33] He does not love Sylvia the less, but he realises that it was by allowing his passion for her to dominate him that he was betrayed into acting the lie which had such fatal consequences:

'Child I ha' made thee my idol; and, if I could live my life o'er again, I would love my God more, and thee less; and then I shouldn't ha' sinned this sin against thee . . .' (Ch. 45)

Philip's recognition that he has done Sylvia 'a cruel wrong', his plea for forgiveness at the last, are met by her own recognition of the wrong she has done him by vowing, on Kinraid's return, that she would never forgive him or live with him as his wife again: 'Them were wicked, wicked words, as I said; and a wicked vow as I

vowed . . .' Sylvia's awareness of her own share of responsibility for
their mutual suffering is not simply the result of an instinctive
response to the dying Philip's appeal for forgiveness. During the
years of her husband's absence her heart had been gradually
softening towards him; she had come to miss the unfailing devotion
she received from no one else in like measure; she had grown in
spiritual awareness through the influence of the Quaker Alice Rose
and her daughter Hester; and she had been startled by the news of
Kinraid's marriage into the recognition that he could never have
loved her as Philip had done: 'For the first time in her life, she
seemed to recognise the real nature of Philip's love.'

The change in her attitude makes it possible for Philip to express
fully, for the first and last time, the depth of his tenderness for her,
the protective love that was always so much a part of his passion. On
the human plane their reconciliation is also a farewell. In the depth
of her remorse Sylvia fears it may be an eternal one, but her
husband, in dying, sees more clearly:

'. . . I niver thought to be so happy again. God is very merciful.'
She lifted up her head, and asked wildly, 'Will He iver forgive me,
think yo'? I drove yo' out fra' yo'r home, and sent yo' away to t'
wars, wheere yo' might ha' getten yo'r death . . . I think I shall
go about among them as gnash their teeth for iver, while yo' are
wheere all tears are wiped away.'
'No!' said Philip, turning round his face, forgetful of himself in
his desire to comfort her. 'God pities us, as a father pities his poor
wandering children; the nearer I come to death, the clearer I see
Him. But you and me have done wrong to each other; yet we can
see now how we were led to it; we can pity and forgive one
another. I'm getting low and faint, lassie; but thou must
remember this; God knows more, and is more forgiving than
either you to me, or me to you. I think and do believe as we shall
meet together before His face: but then I shall ha' learnt to love
thee second to Him; not first, as I have done here upon the earth.'
(Ch. 45)

Sylvia's Lovers might have been, as far as the actual events are
concerned, an unmitigated tragedy of human error. That it is not,
that the great closing scene uplifts rather than depresses, that Sylvia
is left with a hope and a purpose in life, that her child grows up in the
stable moral environment her own youth had lacked, all this is due

to the spiritual dimension that pervades the book as surely as life in Monkshaven is lived within sight and sound of the boundless sea. After *Sylvia's Lovers* Elizabeth Gaskell moved back, in imagination, to the world of her youth, though her view of it was enriched by all the wisdom of her maturity. *Cousin Phillis* is, from this point of view, the preliminary to *Wives and Daughters*. It does not, in its more restricted scope, afford such a wide canvas, but it offers, in the character of Holman, the father of Phillis, what is probably Elizabeth Gaskell's most complete conception of practical Christianity. It was natural that, in making such a study, she should turn to the Nonconformist background of her own life, not from any sectarian bias but because this was, after all, what she most intimately knew.

Holman does not possess, as the local innkeeper makes clear to newcomers, the social status of the Church clergyman. He is both minister and farmer. The combination was not unusual in Dissenting circles at the time, and Elizabeth Gaskell's maternal grandfather, Samuel Holland of Sandlebridge, thought to have served as part prototype of the character, similarly combined preaching with agriculture. Holman does so with complete success, as the innkeeper, also a countryman, recognises:

> '. . . minister Holman knows what he's about, as well as e'er a farmer in the neighbourhood . . . He spends Saturday and Sunday a-writing sermons and a-visiting his flock at Hornby; and at five o'clock on Monday morning he'll be guiding his plough, in the Hope Farm yonder, just as well as if he could neither read nor write.' (p. 7)

For Holman there is no artificial distinction between his religion and his life as a farmer. Both are based on a firm belief in the goodness of God. He can end a day's work in the cornfield with a psalm as unself-consciously as the vintagers in 'Six Weeks at Heppenheim' join in a harvest hymn, and the labourers who live on his farm join in the evening prayers of the family. At their conclusion, while still on his knees, he can turn to a farm servant to recommend treatment of a sick animal: '. . . here was I asking a blessing and neglecting the means, which is a mockery.'

His practical sense and method are the product not only of a clear head but of a vigorous intellect. He has wide intellectual interests, saying with truth: 'I have fewer books than leisure to read them, and

I have a prodigious big appetite.' A 'volume of stiff mechanics' is full of fascination for him, he reads law books 'with relish', and can quote from Virgil's *Georgics*. Such catholicity of taste is not approved by his more circumscribed fellow minister, Brother Robinson. Brother Robinson, of whom Elizabeth Gaskell had no doubt met the equivalent on more than one occasion, is a good man but a limited one, who considers that to quote from the *Georgics* 'savours of vain babbling and profane heathenism'. Holman can take such criticism in his stride. He sees nothing to be ashamed of in using to the full the intellect with which God has endowed him, and is at once at home in the society of Manning, the engineer, father of the narrator of the story, a thinker like himself and like him 'a sturdy Independent by descent and conviction'.

Both physically and mentally impressive, Holman dominates the life at the farm at Heathbridge and it seems as if nothing could trouble its idyllic calm. Trouble comes, however, with the desperate illness of the only daughter. Conscious that he had been mistaken in thinking of her as still a child, and had, for the first time, shown himself unsympathetic to her on discovering her love for the 'stranger' whose brief visit to Heathbridge had shattered her peace, Holman is at first almost broken by the blow. It is while he is enduring the greatest trial of his life that he receives a visit from Brother Robinson and another minister, both well supplied with quotations from the Book of Job. As might be expected, they adjure him to resign himself to the probable death of his child. Holman's attitude in face of calamity is as positive as theirs is negative: his is the vital religion that rejects premature resignation in favour of hope: 'God has given me a great heart for hoping . . . Brethren, God will strengthen me when the time comes, when such resignation as you speak of is needed. Till then I cannot feel it; and what I do not feel I will not express . . .'[34] With similar honesty he refuses to accept their suggestion that it must have been his own sins that have brought this calamity upon him: 'I hold with Christ that afflictions are not sent by God in wrath as penalties for sin.' Brother Robinson's companion fears that this may not be 'orthodox', but Holman is not concerned with problems of theology, he is concerned with life and death and the love of God as revealed in the New Testament.

Elizabeth Gaskell was not an advocate of long sermons, and Holman is never shown in his pulpit, though he is shown on Sunday, thinking over what he has to say, as he and his family make their way to the chapel at Heathbridge through the country lanes. One remembers that Thurstan Benson never preached the sermon he had prepared for Ruth's funeral; he found that only words from the Bible could adequately express what he felt. Elizabeth Gaskell probably retained no distinct memories of the sermons she had listened to in childhood in the little Unitarian chapel at Knutsford, but it was none the less an imperishable part of her memories because of all that it stood for in her life. It lives again in the description of Benson's chapel on the outskirts of Eccleston, where the whitewashed walls reflect the tracery of the ivy growing round the casement windows, sometimes stirred by the flight of one of the many birds whose song emulates the chorus of human praise within. The congregation consists of some who love the place because their fathers had worshipped there, and they knew how much those fathers had suffered for it, some who are Dissenters from conviction, unmixed with ancestral association, and 'many poor, who were drawn there by love for Mr Benson's character, and by a feeling that the faith which made him what he was could not be far wrong'.

9 Form

Elizabeth Gaskell was not primarily concerned with considerations of form. The themes that dominated her work were those that suggested themselves to her naturally, out of her own experience of life, and naturalness was her chief criterion in presenting them to her readers. She expressed herself on paper as fluently as she did in conversation. But it is not as easy to achieve naturalness on paper as in the spoken word. It was only through writing that she learned how to develop the kind of art that was her own, and to progress, in the seventeen years of her literary career, from the powerful but uneven *Mary Barton* to the finished mastery of *Wives and Daughters*. The development of her art is most clearly seen in the works themselves. She was no theorist and one does not find, in her letters to her publishers, the exposition of critical views in which Charlotte Brontë, in the years of her fame, became increasingly competent. They occupy little place even where one would expect them to occupy most, in her own biography of Charlotte Brontë. But one finds, scattered through her letters and sometimes in the works themselves, occasional indications of her personal opinions about art, given not as theories but as facts of her own experience.

She felt, like every artist, the need at times to take refuge in another world but, characteristically, she saw this in the context of the woman's problem as to how to combine creativity with domesticity:

> One thing is pretty clear, *Women* must give up living an artist's life, if home duties are to be paramount . . . I am sure it is healthy for them to have the refuge of the hidden world of Art to shelter themselves in when too much pressed upon by daily small Lilliputian arrows of peddling cares; it keeps them from being morbid as you say; and takes them into the land where King Arthur lies hidden, and soothes them with its peace. I have felt this in writing, I see others feel it in music, you in painting, so assuredly a blending of the two is desirable (Home duties and the

development of the Individual I mean) . . . but the difficulty is where and when to make one set of duties subserve and give place to the other. I have no doubt that the cultivation of each tends to keep the other in a healthy state . . .[1]

The problem of the combination of art with domestic duties, here expressed in a letter to the artist Eliza Fox, seems to have been in her mind when she questioned Charlotte Brontë about her mode of composition, and learnt that Charlotte could write only at those times when 'the progress of her tale lay clear and bright before her, in distinct vision' but that, at such times, she always attended first to her 'household and filial duties'. What concerns Elizabeth Gaskell is to show 'how orderly and fully she accomplished her duties, even at those times when the "possession" was upon her'.[2] But it is doubtful if she would ever have used the word 'possession' with reference to her own mode of composition. Her 'hidden world of Art' had closer affinities with the world of everyday, and it was easier to enter and re-enter it at will.

For her, imagination was not so much a 'strong, restless faculty' as a lively and consoling one. She possessed, like Charlotte Brontë, amazing powers of observation—which, in her case, had been exercised over a wide field—a wonderfully retentive memory and a keen intelligence. Her attitude to her art was typical of the balance of her nature; she enjoyed it, allowed it to develop naturally, and gradually learned how to increase its effectiveness through greater complexity and a greater measure of control, which never endangered its inherent spontaneity.

The story-telling gift was hers from the first, and she did not minimise its importance. In 'Company Manners' she praises the guests of Mme de Sablé's salon for their competence in this field: 'They knew how to narrate, too. Very simple, say you? I say, no! I believe the art of telling a story is born with some people, and these have it to perfection; but all might acquire some expertness in it . . .'[3] And she goes on to criticise those who misguidedly launch into the 'muddled, complex, hesitating, broken, disjointed, poor, bald, accounts of events which have neither unity, nor colour, nor life, nor end, in them, that one sometimes hears'. Five years later, in a letter of advice to a young novelist which has been described as the key to her art, she advised him to make a careful preliminary study of plot. The themes were to be provided by the novelist's own experience and observation, but the shaping of the narration demanded conscious planning as well:

> Every day your life brings you into contact with live men and women . . . Think if you can not imagine a complication of events in their life which would form a good plot . . . The plot must grow, and culminate in a crisis; not a character must be introduced who does not conduce to this growth and progress of events . . . Study hard at your plot . . . really make this sketch of your story a subject of labour and thought.[4']

Her own novels have unity and conscious design. The original rough sketch of her first novel *Mary Barton* still exists to bear witness to the preliminary planning involved. Like any creative artist, she inevitably modified the original plan, but the essential outline of the plot is there.

But for her the writing of fiction involved very much more than this. To use her own metaphor, the outline of the plot was only the 'anatomical drawing' of the artist; he must give it muscle and flesh:

> Then set to and imagine yourself a spectator and auditor of every scene and event! Work hard at this till it becomes a reality to you,—a thing you have to recollect and describe and report fully and accurately as it struck you, in order that your reader may have it equally before him.[5]

One recognises here the most salient quality of her own art, the power to realise not only the great crucial scenes but a multiplicity of smaller ones which are also 'events' in their own right, happenings and conversations which, as in real life, are all in their own way a series of minor crises, unobtrusively but surely helping to shape the onward course of the action.

It is noticeable that at this stage of the creative process the artist has become largely the spectator. The role of spectator is a demanding one; the ideal spectator is observant, familiar with what he sees, or he cannot report on it intelligently, and sympathetic in his attitude to mankind in general, or else his account is likely to be heavily biased. He is not expected to intervene more than is absolutely necessary with comments of his own. Elizabeth Gaskell is emphatic in her counsel on this subject to the young novelist who had asked her opinion of his writing. 'Don't intrude yourself into your description' is her pithy advice. She had already warned him against being too subjective in his attitude to his art:

> . . . I think you must observe what is *out* of you, instead of examining what is *in* you. It is always an unhealthy sign when we are too conscious of any of the physical processes that go on within us; and I believe in like manner that we ought not to be too cognizant of our mental proceedings, only taking note of the results. But certainly—whether introspection be morbid or not,—it is not a safe training for a novelist. It is a weakening of the art which has crept in of late years. Just read a few pages of De Foe . . . and you will see the healthy way in which he sets *objects* not *feelings* before you.[6]

The author who endeavours to restrict his role to that of spectator and reporter, keeping his own personality in the background, is not without his problems, even if he is not introspective by nature. Where it was necessary to introduce the natural setting, or to give information about the social or industrial background, Elizabeth Gaskell encountered no difficulty, since she never dealt with themes in which she was not keenly interested and with which she was not thoroughly familiar. As Cazamian says, with reference to the Manchester tales, 'Mrs. Gaskell instructs as painlessly as she writes'. Where the moral implications of a situation were involved, her concern that they should be correctly understood sometimes betrayed her into a didacticism which brought her into the foreground as a conscious moralist. Charming as she was, in this character she did not please all her Victorian readers and can alienate modern ones.

Yet this moralising strain was intimately connected with her views on the purpose of art, which she saw not only as a pleasure but also as a duty, no less important than her duty to her family. She did not feel that her discussion of the rival claims of home duties and 'the development of the Individual' (in the context, the artist) in her letter to Eliza Fox was complete until she had added, a few days later, a final comment:

> . . . If Self is to be the end of exertions, those exertions are unholy, there is no doubt of *that*—and that is part of the danger in cultivating the Individual Life; but I do believe that we all have

some appointed work to do, which no one else can do so well;
which is *our* work; what *we* have to do in advancing the Kingdom
of God; and that first we must find out what we are sent into the
world to do, and define it and make it clear to ourselves, (that's
the hard part) and then forget ourselves in our work, and our
work in the End we ought to strive to bring about.[7]

There is a conflict, however, implicit in this statement; art is seen as
capable of fulfilling a religious purpose, but the purpose is to take
precedence over the art. Such an attitude ignores the truth that
every work of art is in itself a testimony to the beliefs, whatever they
may be, which have inspired the artist, and would never have taken
shape without them. Elizabeth Gaskell was profoundly influenced
by the Christian ethos, and everything she wrote was in its own way
a declaration of her faith. Her evolution as an artist was largely the
progressive discovery of how best to let her work speak for itself.

Although all her writings throw light on her artistic development,
it is in the full-length novels that it can be seen most clearly. There is
a wide difference between the artistic achievement of *Mary Barton*,
considerable as it is, and the art of *Wives and Daughters*, the story
which Henry James praised for being 'so delicately, so elaborately,
so artistically, so truthfully, and heartily . . . wrought out'.[8]

The growth in artistry is very evident in the increase in power and
originality shown in the composition, which progresses through
some initial uncertainties to the structural mastery of *North and South*
and the finished symphonies of the final novels. *Mary Barton* has,
instead of a wholly integrated action, what is really a combination
of two different plots. In the first part, though dramatic scenes do
occur, the author builds up to the crisis of the murder largely
through a sequence of those seemingly everyday yet significant
scenes in the handling of which lay her truest originality. After the
commission of the murder, at a point little more than halfway
through the action, the interest shifts to Mary's dramatic search for
the missing witness, who must be found within a few days, if her
lover's life is to be saved. Once this is achieved, there is a natural
diminution of tension, and the eventual return and death of the long
absent John Barton have the character of an epilogue rather than
the natural conclusion of the action. *Ruth* has a simpler plot and no
alternative title would have been possible, as in the case of its
predecessor, for the interest is concentrated throughout on the
heroine. Scenes of dramatic confrontation occur, but within a

domestic context. But there is a certain monotony in the linear plot, and readers have questioned the inevitability of the tragic conclusion. Far more assured is the handling of a much more complex subject in *North and South*, where the two main protagonists at the same time represent two widely differing cultures. The Milton environment brings them together, involving Margaret Hale in the industrial unrest which is Thornton's natural element. The complex plot never becomes confused because its basic pattern is established by the gradual growth in understanding between Margaret and Thornton. Dramatic crises do occur but the chief interest lies in the progress towards final reconciliation. The novel first appeared as a serial in Dickens' *Household Words* and Elizabeth Gaskell's refusal to comply with his criticisms, when the demands of serialisation threatened the shape of her narrative, reflects her growing confidence in her own technique. *Sylvia's Lovers* has a simpler plot, the age-old story of the lover who sees another preferred to himself, but its simplicity is endowed with an epic quality by the rugged grandeur of the setting, the intensity of the passions involved and the prestige of a historical epoch, that of the Napoleonic Wars. Unavoidably, violence plays a part in the action but it does not obscure the living presentation of life on a small farm and in a primitive sea-faring community. The composition of *Wives and Daughters* represents a higher level of achievement than in any of the other novels. For over seven hundred pages the author succeeds without apparent effort in holding the reader's interest with her 'every-day story' of the doctor's daughter, where dramatic scenes are few and life moves at a leisurely pace. Her narrative has none the less the 'unity, life and colour' she judged essential and moves so naturally towards its conclusion that, when it breaks off unfinished, no one is left in any doubt as to how it would have ended.

The progressive subordination of the dramatic element in the novels does not mean that Elizabeth Gaskell had not a sense of drama. All born storytellers have. The account of the search for the missing witness in *Mary Barton* is compelling in its force. She possessed to the full the power to awaken suspense, and to prolong it till it becomes almost unendurable. It was perhaps his awareness of this that made Dickens impatient at her refusal to satisfy the normal expectations of the serial-reading public with her over-leisurely instalments of *North and South*. Yet she was right to develop her own technique as a novelist and to judge that there, though not necessarily in her shorter tales, high drama should be, as she had most often found it to be in real life, a matter of relatively rare occurrence. But in relying increasingly, for the interest of her narrative, on a multiplicity of minor events rather than on the number of major ones, she was opting for a technique that made considerable demands on her skill. It was necessary that the minor events should all be felt to have a bearing on the development of the action, and that they should be introduced in such a way as to make their significance clear. To achieve this, she relied to a considerable extent on her great skill in using a pattern of contrast. Her gifts in this direction were already evident in the first part of *Mary Barton*, where the significance of the individual scenes is enhanced by telling juxtaposition: the Bartons' home, warm with firelight and hospitality, is contrasted with the same house at midnight, petrified by the intrusion of death; Barton's account of his experiences in London, where he had gone as a Chartist delegate, is directly followed by Job Legh's recollections of his own past visit to London to bring home his infant granddaughter, selected by Legh himself as a topic 'neither sufficiently dissonant from the last to jar on the full heart, nor too much the same to cherish the continuance of the gloomy train of thought'.[9] Similar effects of contrast and balance recur throughout the novels. After participating in society again at the Thorntons' dinner party, Margaret Hale returns home to find that her mother's illness has taken an alarming turn; Molly Gibson's golden dreams of the coming visit to the Towers are followed by the disillusioning reality.

By such means Elizabeth Gaskell introduces both significance and variety into the narration of the many small crises which only slowly and cumulatively build up to major ones. She also enlivens her narration by frequent variations in tone. Only in *Mary Barton* did the tragic nature of her subject almost preclude the exercise of her gift of humour, though occasionally it asserted itself irrepressibly even there. Normally her balanced attitude to life enabled her to see the comic element latent in many of the occurrences that make up everyday existence. *Ruth* is inherently a sombre story, but life at Eccleston is enlivened by the resilience of Faith Benson and the conversation of the fortright Sally. In *North and South*, sombre though much of the action is, the humour is more pervasive; the characters are subjected to many stresses, but there is often a humorous side to their reactions. Mrs Thornton's monumental incomprehension of Margaret Hale, though distressing to her son, has its comic aspects, the nadir of their relationship being reached when Margaret, rebuked by Mrs Thornton for unbecoming behaviour, sweeps from the room 'with the noiseless grace of an offended princess', leaving her mentor to show herself out. The latter part of *Sylvia's Lovers* is darkened by tragedy, but there is abundant humour in the evocation of life at Haytersbank Farm during Sylvia's happy youth. Daniel Robson's criticism of the culinary operations of his wife, when a bout of rheumatism makes him an unwilling prisoner in the chimney-corner, is endured by her with exemplary patience—'th' feyther's feyther, and we mun respect him'—but his lively young daughter's suggestion 'that his ignorant directions should be followed, and the consequences brought before his eyes and his nose' would have been, as Elizabeth Gaskell points out, a surer means of dispelling his boredom. *Wives and Daughters* represents the greatest triumph in this field also, for here it is one of the major characters who is the most unfailing source of comedy.

Another resource of which she makes good use in her leisurely plots is the importance of the time factor. A sequence of small events gives her the opportunity to convey that sense of being imprisoned in a quagmire of difficulties which most people experience at some time in their lives. Margaret Hale has to endure this in Milton before she is called on to face more dramatic tests of her fortitude: 'They were settled in Milton, and must endure smoke and fogs for a season; indeed, all other life seemed shut out from them by as thick a fog of circumstance . . . She fell asleep, hoping for some brightness, either internal or external. But if she had known how long it would be before the brightness came, her heart would have sunk low down.'[10] The comparative rarity of major happenings can produce an illusory sense that time is standing still. Life flows on smoothly for Ruth in the Benson household during her first years at Eccleston: 'The quiet days grew into weeks and months, and even years, without any event to startle the little circle into the consciousness of the lapse of time.'[11] Yet during this quiet stretch of time the Bensons are growing older, and Ruth matures from the heartbroken girl into the woman who is able to safeguard the future of her child. A different but no less fateful change takes place in Sylvia during the monotonous months when she mourns the supposed death of Kinraid, transforming her from the lively, impetuous creature she had been till then into the apathetic shadow of her former self. But it is Bessy Higgins, the weaver's daughter, once 'a gradely lass enough', who is so sickened of life by her endless days in the carding-room that it comes as a relief to her to know, at nineteen, that she is dying of the disease contracted there:

'If yo'd led the life I have, and getten as weary of it as I have, and thought at times, 'maybe it'll last for fifty or sixty years'—it does wi' some—and got dizzy and dazed, and sick, as each of them sixty years seemed to spin about me, and mock me with its length of hours and minutes, and endless bits o' time—oh, wench! I tell thee thou'd been glad enough when th' doctor said he feared thou'd never see another winter.' (Ch. 11)

Through the leisurely action of her novels, Elizabeth Gaskell lets her characters reveal themselves as they would do in the course of everyday life. One of the triumphs of her characterisation is the way in which she uses the small and apparently trivial to throw light on feeling and motive. Mr Hale blames Margaret for morbid anxiety when her concern for her mother's health brings into the open the fears he himself has been trying to suppress. Sylvia's choice of scarlet duffle for her new cloak displeases Philip who has recommended the more serviceable grey, 'a respectable, quiet-looking article'. Mrs Kirkpatrick appears to sympathise with Molly Gibson when, as a child, she is overcome by the heat and falls asleep during the afternoon at the Towers, but forgets to wake her in time to depart with the other visitors. Even the minor characters, who are only 'minor' in relation to the particular circumstances involved, reveal themselves by small but significant acts. Jenny Morgan, the Welsh landlady, feels Ruth's presence at the inn an embarrassment when her lover falls ill, but sends her food after she has nearly fainted and feels enough real concern to scold her for not eating it.

Dialogue is another unfailing means of characterisation in the Gaskell fiction. When criticising the work of a young novelist, in the letter of advice already referred to, she mentioned, as one of the faults of his book, 'the length of the conversations, which *did not advance the action* of the story'. Earlier in the same letter she had remarked: 'In all conversation there is a great deal of nothing talked.' Neither of these criticisms could be levelled at the dialogue in her own novels. They all advance the action by adding to our knowledge of the protagonists. Some of these do talk 'a great deal of nothing', the most obvious example being Mrs Gibson, but it always has a relevance to the immediate situation. From *Mary Barton* onwards Elizabeth Gaskell uses reported conversation to reveal the minds and hearts of her people. The Barton and Wilson families, Job Legh and his granddaughter express their hopes and fears in their own simple and energetic idiom. Dialogue can also become at times the voice of the community; the neighbours who gather round Barton before his departure for London voice the grievances of their submerged world. In this first work there are occasional faults of tone; Mary sometimes fails to convince when speaking of her love, and Esther's speech can descend to melodrama. But there are few such lapses in the subsequent works. In *North and South* the clash between Margaret and Thornton is expressed primarily in dialogue, with Mr Hale to act as mediator. In *Wives and Daughters* a whole cross-section of society becomes audible and at the same time each character speaks with an individual voice. Mrs Gibson, in plaintive mood, betrays, in the course of one inconsequential speech, her partial disillusionment with her second marriage and her rooted dislike of plain-speaking, especially in her stepdaughter:

'I remember dear Mr Kirkpatrick walking five miles into Stratford to buy me a muffin, because I had such a fancy for one after Cynthia was born. I don't mean to complain of dear papa— but I don't think—but perhaps I ought not to say it to you. If Mr Kirpatrick had but taken care of that cough of his; but he was so obstinate! Men always are, I think. And it really was selfish of him. Only, I daresay, he did not consider the forlorn state in which I should be left. It came harder upon me than upon most people, because I always was of such an affectionate, sensitive nature. I remember a little poem of Mr Kirkpatrick's, in which he compared my heart to a harpstring, vibrating to the slightest breeze.'

'I thought harpstrings required a pretty strong finger to make them sound,' said Molly.

'My dear child, you've no more poetry in you than your father.' (Ch. 41)

When she lets her people express themselves in speech and action, Elizabeth Gaskell's characterisation cannot be faulted. When it becomes necessary to describe their unspoken thoughts and feelings she is, in her first novels, less at ease. The role of omniscient narrator came less naturally to her than that of the interested spectator, concerned to report speech and action. In *Mary Barton* the heroine dismisses her lover and former playfellow Jem Wilson out of social ambition, only to discover that it is he and not his rich rival whom she loves. Elizabeth Gaskell as narrator has to inform the reader of this sudden revolution in Mary's inmost feelings. She does not do so from the lofty vantage point of philosophic detachment; she is anxious to point out that we have all of us experienced such sudden reversals of attitude: '. . . we have every one of us felt how a very few minutes of the months and years called life, will sometimes suffice to place all time past and future in an entirely new light.'[12] None the less the analysis of Mary's feelings does not impress the reader with the sense of a felt reality. In her second novel Ruth's passage from youth to maturity, during the quiet years at Eccleston, is not described in sufficient depth to be convincing. It needs the magnificent confrontation of the former lovers on Abermouth sands to reveal the distance she has travelled since the days at Fordham. There is a great advance in the ability to portray the inner life of the characters from *North and South* onwards. In her later novels Elizabeth Gaskell enters into the consciousness of her central characters not with the intellectual equipment of the philosopher but with the intuitive insight of the painter of genius. We know Margaret Hale and Thornton, Sylvia Robson and Philip Hepburn not only by what they say and do but by what they are in the private world of the individual conscience. Not surprisingly, she shows a particular aptitude for introducing at intervals the interior mono-logue, which allows the characters to express their own thoughts directly, in the intervals of the narrator's commentary. In the crisis of her young life, Molly Gibson is herself her own best interpreter: 'She did not care to analyse the sources of her tears and sobs—her father was going to be married again—her father was angry with her; she had done very wrong—he had gone away displeased; she had lost his love; he was going to be married again—away from her—away from his child—his little daughter—forgetting her own dear, dear mother.'[13]

It was in the relationship of art and ethics that Elizabeth Gaskell encountered her most serious problems. The religious theme is the most basic in her work, the common factor that underlies all the others. In her first novels her anxiety to make her own outlook clear led her at times perilously near to contradicting, by explicit moralising statements, the impression given by the work in general. In *Mary Barton* her early account of Barton's resentment when he sees employers continuing to live in comfort while economic depression brings the workers to destitution is immediately followed by a qualifying statement: 'I know that this is not really the case; and I know what is the truth in such matters; but what I wish to impress is what the workman feels and thinks.'[14] This remark is obviously motivated by the desire to be fair to both sides, and above all by the fear of appearing in any way to incite class warfare, which is in opposition to the Christian ideal of reconciliation. But it is ineffective in the context and is contradicted by the whole tenor of the novel; there is no sign that the Carsons and their fellow mill-owners are deprived of any material comfort, and every evidence of the extreme privation of the workers. In *Ruth* the chief emphasis is on the courageous moral recovery of the seduced girl, who becomes a devoted mother and a valuable member of society, but the language used is sometimes, as W. R. Greg understandably complained, 'at war with this impression', suggesting that 'the sin committed was of so deep a dye that only a life of atoning and enduring persistence could wipe it out'.[15] In *North and South* ethical viewpoints are skilfully combined with dialogue and thus become an organic part of the whole structure. Even here, however, Margaret Hale's relationship with the dying Bessy Higgins is complicated by her fear of encouraging complaints which might be construed as directed against religion, although the girl's illness has clearly been caused entirely by the industrial conditions which are criticised throughout the novel. In *Sylvia's Lovers* moral issues are seen in a historical perspective and Elizabeth Gaskell, in one of her occasional authorial comments, shows her growing recognition of the inconsistencies that characterise all human endeavour:

> Will our descendants have a wonder about us, such as we have about the inconsistency of our forefathers, or a surprise at our blindness that we do not perceive that, holding such and such opinions, our course of action must be so and so, or that the logical consequence of particular opinions must be convictions which at present we hold in abhorrence? (Ch. 6)

Wives and Daughters, the final masterpiece, contains no ethical discussion. Molly Gibson is alarmed when told she has been talking metaphysics. Only Mrs Gibson moralises, sometimes astonishing herself by the depth of her remarks. But the reader is never left in any doubt as to the unselfishness of Molly or the selfishness of her stepmother, nor as to the fact that Molly is infinitely the more attractive of the two.

Elizabeth Gaskell was in full possession of her powers as a novelist when she faced the challenge of the biographer's task in *The Life of Charlotte Brontë*. To a large extent she had only to apply to the writing of biography the method of composition she had found most appropriate to the novel. Her storyteller's instinct was aroused by what she heard from Lady Kay-Shuttleworth, and from Charlotte herself, at their first meeting, of the unusual household at Haworth. When asked, after her friend's death, to undertake her biography, she welcomed the opportunity. She was able to assume the role she preferred, that of spectator narrator. She visited, or revisited, the places connected with Charlotte, first and foremost Haworth itself, though she also went as far afield as Brussels. And she was able, thanks to Ellen Nussey, to quote from Charlotte's correspondence, preferring, as always, to let her heroine reveal herself, as far as possible, by her own words and actions. The reader is able to follow Charlotte, stage by stage, on the often monotonous but sometimes dramatic journey which led, through much hardship and brief fame, to death in the same remote environment where she had lived. Inevitably there were differences between the position of the biographer and that of the novelist, but Elizabeth Gaskell, with her aptitude for realistic observation and her love for informative facts, was stimulated rather than daunted by the need for exact documentation. In the use of her material she was limited, as the novelist is not, by the need for discretion where reference to living people was involved and, in her sympathy for her heroine, did not always observe this sufficiently, as she found to her cost. But her assessment of the circumstances of Charlotte's life was on the whole a remarkably fair one, which could still be used by Margaret Lane as the basis of *The Brontë Story*.

It was not, in any case, the danger of being unjust to Lowood School or to the wife of Branwell's employer or even to the, on the whole, remarkably patient Mr Brontë that was the chief hazard Elizabeth Gaskell encountered in her biography. It was the fact that she really had two subjects: Charlotte Brontë and Currer Bell. It was her wish to 'make the world honour the woman as much as they have admired the writer', but in the process the writer sometimes receded too far into the background. Charlotte's intense sensitivity, her at times morbid introspection were not just the price she paid for her genius, they were part of it. Elizabeth Gaskell fully recognised the existence of these qualities in her, but she did not admire them as she did Charlotte's fortitude, her common sense, her sense of duty, her passionate loyalty to her family and her home. In sympathising with what she felt almost as weaknesses, caused by physical frailty and unnatural conditions, she does not seem altogether to have realised that they might be a valuable source of inspiration for an artist of a nature different from her own. She herself did not feel she had always penetrated to the depths of her subject, but she allowed Currer Bell to speak for herself in her letters, and her biography, based not only on scrupulous documentation but on love, admiration and personal knowledge, will always remain the best introduction to the life of Charlotte Brontë.

The biography shares in the popularity enjoyed today by most of Elizabeth Gaskell's novels, notably *Mary Barton, North and South* and, above all, *Wives and Daughters*. But it is possible that *Cranford* still has more admirers than any. *Cranford* is the most distinguished representative in her work of a different genre, the collection of related episodes, held together by a first-person narrator and a common social setting, which she had first essayed in 'Mr Harrison's Confessions' and to which she returned, the year after the publication of the *Life of Charlotte Brontë*, in *My Lady Ludlow*. The first-person narration, the form most often used by Charlotte Brontë, was one she used less frequently, never in her full-length novels and never for subjective reasons. But the presence of a personal narrator offered certain advantages to an author who was anxious to appear thoroughly familiar with the setting and society described and yet to avoid any undue assumption of omniscience. The narrator in each of these works is someone who comes originally from outside and is at first aware of the novelty of different surroundings, but who very soon absorbs the atmosphere of the place to the point of becoming almost as much a part of local society as anybody else. Such a formula conforms to Elizabeth Gaskell's wish that the author should not intrude himself into his description and yet affords opportunity for social comment more directly humorous, or compassionate, or both, than is possible in the third-person narrative. 'Mr Harrison's Confessions', which has a masculine narrator, is the least successful of these eye-witness accounts of provincial society. The young and eligible doctor becomes, in spite of himself, too much involved in the life of Duncombe to see it with the necessary detachment and his picture of the little town varies somewhat unpredictably from the farcical to the serious, with the result that it is not seen in the same steady illumination as Cranford or Hanbury. *Cranford* began as a self-contained sketch,

'Our Society at Cranford', but the succeeding episodes effortlessly maintain the same atmosphere and the same ethos. In the little community itself the central character is undoubtedly Miss Matty, not the narrator, Mary Smith. Yet unobtrusively it is Mary Smith who directs our attention, answers our questions, shows us what calls for laughter or compassion. Though a very self-effacing narrator, she is something more than the 'prim little Mary' that Mr Peter considers her. She is nearer to the 'well-to-do and happy young woman' she once calls herself. She is nearer still to Elizabeth Gaskell as she surveys the human comedy in her letters, wise, witty and compassionate. *Cranford* is not a subjective work, but perhaps in that hidden affinity lies the true secret of its charm.

My Lady Ludlow is another eye-witness account of provincial society, but it is not as successful an example of the genre as *Cranford* because Margaret Dawson sees the village of Hanbury from the vantage point of the Court, and the old house and its chatelaine still belong essentially to the eighteenth century. Lady Ludlow does eventually recognise that times are changing, and that her feudal village is changing with them, but even the introduction of the buoyant Miss Galindo, who moves freely between both worlds, cannot efface the melancholy impression given by the spectacle of an ancient family on the verge of extinction. The emphasis on the old order is implicit in the choice of title, though the future is evidently with Hanbury rather than with its manor-house. The most serious weakness of *My Lady Ludlow* is, however, the introduction, insufficiently motivated, of the long tale of the French Revolution, recounted by my lady, which occupies a third of its entire length, and portrays a very different world from that shown in the quiet chronicles of Hanbury.

Elizabeth Gaskell did not confine herself to the full-length novel, the biography or the social sketch. No doubt there were practical reasons, as well as aesthetic ones, for the variety of forms in which she chose to express her creative gifts. The growing popularity of serialisation afforded an opportunity for authors to experiment with stories of varying lengths. Doubtless also the pressure under which she frequently worked, especially when at home in Manchester, made her welcome on occasion the opportunity for shorter works. 'If I had a library like yours, all undisturbed for hours', she wrote to her friend Norton, 'how I would write! . . . But you see everybody comes to me perpetually . . .'[16] She made no secret of the fact that some of her short stories were written for money, to help her family.

The true reason for her versatility lies deeper, however, than in any purely practical considerations. It was part of her nature to welcome variety and improvisation. Spontaneity attracted her more than perfection; like the guests in Madame de Sablé's salon, she enjoyed being carried away by 'the humour of the moment'. The nouvelle, the short story and the essay were part of her art, and to fail to appreciate the use she made of these differing genres would be to do less than justice to the extent of her artistic resources.

The nouvelle, or short novel, has indeed an important place in her total achievement. The shorter form presented hazards for an author with her need to evoke clearly the physical and social environment but offered, if handled successfully, corresponding advantages by encouraging concision in one so naturally fluent as to be sometimes diffuse. 'The Moorland Cottage', her first treatment of the genre, avoids the danger of too leisurely a start and anticipates *Wives and Daughters* in its subject matter, but it is marred by an obviously hurried and melodramatic conclusion. The poignant tale 'Lois the Witch' is, however, a powerful example of the short novel. It belongs to the period between the *Life of Charlotte Brontë* and *Sylvia's Lovers*, when the tone of Elizabeth Gaskell's work tended in any case to be sombre, but it is unique in its tragic force, to which the greater concision of its form certainly contributes. The note of doom is clearly struck near the outset, with Lois's recollection of the Barford witch's prediction of her fate, and events follow each other inexorably up to the time of its grim fulfilment. Every detail of the physical and mental environment points to the inevitability of disaster from the moment when she arrives at the home of her New England relatives. The brief epilogue, combining realistic acceptance with the sense of incurable grief, is the fitting conclusion to a tale of almost unbearable poignancy. 'A Dark Night's Work', written a few years later, has neither the same force nor the same artistic cohesion, though its subject matter is not lacking in interest. The action takes too long to get under way, the dramatic crises are unevenly distributed in the course of the usually uneventful narrative and there is a lack of inevitability about the artificially cheerful conclusion. None of these criticisms apply to *Cousin Phillis*, whose art shares the maturity of the final masterpiece, *Wives and Daughters*, and yet has qualities of its own, due to the difference in form. Where *Wives and Daughters* involves us slowly, without our knowing it, in the tissue of the story, *Cousin Phillis* allows us the pleasure of consciously appreciating the perfect symmetry of a tale whose unfolding stages are clearly marked by basic harmonies. The love of Phillis and Holdsworth ripens with the summer days; the departure of Holdsworth is followed by the winter of discontent and the spring which is a false spring; the July thunderstorm sychronises with the news of Holdsworth's marriage and heralds the illness from which Phillis emerges to face life anew. The use of a first-person narrator enhances the unity of this quiet idyll but here the young narrator, unobtrusive though he is, develops through his sympathy with Phillis, and becomes increasingly skilled in interpreting the emotions she strives to conceal. This exquisite pastoral, which has Virgilian overtones and something of the afterglow of an Italian summer, is perhaps the most finished example of Elizabeth Gaskell's art.

   She was also attracted to the short story. Her first published essay in the genre, 'Libbie Marsh's Three Eras', appeared prior to *Mary Barton* and throughout her writing career she frequently returned to it. It was, however, what might be termed paradoxically the long short story which attracted her most, for even here she needed a certain amount of space for the development of her themes. The regional setting is always important, though in these tales Manchester and Knutsford, or their counterparts, are rather less in evidence than localities remembered from holidays at home or on the continent ('The Grey Woman' and 'Six Weeks at Heppenheim' are both set in Germany). The time of the action, like the place, shows more variation than in the novels. The first episode of 'Morton Hall' takes place at the Restoration, 'The Poor Clare' begins early in the eighteenth century, and 'My French Master' and 'The Grey Woman' during the later years of the same century. The completed action frequently comprehends a considerable time span. 'Morton Hall' covers the longest period, continuing the story of the Mortons up to the era of the Industrial Revolution. Stories like 'Libbie Marsh's Three Eras' (where the action lasts from one autumn to the next) or 'Six Weeks at Heppenheim' are the exception rather than the rule. Elizabeth Gaskell normally prefers, even in these shorter tales, to study not simply a crisis but the conditions which led up to it and its perhaps long delayed repercussions.

   This conception of the 'short' story makes considerable demands on the resources of the narrator. The short story writer who is content to deal only with one situation, or perhaps simply to evoke an atmosphere, may be quite as great an artist, but he does not face the same problem of how to compress his material into a form which is structurally satisfying. Elizabeth Gaskell is most successful when she adopts as the pattern of her story the natural stages of a human life. In 'Lizzie Leigh', 'The Well of Pen-Morfa', 'The Heart of John Middleton' and 'Half a Lifetime Ago' the story develops naturally through the hopes and illusions of youth and the conflicts of adult life to the final acceptance which characterises maturity. 'Half a Lifetime Ago', an unforgettable study of the quiet heroism of a Cumbrian 'Stateswoman', is probably Elizabeth Gaskell's finest achievement in this genre.

In others of these tales she sometimes shows less familiar aspects of her genius, but is not always successful in combining them with the necessary firmness of structure. The historical sense which she was to reveal fully in *Sylvia's Lovers* is already evident in 'Morton Hall' and 'My French Master', but in the former there is a lack of correlation between the different episodes, and in the latter the central character is not drawn vigorously enough to bear the weight of historical significance he might otherwise possess. 'Crowley Castle', an eighteenth-century tale, also has potential historical interest, not least in the contrast between the sophistication of the one heroine 'with her Parisian experience of the way in which women influenced politics' and the domestic virtues of the other. Unfortunately in this story dramatic events are multiplied to the point of melodrama, thus depriving it of any true artistic merit.

The love of drama was natural to Elizabeth Gaskell. Even the ladies at Cranford experienced a kind of pleasure when they 'rummaged up, out of the recesses of their memory, such horrid stories of robbery and murder . . .'. But her dramatic sense really finds its best expression in the novels, where scenes of violent confrontation are powerfully handled and secrets in the past lives of the characters unexpectedly revealed, but never without such crises having been in fact skilfully prepared. In some of the 'long' short stories, like 'Crowley Castle', the emphasis falls all too heavily on the sensational. 'The Grey Woman', after a realistic beginning, develops into a sequence of murders and hairbreadth escapes, the intrusion of melodrama diminishes the tragic effect of 'The Doom of the Griffiths', and even of the final trial scene in 'The Crooked Branch', and disturbs the balance of the otherwise well constructed 'Manchester Marriage'. Elizabeth Gaskell is happier when she combines drama with the occult. 'The Old Nurse's Story' is a remarkable artistic achievement. The gradual awakening of the narrator to the presence of the occult in the shape of ghostly music, 'which did one no harm', is followed by her experience of the presence of the phantom child, who possesses the power to lure her own charge to her death on the fells. The suspense is comparable in degree to that evoked by Henry James in 'The Turn of the Screw', which may well owe something to the earlier tale. As Miriam Allott has said, James's 'haunted children', Miles and Flora, are also under the spell of 'a restless and predatory power'.[17] But in the Gaskell tale evil is defeated. Her stories of the supernatural illustrate in their structure the same pattern of reconciliation as the novels.

The short story properly so called was less suited to Elizabeth Gaskell as a writer than the more extended version. She was known to her friends as a born raconteur. 'No one ever came near her in the gift of telling a story'[18]—and the best of her really short stories are in fact the interpolated anecdotes and reminiscences in her longer works, where they occur naturally in the course of reported conversation. It is with the authentic accent of the oral storyteller that Job Legh recalls his return from London or Sally tells of her lovers. There is an effort to capture the same tone, evidently with a young audience in mind, in the tales 'Hand and Heart' and 'Bessy's Troubles at Home' but, like the earlier 'Christmas Storms and Sunshine', they are also intended to point a moral, and do so all too obviously, though with evident sincerity. 'The Squire's Tale' has a convincing social context and a certain interest as an early detective story, but the principal character never comes altogether to life. 'Right at Last' is also an early detective story, this time in uneasy combination with a study of moral conflict. Elizabeth Gaskell is much more successful, in this genre, when she concentrates on a single situation. 'The Sexton's Hero' and 'The Half-Brothers' build up rapidly to an eye-witness account of catastrophe, against an impressive natural background, and leave the reader with a unified impression of heroic sacrifice.

The desire to narrate was the mainspring of Elizabeth Gaskell's art, but her keen interest in social phenomena in general, both in the present and in the past, inspired a number of articles, the majority of which were first published in Dickens' *Household Words*, which constitute another example of the versatility of her genius. In the letter of advice to a young novelist which is so informative for her own views, she remarks that if the narrative form is used simply to convey 'certain opinions and thoughts', they would be more appropriately condensed into the shape of an essay. It is noticeable that she distinguishes between the thought that is the result of introspection and that which is the result of experience, and praises the latter as 'the best and likely to be the most healthy'. Certainly it is experience and not abstract reflection that is the key to all that is best in her non-fictional writings. They can hardly be said, however, to conform to the standard of concision which she theoretically considers desirable for the essay. They are better considered as studies of manners, where the nature of the content determines the length of the whole.

She is happiest when she writes directly out of her own personal experience. 'Cumberland Sheep-Shearers' reconstructs her memory of a Lakeland summer day and in doing so becomes a synthesis of the virtues of the pastoral life. In 'Company Manners' her recent visits to the Parisian salons blend with her past experience of society at home to form a synthesis of the virtues which characterise life in society at its best. 'French Life', which is much the longest of her non-fictional writings, compresses into diary form the material gained during several visits to France; from an intimate view of a bourgeois interior in the heart of Paris, the angle of observation widens to embrace provincial life, first in the region of Brittany associated with Mme de Sévigné and then in Provence, where the mistral sweeps through the historic streets of Avignon. The result is an admirable amalgam of past and present French civilisation, given form through the personal experience of a perceptive and open-minded observer.

Elizabeth Gaskell is less successful when her studies of manners, present and past, depend on information gained at second-hand. 'The Shah's English Gardener' owes its straightforward development to the fact that she is reporting the experience of a single individual. In 'Disappearances', however, where she is dealing with a number of tales of unsolved mysteries, most of them gathered from conversation with friends, she fails to co-ordinate them into a satisfying pattern. In 'Traits and Stories of the Huguenots' she is again dealing with a whole nexus of tales, the majority supplied by a friend who was herself a descendant of Huguenot immigrants, and once more her gifts as narrator hardly compensate for the lack of a clear design. The same lack is even more evident in 'An Accursed Race', where the numerous tales, originating probably in material supplied by friends in France, of the persecutions sustained by the unfortunate 'Cagots' present on the whole a confused picture.

'Modern Greek Songs' relies for its development on a discursive
account of the original work by Fauriel, occasionally introducing
parallels between the beliefs of countryfolk in modern Greece and in
Lancashire or Scotland. In 'An Italian Institution', a sketch of the
methods of the 'Camorristi' in nineteenth-century Naples, there is
rather more concision, for here the author is dealing with a more
limited topic and one about which she had more precise information, no doubt obtained during her visits to Italy. One recognises in
these essays the characteristic preoccupations of the author, her
interest in the mysterious, her love of the ballad, her aversion to
fanaticism and tyranny. What remains in the memory after reading,
however, is less an increased knowledge of the subject than an
exciting narration, a humorous anecdote or a vivid description.

All in all, these non-fictional writings, though always themati-
cally interesting, show that Elizabeth Gaskell is primarily a narrator
rather than an essayist. Where her material calls for a plan involving
abstract considerations, she is not entirely at home. She does not
attempt to give a historical account of the persecution of the
Huguenots; she gives us 'Traits and Stories of the Huguenots' with a
minimum of historical information which is not really adequate
even as a background.[19] In her fiction, on the contrary, she proves
herself both sociologist and historian, able to reproduce the very
structure of life in contemporary Manchester or Knutsford, or in
eighteenth-century Whitby. As Edgar Wright says, 'she is not
concerned with society in the abstract, with analysing or criticising
the remote forces which mould or alter it'.[20] Her views on society
and history find their natural place in her fiction, from which they
emerge with admirable clarity.

Elizabeth Gaskell's use of language is governed by the same belief
in naturalness which is her basic guide in the composition of her
work. She distrusted the 'unusual fineness of language' which some
people assume in society, and which effectively puts an end to any
natural conversation. She was equally an enemy of the pedantic,
sympathising, one may surmise, with the homely narrator of
'Morton Hall' who knows her sister is mistaken in maintaining that
'the long chapters in the Bible which were all names, were
geography' but, having forgotten the right word herself, forbears to
correct her on the grounds that 'one hard word did as well as
another'. This did not mean that hers was a careless style. On the
contrary, her criterion of naturalness meant that it must always be

appropriate to the situation. And since she dealt with a variety of situations, she was as versatile in her style as she was in her methods of composition.

The use of regional setting and atmosphere necessarily involved variations in spoken language. Regional dialect is a sustained feature of her style whose importance has already been commented on. From *Mary Barton* onwards it recurs, attaining its highest development in *Sylvia's Lovers*, but appearing also in many of the shorter works. In 'The Crooked Branch', for instance, the Yorkshire farmer and his family use the idiom of their countryside and do not fail to notice the alien speech and accent of the son on his return from London: '. . . he minces his words, as if his tongue were clipped short, or split like a magpie's.'[21] The contrast between dialect and educated English emphasises contrasts in culture and outlook. Philip Hepburn's speech is more correct than his cousin Sylvia's, but it is not, as he knows, 'the high English that parsons and lawyers speak'. The language spoken by Elizabeth Gaskell's characters shows indeed all the subtle variations that exist between the speech of different social groups. After her visit to Hamley Court the loyal Molly Gibson is dismayed to find herself noticing defects hitherto unperceived in her old friends the Miss Brownings, 'the coarser and louder tones in which they spoke, the provincialism of their pronunciation, the absence of interest in things, and their greediness of details about persons.'[22]

When, instead of reporting the conversation of her characters, Elizabeth Gaskell writes in the capacity of narrator, her style is guided by the same ideal of naturalness. At its best and most characteristic, it shows no straining after effect, no self-consciousness. The interest is concentrated on 'the thing let seen'. Her fluency had its dangers, however, and, when not writing at her best, she could sometimes become diffuse. Lack of time for revision, especially in the writing done for periodicals, may have been partly responsible, but economy was not a virtue natural to her as an artist. Experience, and her own love of order, gradually showed her how to exercise a firmer control when describing situations that held possibilities of sentimentality and melodrama. In her first novel Mary Barton's despair after rejecting Jem Wilson is described in tones of high tragedy: '. . . she lay half across the dresser, her head hidden in her hands, and every part of her body shaking with the violence of her sobs.'[23] The grief of Molly Gibson at the news of her father's coming marriage finds similar physical expression, in itself as uncontrolled, but the firmness of a mature art is evident in every line of the description:

> She had cast herself on the ground—that natural throne for violent sorrow—and leant up against the old moss-grown seat; sometimes burying her face in her hands; sometimes clasping them together, as if by the tight painful grasp of her fingers she could deaden mental suffering. (Ch. 10)

The lack of artistic restraint, in the earlier works, is most evident where the author's intense moral seriousness, and her genuine compassion, cause her to intervene personally to point a lesson with unnecessary emphasis. It is clear that the respect shown to Mr Benson in the little Welsh community where he spends his holidays is due to his known goodness, but the fact becomes a peg for an unneeded homily:

> People may talk as they will about the little respect that is paid to virtue, unaccompanied by the outward accidents of wealth or station; but I rather think that it will be found that, in the long run, true and simple virtue always has its proportionate reward in the respect and reverence of every one whose esteem is worth having . . . (Ch. 10)

Mr Hale inspires respect and liking for the same reason, when he moves to Milton, but the good relations between himself and the weaver Higgins are made clear without the addition of any generalisations:

> In the first place, the decorous, kind-hearted, simple, old-fashioned gentleman had unconsciously called out, by his own refinement and courteousness of manner, all the latent courtesy in the other.
> Mr. Hale treated all his fellow-creatures alike: it never entered into his head to make any difference because of their rank. He placed a chair for Nicholas; stood up till he, at Mr. Hale's request, took a seat; and called him, invariably, 'Mr. Higgins', instead of the curt 'Nicholas' or 'Higgins', to which the 'drunken infidel weaver' had been accustomed. (Ch. 28).

The greater control which Elizabeth Gaskell gradually acquired as a narrator was something she never needed to learn where description was concerned. The part her descriptive genius played in her evocation not only of setting but of atmosphere, mood and feeling has already been mentioned. The sheer felicity of her language, whether she paints the interior of a dingy court or a summer day in the Welsh mountains, never fails. It is seen in her work from the beginning. The early story 'The Sexton's Hero', published a year before *Mary Barton*, has for framework a country churchyard near the coast of Morecambe Bay. The opening description captures, with a perfection which might almost be called Wordsworthian and yet which is all her own, the colour, the peace and, at the same time, the scintillating life of the postmeridian scene:

> Of the view that lay beneath our gaze, I cannot speak adequately. The foreground was the grey-stone wall of the vicarage garden; rich in the colouring made by innumerable lichens, ferns, ivy of most tender green and most delicate tracery, and the vivid scarlet of the crane's-bill, which found a home in every nook and crevice—and at the summit of that old wall flaunted some unpruned tendrils of the vine, and long flower-laden branches of the climbing rose-tree, trained against the inner side. Beyond, lay meadow green and mountain grey, and the blue dazzle of Morecambe Bay, as it sparkled between us and the more distant view.[24]

The same descriptive power continues to manifest itself in all the many landscapes and interiors of her novels and tales, and never more charmingly than in the last work, *Wives and Daughters*. It was so much a part of her genius that she exercised it whenever she could, in her occasional articles as well as in her fiction. 'French Life', which appeared the same year as the first chapters of *Wives and Daughters*, and which incorporates material acquired during several visits to France, contains some of the most subtle and delicate examples of her landscape painting. Though she never wrote her projected Life of Madame de Sévigné, she records her impressions of the rural charm of the home of the Marquise, seen during a visit to Brittany, characteristically noting at the same time the humour of a conversation with an old servant, who boasted of his noble ancestry. Months later, back in Paris, she met the contemporary chatelaine of Les Rochers in a Parisian salon, and she describes how the chance meeting was enough to conjure up in her memory the original scene, less detailed but as vivid, as living, as faithful in all essentials to the sunlit reality:

> After she was gone, I recollected where I had heard the name. She was the present lady of Les Rochers, whose ancient manor-house we had visited in Brittany the year before. Instead of a Parisian drawing-room, full of scented air, brilliant with light, through which the gay company of high-born revellers had just passed, the bluff of land overlooking the Bocage rose before me; the short sweet turf on which we lay fragrant with delicate flowers; the grey-turretted manor-house, with here and there a faint yellow splash of colour on the lichen-tinted walls; the pigeons wheeling in the air above the high dove-cot; the country-servants in their loosely-fitting, much-belaced liveries; and old De la Roux in his blouse, shambling around us, with his horn snuff-box and story of ancestral grandeur.[25]

Naturalness is the essence of Elizabeth Gaskell's art. In the form of her work, as in its matter, she had the same aim, to reproduce life as she saw it. She believed that it was a unity, but a unity in diversity. She did not attempt to impose any artificial pattern; she allowed her themes, and they were always the same basic themes, to express themselves in the ways that seemed most appropriate, confident in the underlying harmony that was audible to her even in moments of crisis. Other writers have been more devoted to art for itself, or more concerned to use it in the service of a philosophy. For her it was part of life, as life was part of a more divine whole. She could paint all that met her eyes 'with the careless, triumphant hand of a master', but her greatness stems even more surely from her unfailing belief in what she described as 'the infinite and beautiful capacities of human nature'.

Notes

CHAPTER I

1. *Ruth*, p. 150.
2. L 616.
3. See Winifred Gérin, *Elizabeth Gaskell. A Biography*, p. 38.
4. Cit. A. B. Hopkins, *Elizabeth Gaskell. Her Life and Work*, p. 41.
5. *Mary Barton*, p. 67.
6. See L 42.
7. See A. W. Ward, Biographical Introduction to *Mary Barton*, p. xxviii.
8. See L 384.
9. See L 61.
10. L 550.
11. L 69. 'Communist' has not in this context the modern connotations; it suggests sympathy with the ideals of Robert Owen.
12. Cit. Edgar Wright, *Mrs Gaskell: The Basis for Reassessment*, p. 26.

CHAPTER 2

1. L 48.
2. 'Cumberland Sheep-Shearers', *Ruth*, p. 470.
3. 'The Crooked Branch', *Cousin Phillis*, p. 237.
4. L 515.
5. *Sylvia's Lovers*, p. 361.
6. *Cousin Phillis*, p. 77.
7. 'The Half-Brothers', *My Lady Ludlow*, p. 400.
8. L 4.
9. 'My French Master', *Cranford*, p. 506.
10. *Ruth*, p. 64.
11. L 9.
12. *Ruth*, p. 63.
13. *Life*, p. 4.
14. Ibid., p. 618.
15. *Sylvia's Lovers*, p. 2.
16. L 9.
17. See ibid.
18. See J. G. Sharps, *Mrs Gaskell's Observation and Invention*, pp. 387–8.
19. L 72a.
20. Quoted by Graham Reynolds, *Constable, the Natural Painter*, p. 72.
21. L 384.

22. *Sylvia's Lovers*, p. 176.
23. L 8.
24. *Ruth*, p. 311.
25. 'Half a Lifetime Ago', *My Lady Ludlow*, p. 278.
26. *Ruth*, pp. 301–2.
27. 'The Doom of the Griffiths', *My Lady Ludlow*, p. 277.
28. *Ruth*, p. 307.
29. *Sylvia's Lovers*, p. 20.
30. Ibid., p. 380.
31. Ibid., p. 106.
32. L 550.
33. *Wives and Daughters*, p. 129.
34. See L 12.
35. Ibid.
36. 'Modern Greek Songs', *Ruth*, p. 481.
37. Ibid., p. 490.
38. See Edgar Wright, op. cit., pp. 258–63.

CHAPTER 3

1. 'The Last Generation in England' was originally published in *Sartain's Union Magazine*, USA, July 1849.
2. *Cranford and Cousin Phillis*, Peter Keating (ed.), Penguin English Library, 1976, Appendix A, 'The Last Generation in England', p. 319.
3. Ibid.
4. L 562.
5. *Cranford*, p. 167.
6. Ibid., p. 150.
7. See Gérin, op. cit., pp. 123–4.
8. 'Mr Harrison's Confessions', *My Lady Ludlow*, p. 412.
9. *Cranford*, pp. 79–80.
10. Ibid., p. 4.
11. L 562.
12. L 55.
13. *My Lady Ludlow*, p. 205.
14. Ibid., p. 59.
15. *Wives and Daughters*, p. 4.
16. Ibid., p. 157.
17. Ibid., p. 184.
18. Ibid., p. 185.
19. *My Lady Ludlow*, pp. 15–16.
20. *North and South*, p. 486.
21. L 44a.
22. See *Life*, p. 370.
23. Ibid., p. 428.
24. 'Mr Harrison's Confessions', *My Lady Ludlow*, pp. 415–16.
25. See L 222.
26. 'French Life', *Cousin Phillis*, p. 617.

27. See Gérin, op. cit., p. 155.
28. Victor Cousin, *Madame de Sablé: Etudes sur les Femmes Illustres de la Société du XVIIe Siècle*, Paris, 1854.
29. 'Company Manners', *Ruth*, p. 498.
30. Cit. Margaret Josephine Shaen, *Memorials of two Sisters: Susanna and Catherine Winkworth*, 1908, p. 24.
31. 'Company Manners', *Ruth*, p. 508.
32. L 206.
33. 'French Life', *Cousin Phillis*, p. 642.
34. 'Company Manners', *Ruth*, pp. 505–6.

CHAPTER 4

1. L 25a.
2. *Mary Barton*, p. 284.
3. See R. H. Mottram, 'Town Life', *Early Victorian England I*, p. 167.
4. She had, however, read Adam Smith. See Ward, op. cit., introdn, lii.
5. *Mary Barton*, p. 66.
6. L 42.
7. Cit. Sharps, op. cit., p. 57.
8. *Mary Barton*, p. 196.
9. Ibid., pp. 7–8.
10. See L 39.
11. See Coral Lansbury, *Elizabeth Gaskell. The Novel of Social Crisis*, p. 37.
12. L 36.
13. L 72a.
14. L 42.
15. See L 55, L 61, L 63.
16. See L 72a.
17. See Ward, *North and South*, introdn, xx.
18. *North and South*, p. 180.
19. Ibid., p. 273.
20. Ibid., p. 77.
21. Ibid., p. 78.
22. Ibid., p. 98.
23. Ibid., p. 398.
24. Ibid., p. 93.
25. Ibid., p. 194.
26. Ibid., p. 364.
27. Ibid., pp. 479–80.
28. L 211.
29. L 421.
30. L 51.
31. L 384.
32. Ibid.
33. L 453.
34. 'Libbie Marsh's Three Eras', *Mary Barton*, p. 474.

CHAPTER 5

1. L 515.
2. L 51.
3. Wright, op. cit., p. 53.
4. L 276.
5. L 69.
6. 'Lizzie Leigh', *Cranford*, p. 206.
7. *Ruth*, p. 152.
8. Ibid., p. 418.
9. *Wives and Daughters*, p. 284.
10. See Wright, op. cit., p. 54.
11. *Wives and Daughters*, p. 33.
12. *North and South*, p. 109.
13. L 330.
14. See 'Concluding Remarks', *Wives and Daughters*, p. 760.
15. 'My Diary', cit. Wright, p. 65.
16. 'Half a Lifetime Ago', *My Lady Ludlow*, p. 303.
17. *Mary Barton*, p. 26.
18. Cit. Aina Rubenius, *The Woman Question in Mrs Gaskell's Life and Works*, p. 157.
19. 'French Life', *Cousin Phillis*, p. 609.
20. *Ruth*, p. 174.
21. L 267.
22. *Life*, p. 305.
23. Cit. ibid., p. 416.
24. Cit. ibid., p. 298.
25. Cit. ibid., p. 411.
26. *Life*, p. 184.
27. Cit. ibid., p. 374.
28. *Life*, p. 634.
29. Ibid., p. 61.
30. Ibid., p. 186.
31. Ibid., p. 80.
32. Ibid., p. 55.

CHAPTER 6

1. Cit. Rubenius, op. cit., p. 27.
2. *Cranford*, p. 158.
3. Ibid., p. 174.
4. 'The Moorland Cottage', *Cranford*, p. 294.
5. *Mary Barton*, p. 196.
6. 'The Heart of John Middleton', *Cranford*, p. 387.
7. *Ruth*, p. 176.
8. 'The Crooked Branch', *Cousin Phillis*, p. 213.
9. 'The Moorland Cottage', *Cranford*, p. 295.
10. L 143.
11. L 93.

12. 'A Dark Night's Work', *Cousin Phillis*, p. 501.
13. *Ruth*, p. 415.
14. *Wives and Daughters*, p. 167.
15. *Cranford*, p. 127.
16. See 'French Life', *Cousin Phillis*, pp. 651–3.
17. See M. C. M. Simpson, *Letters and Recollections of Julius and Mary Mohl*, pp. 189–90.
18. 'Libbie Marsh's Three Eras', *Mary Barton*, p. 484.
19. See Martin Dodsworth, 'Women without Men at *Cranford*', *Essays in Criticism*, vol. 13, 1963.
20. L 453.
21. Patricia A. Wolfe, 'Structure and Movement in *Cranford*', *Nineteenth-Century Fiction*, vol. 23, 1968.
22. 'A Dark Night's Work', *Cousin Phillis*, p. 415.
23. *Life*, p. 169.
24. Ibid., p. 202.
25. Cit. ibid., p. 156.
26. L 68.
27. Miriam Allott, *Elizabeth Gaskell*, p. 12.
28. Martin Dodsworth, introdn to *North and South*, Dorothy Collin (ed.), Penguin English Library, 1970, p. 15.
29. *Ruth*, p. 93.
30. *Life*, p. 26.
31. Ibid., p. 12.
32. See Gérin, op. cit., p. 1.
33. 'The Heart of John Middleton', *Cranford*, p. 400.
34. 'Half a Lifetime Ago', *My Lady Ludlow*, p. 280.
35. Ibid., p. 323.
36. *Life*, p. 340.
37. Ibid.
38. *North and South*, pp. 249–50.
39. *Wives and Daughters*, p. 426.
40. *Life*, p. 202.

CHAPTER 7

1. 'Modern Greek Songs', *Ruth*, p. 490.
2. See Sharps, op. cit., p. 191, n. 3.
3. 'The Old Nurse's Story' in 1852 and 'The Poor Clare' in 1856. Subsequently included in *Cranford* and *My Lady Ludlow* respectively.
4. L 48.
5. 'The Old Nurse's Story', *Cranford*, pp. 444–5.
6. 'The Poor Clare', *My Lady Ludlow*, p. 348.
7. See Ward, *Cousin Phillis*, introdn, pp. xxi–xxii.
8. Ibid.
9. 'Lois the Witch', *Cousin Phillis*, p. 147.
10. Ibid., p. 207.
11. 'Disappearances', *Cranford*, pp. 410–11.

12. *Household Words*, 1853. Subsequently included in *Cranford*.
13. 'The Squire's Story', *Cranford*, p. 540.
14. *All the Year Round*, 1859. Subsequently included in *Cousin Phillis*.
15. See Ward, *Cousin Phillis*, introdn, p. xxiv.
16. L 384.
17. See Sharps, op. cit., pp. 335–6.
18. *The Cornhill Magazine*, 1860. Subsequently included in *Cousin Phillis*.
19. Cf. M. E. Storer, *La Mode des Contes de Fées (1685–1700)*, Paris, Champion, 1928.
20. Cf. *Mrs Gaskell's Tales of Mystery and Horror*, Michael Ashley (ed.), introdn to 'Curious if True', p. 217.
21. 'Curious if True', *Cousin Phillis*, p. 262.

CHAPTER 8

1. Mrs Chadwick, *Mrs Gaskell*, pp. 71–2.
2. *Life*, p. 191.
3. *My Lady Ludlow*, pp. 206–7.
4. Cit. Wright, op. cit., p. 26.
5. 'The Moorland Cottage', *Cranford*, p. 293.
6. *Sylvia's Lovers*, p. 79.
7. *Ruth*, p. 174.
8. *Sylvia's Lovers*, p. 444.
9. L 414.
10. *Mary Barton*, pp. 430–1.
11. *Ruth*, p. 121.
12. *Wives and Daughters*, p. 417.
13. *Mary Barton*, p. 102.
14. 'The Well of Pen-Morfa', *Cranford*, p. 260.
15. See Valentine Cunningham, *Everywhere spoken against*, p. 134.
16. *Mary Barton*, p. 209.
17. Ibid., pp. 63–4.
18. *Wives and Daughters*, pp. 125–6.
19. Ibid., p. 200.
20. L 16.
21. *Life*, p. 127.
22. Ibid.
23. *Cranford*, p. 54.
24. *Mary Barton*, p. 315.
25. *Sylvia's Lovers*, p. 70.
26. *Mary Barton*, p. 81.
27. *My Lady Ludlow*, p. 169.
28. L 220.
29. *Mary Barton*, p. 435.
30. *Wives and Daughters*, p. 649.
31. *Mary Barton*, p. 426.
32. *Sylvia's Lovers*, p. 526.
33. Ibid.
34. *Cousin Phillis*, p. 104.

CHAPTER 9

1. L 68.
2. *Life*, p. 315.
3. 'Company Manners', *Ruth*, p. 508.
4. L 420.
5. Ibid.
6. Ibid.
7. L 68.
8. Cit. A. Pollard, *Mrs Gaskell*, p. 247.
9. *Mary Barton*, p. 115.
10. *North and South*, pp. 75–7.
11. *Ruth*, p. 199.
12. *Marry Barton*, p. 149.
13. *Wives and Daughters*, p. 128.
14. *Mary Barton*, p. 24.
15. Cit. Ward, *Ruth*, introdn, p. xviii.
16. L 384.
17. See Allott, op. cit., pp. 39–40; Wright, op. cit., p. 165, n. 2; E. L. Duthie, 'Henry James's "The Turn of the Screw" and Mrs Gaskell's "The Old Nurses's Story" ', *Brontë Society Transactions*, XVII, pt. 87.
18. Cit. Shaen, op. cit., p. 25.
19. See Ward, *Cranford*, introdn, p. xxxi.
20. Wright, op. cit., p. 120.
21. 'The Crooked Branch', *Cousin Phillis*, p. 22.
22. *Wives and Daughters*, p. 168.
23. *Mary Barton*, p. 149.
24. 'The Sexton's Hero', *Mary Barton*, p. 490.
25. 'French Life', *Cousin Phillis*, p. 645.

Selective bibliography

Allott, Miriam, *Elizabeth Gaskell*, 'Writers and Their Work', No. 124. Published for the British Council and the National Book League by Longmans, Green & Co., 1960.

Basch, Françoise, *Relative Creatures: Victorian Women in Society and the Novel, 1837–1867*, translated by Anthony Rudolf (Allen Lane, 1974).

Beer, Patricia, *Reader, I Married Him, A Study of the Women Characters of Jane Austen, Charlotte Brontë, Elizabeth Gaskell and George Eliot* (Macmillan, 1974).

Briggs, Asa, *Victorian Cities* (Odhams, 1963).

Cazamian, Louis, *Le Roman social en Angleterre* (Paris, 1903). Translation by Martin Fido, *The Social Novel in England, 1830–1850* (Routledge & Kegan Paul, 1973).

Cecil, David, *Early Victorian Novelists* (Constable, 1934).

Chadwick, Mrs E. H., *Mrs Gaskell: Haunts, Homes and Stories* (Pitman, 1913).

Chapple, J. A. V. and Arthur Pollard (eds), *The Letters of Mrs Gaskell* (Manchester University Press, 1966).

Collins, H. P., 'The Naked Sensibility: Elizabeth Gaskell', *Essays in Criticism*, vol. 3 (Jan. 1953).

Craik, W. A., *Elizabeth Gaskell and the English Provincial Novel* (Methuen, 1975).

Cunningham, Valentine, *Everywhere Spoken Against: Dissent in the Victorian Novel* (Clarendon Press: Oxford University Press, 1975).

Dodsworth, Martin, 'Women without Men at Cranford', *Essays in Criticism*, vol. 12 (April 1963).

Easson, Angus, *Elizabeth Gaskell* (Routledge and Kegan Paul, 1979).

Ffrench, Yvonne, *Mrs Gaskell* (Home and Van Thal, 1949).

Ganz, Margaret, *Elizabeth Gaskell: the artist in conflict* (Twayne Publishers, New York, 1969).

Gérin, Winifred, *Elizabeth Gaskell, A Biography* (Clarendon Press: Oxford University Press, 1976).

Haldane, Elizabeth, *Mrs Gaskell and her Friends* (Hodder & Stoughton, 1931).

Hopkins, A. B., *Elizabeth Gaskell: Her Life and Work* (John Lehmann, 1952).

Lane, Margaret, *The Brontë Story* (William Heinemann, 1953).

Lansbury, Coral, *Elizabeth Gaskell, The Novel of Social Crisis* (Paul Elek, 1975).

Lucas, John, *The Literature of Change: Studies in the Nineteenth-Century Provincial Novel* (The Harvester Press, Sussex and Barnes & Noble, New York, 1977).

McVeagh, John, *Elizabeth Gaskell* (Profiles in Literature) (Routledge & Kegan Paul, 1970).

O'Meara, Kathleen, *Madame Mohl, Her Salon and Her Friends* (Richard Bentley & Son, 1885).

Pollard, Arthur, *Mrs Gaskell—Novelist and Biographer* (Manchester University Press, 1965).

Rubenius, Aina, *The Woman Question in Mrs Gaskell's Life and Works* (Copenhagen and Cambridge, Mass., 1950).

Sanders, G. de Witt, *Elizabeth Gaskell* (Oxford University Press, 1929).

Shaen, Margaret J., *Memorials of Two Sisters: Susanna and Catherine Winkworth* (Longmans, Green & Co., 1908).

Sharps, J. G., *Mrs Gaskell's Observation and Invention* (Linden Press, 1970).

Showalter, Elaine, *A Literature of Their Own. British Women Novelists from Brontë to Lessing* (Princeton University Press, 1977).

Simpson, M. C. M., *Letters and Recollections of Julius and Mary Mohl* (Kegan Paul, 1887).

Tarratt, Margaret, '*Cranford* and "the Strict Code of Gentility"' *Essays in Criticism*, vol. 18 (1968).

Tillotson, Kathleen, *Novels of the Eighteen-Forties* (Oxford Paperbacks, 1961).

Whitfield, A. S., *Mrs Gaskell: Her Life and Work* (George Routledge & Sons, 1929).

Wolfe, Patricia, A., 'Structure and Movement in *Cranford*', *Nineteenth-Century Fiction*, vol. 23 (1968).

Wright, Edgar, *Mrs Gaskell: The Basis for Reassessment* (Oxford University Press, 1965).

Cf. also the introductions to the Penguin English Library editions of Elizabeth Gaskell's novels (*Mary Barton*, edited with introduction by Stephen Gill; *Cranford and Cousin Phillis*, edited with introduction by Peter Keating; *North and South*, edited by Dorothy Collin with introduction by Martin Dodsworth; *Wives and Daughters*, edited by Frank Glover Smith with introduction by Laurence Lerner) and to the selection *Mrs Gaskell's Tales of Mystery and Horror*, edited by Michael Ashley, Gollancz, 1978.

Index